IMPROVISING in STYLES

A Workbook for Music Therapists, Educators, and Musicians

IMPROVISING in STYLES

A Workbook for Music Therapists, Educators, and Musicians

Colin Andrew Lee

and

Marc Houde

with contributions from Carolyn Arnason, Diane Austin, Rosemary Fischer, Janet Graham, Ian Hayter, Monique McGrath, Ruth Roberts, Sung-yong Shim, and Michelle Song

Barcelona PUBLISHERS

Improvising in Styles:
A Workbook for Music Therapists, Educators, and Musicians

Copyright © 2011 by Barcelona Publishers

ISBN: 1-891-278-58-4
ISBN 13: 978-1-891-278-58-7

Distributed throughout the world by:
Barcelona Publishers
10231 Plano Rd.
Dallas TX 75238
www.barcelonapublishers.com
SAN 298-6299

Cover illustration and design: © 2011 Frank McShane
Music editing and engraving: Ian Hayter
Copy-editor: Jack Burnett

To Rosemary Fischer

PERMISSIONS

ACKNOWLEDGMENTS

This book has been the vision and inspiration of many music therapists. We are grateful to all the authors, who allowed us to use their work. Thank you also to the other professionals, and students who have given us feedback and comments as the writing of the book progressed, and to our music editor, Ian Hayter, who dedicated many hours to formatting the book and who was there to lend a critical ear and give us concrete suggestions. His professional insight was integral to the layout and accessibility of the text. Thanks to Kenneth Bruscia, whose vision through Barcelona Publishers allows music therapists to speak and find their unique voices. His enthusiasm and support for this project has been much appreciated. In the completion of the CD audio examples, we wish to thank Marrisa Feria, Deborah Seabrook and Monique McGrath for their support during the recording sessions.

Colin Andrew Lee

The idea of writing a teaching text for clinical improvisation has been a project throughout my career that I have aspired to complete. Rosemary Fischer and I dialogued over many years on how this book might look. Her groundbreaking ideas on modulation and sonata form are included, and I am grateful for her dialogue and unwavering support as the work developed. Working with Marc Houde, a graduate student who specialized in jazz and popular music, gave me the impetus to begin this collaborative project. His playing and knowledge of popular styles expanded the writing, as well as our joint interest in world music.

Improvisation in therapy is balanced between artistic integrity and human empathy. It is this balance that makes good clinical musicianship. Important musical figures have been influential in finding this balance during my 25 years as a practicing therapist and educator. Paul Nordoff's inspiration and kindred spirit allowed me to find my true creative self as both a composer and a music therapist. Rachel Verney taught me that the smallest and simplest music can be the most effective and, if played with intent and meaning, can produce powerful results. During my time in Boston, working with Kimberly Khare gave me the opportunity to share my beliefs and ideas both during sessions and scribbling on napkins in coffee shops. Her continued dedication to music-centered practice helps me to keep grounded and continue believing in the power of music.

I would like to thank the following people who during my education as a Nordoff-Robbins music therapist in London guided and inspired me: Sybil Beresford Pierce, Robin Howat, Jane Edwards, and Alyson Carter. Thanks to my fellow students, especially Cathy Bowker, who was my co-partner in sessions, and to Pauline Etkin, Julie Sutton, and Gary Ansdell, who supported me after my training and during my early years in the field. Other therapists have been influential: in Germany, David Aldridge and Lutz Neugebauer; in New York, Barbara Hesser, Alan Turry, and Kenneth Aigen; in Boston, Michele Forinash, Suzanne Hanser, Karen Wacks, and Donna Chadwick.

Settling in Canada, I would like to give special thanks to Heidi Ahonen for her collaboration and inquiring into music-centered psychotherapy, and also to Carolyn Arnason and Debra Martz Melanson for their professional support. Thanks to all of the students I have worked with at Berklee College of Music and Wilfrid Laurier University. Your enthusiasm and enquiring minds have helped to shape this book on many levels.

Two figures have been my mentors and guides, providing unwavering support over the years. I remember Carol Robbins with the greatest affection and deepest gratitude. Her clinical-musical clarity and presence with children contained a beauty that is at the core of Nordoff-Robbins music therapy. Clive Robbins's voice of wisdom and gentle spirit continues to provide stability in my professional world. Thank you for our continued dialogue on Paul Nordoff's art music and sharing my times of heightened inspiration as we uncover ever more great works that need and deserve to be on the concert platform.

Finally, I would like to thank my partner, Rainier Liboro, for his unwavering love and for allowing me to be who I am, warts and all.

Marc Houde

During my studies at Wilfrid Laurier University, I never thought that I would have the opportunity so early to work on a book publication. What started out as a master's thesis on the blues was eventually converted to a chapter of this book. Never would I have imagined such a possibility if it were not for the encouragement and support of my professors, colleagues, family, and friends. In particular, it was the dedication and inspiration of my teacher Dr. Colin Andrew Lee that roused my enthusiasm and sense of adventure regarding this project. His unwavering passion and vision for music therapy has had a profound impact on my philosophy and practice. I wish to thank him not only for his mentorship and for supervising my research paper, but also for giving me a chance to work with him as coauthor of this book.

I would also like to extend thanks to all of the faculty of the music therapy program — Carolyn Arnason, Heidi Ahonen, and Debra Martz-Melanson — for playing a crucial role in my education and for contributing to this project. Also, thanks go to all of my supervisors — Susan LeMessurier-Quinn, Aaron Lightstone, Brian McBay, Janet Zadorsky, and Karie Bilger — for helping meto get to know myself as a student music therapist.

During my studies, I was lucky to meet an inspiring and caring group of classmates: Liz Mitchel, Cheryl Jones, Jennifer Kong, Marissa Feria, Robert Harris, Debra Seabroo,k and Carolyn Williams. Their friendship gave me the energy to begin this project. Their input and encouragement along the way will not be forgotten. A special thanks, also, goes to my partner, Marissa Feria, who has never stopped supporting me with dedication, patience, and love in all aspects of life in addition to the recording of the CD and feedback about the book.

In addition, I wish to thank Rebecca Hill, who gave me helpful feedback on choosing content for the book and for being a great mentor as I learned to practice music therapy in the hospital setting.

My greatest passion in music is improvisation, especially jazz. My interest in this direction would not have occurred without having lived in Montreal while obtaining my undergraduate degree at McGill University, where I met some of the most wonderful musicians and teachers, who not only had a mastery of their craft but also were unforgettable characters. I wish to thank my piano teacher, Tom Plaunt, who helped me to develop both musically and personally. Professors Jan Jarczyk and André White took the time to give me a solid foundation for approaching jazz improvisation. Thanks also to all my piano teachers Robert Miron, Ian Hepburn, Debbie Laundry, and Professor Louis-Philip Pelletier.

Finally, to my family, thank you for your interest and support in my education and in the process of working on this publication. It is because of your love and your belief in me that I was able to pursue my path as a musician and music therapist. I want to thank especially my grandpapa Jerome for his passion for music and his interest in music therapy. He has had an influence on me both personally and musically since my childhood, so I wish to in part dedicate this book to him.

TABLE OF CONTENTS

PART THREE: POPULAR

PART FOUR: WORLD

CONTRIBUTORS

Contributions for invited authors were submitted and edited to fit within the format and style of the book.

AUDIO EXCERPTS

CD 1

page

Chapter 2

Chapter 3

Chapter 4

Chapter 5

CD 2

Chapter 6

Chapter 7

Chapter 8

Chapter 9

Chapter 10

Chapter 11

PREFACE

This is a practical, hands-on book dedicated to teaching how to incorporate specific musical styles in music therapy. Educators and musicians interested in learning how to improvise in idiomatic styles can also use this book to increase their musical vocabulary and expand their sense of creativity. Although the book is addressed primarily to music therapists, readers of other professions may substitute "music therapist" for "musician" in the majority of the text. General musicians may choose to focus on the aesthetic and technical aspects of each style, but can also benefit from some music therapy–oriented exercises — which are geared toward self-reflection and the clinical uses of music — as these are likely to impact their conceptions of music and music-making. Music therapists, through detailed practising, can bring to their work specific resources that constitute different styles, which in turn may affect the emotional and empirical content of sessions. No one style can be developed in isolation, and this book further looks to integrating diverse ways of playing that will enhance all aspects of clinical practice.

This book has been many years in the making. It is the culmination of music-centered thinking, Aesthetic Music Therapy, and Nordoff-Robbins practice that have been realized and developed by both authors. To these fundamental ideas and philosophies, other like-minded therapists have added either complete chapters or smaller, yet significant, sections. The flow of the book is balanced between individual and collective ideas and inspirations. We hope that these musicological inspirations will contribute to the forming of an indigenous theory of music therapy (Aigen, 2006) and help to move the profession towards new levels of musical understanding.

The text is straightforward and provides step-by-step instructions on how to practise and incorporate each style into clinical improvising. The exercises are balanced between solos and duets, placing an emphasis on the relationship between two players. It makes philosophical and practical links between each style and the possible applications to music therapy practice.

Part One, Introduction and How to Practise, provides a template for how to approach practically the main sections of the book. It proposes structured ways of practising to ensure that a method is taken in building each style. Defining a timetable of practice is fundamental to ensuring that each style is clearly added to the therapist's developing musical tools.

Part Two, Western Classical Music, is divided into four sections covering music from the baroque era to the present day. It examines musical structures from tonality through chromaticism to atonality. Compositions from composers are taken as the main vehicle for extracting components of each style. With this in mind, each composition is extracted differently depending on the piece and the potential clinical application. Suggestions on how the music can be incorporated into improvising are analyzed at various levels, the main focus being the seminal content of the music and the consequences of taking each composition into therapy.

Part Three, Popular Music, explores the relevance of blues, jazz, and pop music. These are the styles most integrated into societies from around the world. For this reason, their familiarity can become an asset in the clinical setting and a key factor in clients' emotional responses. Many therapists have at some point created a song with a client using popular idioms. This chapter is designed to expand therapists' awareness of the potential of improvising in the pop idiom and to develop new possibilities in song creation. The following chapters, blues and jazz, are the founding styles that defined American popular music in the 20th century and are the root of many of today's most well-known genres, such as rock, hip-hop, soul, R&B, and country. Studying these styles will yield insight into today's music and inform therapists and musicians on the emotional world that each contemporary style brings, along with its social implications.

Part Four, World Music, looks at three distinctly different styles from disparate parts of the world. The cultural implications of these styles are discussed, looking to their socio-economic and spiritual backgrounds. From the intoxication of using tangos to the simplicity of Korean folk song and the serenity and inward-looking nature of ragas, this part provides a depth of musical expression that further expands the bounds of the book. The findings presented here are just the beginnings of embracing world styles in clinical practice.

Part Five, Authenticity, provides the platform for the therapist to amalgamate different resources and styles. Exercises that encompass broader musical perspectives are offered, to build ever more exciting and visionary ways of creating improvisations. Finding our own unique musical voice that is free from, but dependent on, formalized musical structures provides the balance for the competent clinical improviser.

We hope that this book will inspire clinicians and general musicians alike to look at new musical areas. By taking time to practise, understand, and assimilate different styles of music, we believe that clinicians will gain the ability to make deeper connections between music and therapy and offer clients a more varied array of musical interventions. By knowing equally musical and clinical dimensions, balanced music therapy practice becomes a reality to which every therapist can aspire.

Colin Andrew Lee and Marc Houde

Part of the proceeds from the authors' royalties will go toward promoting concerts and recordings of the art music of Paul Nordoff.

PART ONE

INTRODUCTION

CHAPTER 1

How to Practise

Although improvisation is a therapeutic method that has been known and used in many music therapy settings, it is surprising that there are only a few published practical guides on how to learn to clinically improvise (Nordoff & Robbins, 2007; Wigram, 2004). This publication aims to redress this gap by providing a workbook specifically designed to give music therapists the tools to successfully improvise in their work. In terms of education, it seems that some courses include in-depth teaching on improvisation while others include none. Whatever your theoretical and/or philosophical stance, this book will be of use in your clinical practice. It is designed to be used by music therapists who have extensive experience in improvising as well as by those who are just beginning. This is a practical text designed and laid out for everyday use as well as reference. We will focus deeply on musical content and its potential applications in clinical improvisation. More specifically, we will explore the aesthetics and therapeutic potential of using musical styles as a means to add to the depth and richness of our practice. Aigen (2002) plainly explains the rationale for such an approach:

> Nordoff-Robbins work is predicated on a belief that the properties, which define musical styles and scales, are reflective of their cultural contexts. By this it is meant that different kinds of music, from different cultures and time periods, have essential, defining qualities which are shaped by, interact with, and embody the experience and world view of the original creators and performers of such music. These personal and communal experiences — these ways of being in relation to other people and the external world — find expression through the appropriate musical forms and tonal relationships, and because they are archetypal experiences, their significance can often transcend cultural boundaries and the limitations imposed by disability. (pp. 11–12)

Music appears to have some objective properties that tend to yield similar subjective experiences in listeners, whether it is the urge to dance to intoxicating swing rhythms or to find our deepest longing expressed in a lyrical ballad. Does anyone ever get the urge to dance at a funeral (in most western countries)? Not only is it socially and emotionally inappropriate, but also it is not warranted by the quality of the music. In other words, different styles of music can affect us not only by their musical properties but also by their unique cultural aspects and the context in which they are performed. It would be naïve, however, to assume that everyone's experience of a particular style is the same or that specific musical components can be associated with specific responses from listeners. For example, some people love country music while others despise it! What is important to remember, as Aigen points out, is that "different styles of music lend themselves to particular types of expression and experiences, and the music therapist who can employ a variety of styles in the improvisational setting is better equipped to create a variety of moods and experiences individually suited for particular clients and circumstances" (p. 14).

Garred (2006) echoes the thoughts of Aigen:

> Using an idiom or style implies an expressive potential. Using an idiom is not solely about knowing a certain scale and how to apply it technically/musically, but also what it represents, what its qualities are. Knowing several idioms or styles *both* technically *and*

aesthetically serves as a basis for finding the "right" music, in therapy, which the client can relate to. (p. 270)

As this book is focused on styles of music, it is by implication concerned with musical frameworking. The term "framework," put forth by Tony Wigram (2004), refers to a set of musical conventions that create a specific type of musical structure, which serves to provide familiar elements that can inspire "the development of more expressive and creative playing by the client" (p. 118). Wigram states that a framework can have the function of "inspiring and encouraging, or it might equally have the function of stabilizing and containing" (p. 118). A style of music can serve many functions simultaneously, and therefore it is important to think about the unique advantages that each one can bring on a clinical level. The exercises in this book should be approached within this mind-set.

While meditating on musical properties, the main focus here is on recognizable stylistic idioms, rather than the fundamentals (intervals, chords, scales, etc.).[1] This is not to say that our experience of the fundamentals have become outdated or invalid. On the contrary, they serve as a foundation for the work in this book. In *Healing Heritage* (Robbins and Robbins, 1998), Paul Nordoff talks of musical archetypes. In a similar vein, each style in this book can be seen as a type of musical archetype, although at a higher perceptual level than that of intervals and scales. It is therefore assumed that some musical archetypes can only be perceived when a particular combination of stylistic elements is played within a specific context. The purpose of this book is to begin exploring music in this way.

There are no quick fixes in learning to improvise in styles. It would be absurd to believe that a style of music can be mastered overnight or even within the period of a few months. This book does not promise to make anyone an authentic jazz musician, baroque improviser, or expert in Indian ragas. It will, however, provide musical seeds that are meant to grow as therapists continue to explore music on their own. We have done our best at extracting the essence of each style and providing the most salient and practical stylistic components for potential use in clinical improvisation. The content within the book is not meant to be dogmatic, prescriptive, and all-encompassing, but rather opens the door for further ideas. The content is designed with the view that all therapists can have access to a variety of styles of music in order to inspire their clients. It is a book of ideas, in the sense that it encourages therapists to be creative and (pardon the cliché) "think outside the box" when it comes to using styles of music in therapy. Ultimately, it is hoped that this workbook will help therapists to expand their creative boundaries by not only increasing their musical vocabulary but also stretching their imagination and ultimately their clinical thinking.

What Is Style?

The term *style* is often associated with similar words such as *idiom*, *convention*, and *framework*. For the purpose of this book, a style can be defined more broadly as a set of musical idioms and conventions that can be identified as belonging to a particular musical culture. According to Todd (2002),

> Style includes everything related to the organization of musical sound itself: pitch elements (scale, melody, harmony, tuning systems), time elements (rhythm, meter), timbre elements (voice quality, instrumental tone color), and sound intensity (loudness/softness). All depend on a music-culture's aesthetics (p. 26).

---

[1] For an in-depth exploration of the fundamental musical elements of clinical improvisation (scales, chords, arpeggios, etc.), the reader is referred to *Creative Music Therapy* (Nordoff & Robbins, 2007), Chapter 19: Developing Musical Resources.

The term can also refer to a composer's particular approach within a style of music. For example, within the baroque style, J. S. Bach has his own defining style, for indeed his music sounds different from that of Couperin or Handel. Some of the book's chapter titles refer to more specific styles associated with well-known personalities — such as Chapter 2 (J. S. Bach) and Chapter 11 (Piazzolla) — while other chapters refer to the broader styles of music under which several individual styles would fall, such as Chapter 4 (Romantic Era) and Chapter 8 (Jazz). This workbook uses the term in both senses.

A style of music can contain several idioms, which are a set of defining musical characteristics or components that work together. For example, the blues style may contain descending syncopated phrases using the blues scale, which can be considered idiomatic but is not complete enough to be called the blues style. A full, authentic rendition of blues would also include a proper groove and most likely a 12-bar form.

Styles do not exist in isolation. They often borrow elements or even evolve directly from one another. What makes each unique, however, is that each emphasizes musical elements or mannerisms more so than another and thus becomes highly identifiable based on the configuration it takes. An extreme example would be to compare the music of J. S. Bach and that of jazz saxophonist Charlie Parker. At first glance, there doesn't appear to be much in common between the two styles of music. However, upon closer inspection, both include similar elaborate melodic lines, walking bass lines, theme and variation, and predictable harmonic sequences. To be more specific, the same voice-leading rules can apply for both jazz and J.S. Bach. In jazz, the 7th and flat 9th still resolve down a half-step as in J.S. Bach's music. Jazz harmony, however, is informed by later harmonic developments from the 1800s (classical and romantic music), and thus harmonies and melodies tend to include more chromaticism and extensive modulations and tonicizations. Jazz is also performed differently and usually with a different intent than that of baroque music. Charlie Parker's music nevertheless owes as much to Bach as many other styles in history.

One of the major aspects of evoking a style is considering *how* the music is to be played. This includes following the "rules" of instrumentation, tempo, timbre, form, timing, and other such conventions. Returning to the above example, when we think of jazz, we think of exciting syncopated rhythms, swinging grooves, and dense, colourful harmonies. In contrast, the first thing that comes to mind when describing baroque music is serenity, order, and a yearning for the divine. In terms of *feeling*, baroque and jazz are very different. The differences are due in large part to the way in which the music is realized. When studying the styles in this book, you will be referred to similar aspects that are part of another chapter. We are convinced that studying one style in depth will lead to a quicker assimilation of another. In Chapter 12, we explore further ideas so that you can become more aware of your own musical personalities and develop your own voices as improvising music therapists. This is a chapter of ideas to help therapists formulate their own long-term aims.

It is important to listen to *authentic* sources in order to learn the stylistic conventions that cannot be represented on paper with traditional notation. To gain a true understanding of each style, it is insufficient to play only the exercises in the book. It is equally important to listen and immerse yourself in authentic renditions from recordings in order to grasp the subtleties of performance and the way each musical component relates to the overall context. Similar to Paul Nordoff's approach in *Healing Heritage* (Robbins and Robbins,1998), the book's content will refer to original notated musical sources (where applicable) but with the addition of a list of suggested recordings to which to listen. We believe that the marriage between listening and playing is the key to absorbing each style proficiently.

Stylistic vs. Generic Improvisation

Aigen (2002) makes a distinction between improvising in an authentic style of music such as that from the Romantic era versus using a specific musical element of a style — for example, using loud chords in the extreme register. This means that therapists can use the techniques of this book in an integrated way or individually, depending on clinical situations. For example, if a client becomes engaged by experiencing Romantic style as a whole, it may be useful to have a more complete mastery of all explorations of the Romantic chapter in order to be able to provide an authentic rendition of the music, rather than simply playing loud, resonating chords in the extreme registers of the keyboard. In other words, it may take more than one musical element to awaken the client's perception of the style. A combination of several aspects by adding chromatic harmony and long melodic lines might drastically change the client's perception and consequently affect their engagement in music. By mastering and integrating several stylistic elements, you will affect the *quality* of the music you offer, and this in turn will affect the therapeutic process.

This book allows therapists to do both stylistic and generic improvisation, as each chapter separates the defining elements and contains exercises that focus only on one or two elements at a time. Although the chapters leave the opportunity for therapists to integrate each component into a more authentic performance, it also encourages the breaking down of styles and recombining of components from several styles to create more generic clinical improvisations.

Aesthetic Music Therapy

Central to the development of Aesthetic Music Therapy (AeMT) (Lee, 2003) is the idea of analyzing precomposed music with the aim of extracting components and styles for advancing the range and aesthetic quality of clinical improvisation. This is what differentiates AeMT from other music-centered theories and is a central component of this book. The idea of improvising in a music therapy framework of "Schumann," "ragas," or "jazz" may at first seem whimsical, for indeed music in therapy is ever changing and cannot be so easily classified musically. Understanding Schumann, however, as a humanitarian and composer can provide clues as to how to adapt his music clinically. Similarly, listening to the improvisations of Keith Jarrett and understanding his philosophical connections between music and life will give us altogether different clues. Music from other cultures provides us with a different range of experiences that generate unique colours and styles. Focussing on one composer's style or genre, learning and knowing it intimately, is a challenge in itself. To then take this music and create a style of improvising that is appropriate in sessions is a further challenge. It is our belief that if we can master different composers' styles and/or genres and amalgamate them into the therapeutic process, then the potential benefits could be immeasurable.

AeMT does not pretend to be a new theory of music therapy. Rather, it provides a philosophical and musicological framework, trying to understand with greater clarity the balance between "art" and "clinical" music. This book in many ways is a testament to the musicality of our work. The quality of our musical interventions should be paramount and equal in no less part to our nonmusical interpretations. To interpret a phenomenon without understanding the nature of the phenomena in question would seem foolish, and yet in music therapy we make significant judgements with little or no analytic knowledge of the medium we are working with. AeMT is a composer/music therapist's plea to embrace all that is musical into our work, to consider music therapy equally in musical and nonmusical terms. Both authors use the principles of AeMT in their work. This book, then, is an expression of all that is central to AeMT.

Very much like the music therapy process, composing lives through the unforeseen. This is both the dilemma and the potential spark for creativity. Allowing the presence of, and being affected by, the moment-to-moment passage of tones contains the spirit of musical reality. To compose is to be open to all possibilities. The blank page provides limitless potential to explore and conceive individual expression; this is the challenge to all artists. Being musical should not be limited by knowledge, and composing should not be confined by rules. Our clients face ambiguity, that of balancing their lives between order and chaos, illness and life. Music can redress this discrepancy and provide human strength. What can composers say to music therapy? Are there similarities between the compositional and therapeutic process? What does it mean to think of clients as composers and artists? The client as composer then becomes the blank page of the therapeutic process. This is the essence of AeMT. As together the client and therapist uncover the design and direction of the relationship, so this is reflected through musical potential. Just as my path as composer is driven by exhilaration and apprehension, so in my growth as a music therapist I must balance that which is known against that which can never be fully understood. If we can find that delicate balance between freedom and structure in clinical improvisation, then maybe our understanding of the bridge between the clinical and artistic will become ever more clear. (Lee, 2003, p. 223)

Cultural Awareness

The topic of culture is one that cannot be ignored in contemporary music therapy practice, especially considering that clients of a variety of ethnic backgrounds can often be found in the same clinical setting. Clients' cultural backgrounds play an important, if not crucial, part in the therapeutic process. Stige (2002) provides a detailed philosophical discussion of the multilayered facets of culture and how they impact the therapeutic relationship and the practice of music therapy. The styles explored in this workbook are presented and filtered through the authors' own cultural milieus. We acknowledge that there are different views on each style and that our perspectives are necessarily incomplete. Although styles of music tend to be associated with particular world cultures, therapists should be careful when using them in a stereotypical fashion. Working with a client from an Indian ethnic background, for example, it is not necessarily the case that ragas or Indian music is the best choice. Therapists should be even more careful when using music associated with a client's culture, as they may be more sensitive and knowledgeable than the therapist, especially if the therapist has only a rudimentary mastery and understanding of the style. Although this book does not go beyond the basic aspects of each style, we believe that it is still possible to offer the beauty that each musical culture has to offer and that clients of all backgrounds have the ability to perceive and respond to the aesthetics of each style. It is the responsibility of the therapist to intervene wisely with the awareness that each style brings its own culture into sessions.

Who Can Use This Book?

This book has been designed as a text to be used by teachers, students, and music therapists, as well as educators and musicians who are interested in developing styles of music in improvising. The pedagogy of its layout means that it can be used in whole or part as a curriculum for teaching improvisation. The aspect that differentiates this book from other teaching texts is the emphasis on duet playing that directly mirrors the therapeutic relationship. The duet exercises can also mirror the relationship between student and teacher or musician and fellow musician. Because the focus is on musical communication, this book can be adapted for all musicians who want to consider the relational qualities of improvised music. Passages from each chapter can be assigned for students to practise before the style is demonstrated in class. Students can also be assigned sections to be worked on their own and then fed back into teaching for further detailed consideration. For the practising music therapist, this book can be a constant daily guide. Referring and exploring can assist the therapist in finding new musical parameters for ongoing clinical work. For educators and general musicians, the exercises offered can be a valid way of exploring and distilling styles for use in all aspects of creative music-making.

Recommended Musical Skills

Although this book is designed to keep musical principles simple and attainable for all levels of musicianship, it requires basic keyboard skills. The exercises were created with piano and keyboard primarily in mind, although we do offer possibilities for guitar and orchestral single-line melody instruments, too. We offer chord symbols wherever possible for players who are more familiar with this form of notation. If you are a nonpianist, it is assumed that you have mastered all major and minor scales along with all triads and their inversions. If not, it is highly recommended that you supplement your practice with this basic technique. For pianists, it will benefit you to practise an additional set of technical exercises, such as arpeggios, diminished and augmented triads, dominant 7th chords, and modal scales. These will most likely be applied at some point within this workbook. Start your practice with a technical warm-up consisting of scales and arpeggios played in all 12 keys. This not only serves to solidify your technique but also will be a way to centre yourself for in-depth listening.

Along with practising basic keyboard skills, it would benefit therapists to work with a complimentary set of literature on clinical improvisation such as the Nordoff and Robbins resources chapter from *Creative Music Therapy* (2006) or *Healing Heritage* (1998). These include explorations of basic musical elements such as intervallic relationships, scales, modes, and triads and how to develop an increased sensitivity and perception towards them. In addition, Wigram's book, *Improvisation: Methods and Techniques for Music Therapy Clinicians, Educators and Students* (2004), contains helpful discussions about how to approach clinical improvisation in therapy on a broader level and provides a variety of examples and exercises.

How to Use This Book

It is important to develop a systematic approach to practising. This applies not only to professional performers but also to music therapists who seek to acquire and master new clinical improvisation skills. According to AeMT and music-centered music therapy, "musicing," the act of engaging in any type of musical activity or experience (Stige, 2002, p. 79), is the primary means of attaining therapeutic aims, if not the aim itself. It is important, therefore, to build a rich musical palette to accommodate the musical needs of a wide variety of clients. The purpose of this book is to help therapists to enrich their knowledge of the style (including social and historical context) as well as expand their musical boundaries to unleash their creative flow. The exercises are not fixed or complete but serve as seeds from which to draw inspiration or to expand and adapt your own clinical aims.

There are two ways of practising. The first is general, nonspecific; the second is specific to a clinical case. The musical resources presented can be used in both ways. In general, nonspecific practice, the idea is to explore sound for its own sake and develop musical sensitivity, to expand musical boundaries and clinical thinking. For such practice, this book can be used on a regular basis with a view toward acquiring new skills and routines. An example would be to explore all the possibilities of the Indian raga scales by playing them in various registers, in octaves, harmonized in 4ths or 5ths, and thinking of various possible clinical applications. In clinical case improvisation practice, on the other hand, the idea is to develop and master a part of the resources that will help to address an actual clinical problem. The book, in this case, acts as a reference guide. For example, if a therapist is used to playing the blues with a strict pulse, which prevents a client from being part of the music, it may be beneficial to refer to sections that discuss lyrical aspects of the idiom.

We encourage you to use any chapter as a starting point (depending on your level of expertise and interest), as each chapter is self-contained and includes exercises for all levels of experience. You may notice, however, that many chapters refer to other chapters that include similar techniques. Although it is beneficial to focus on a single chapter for a period of time, it is also a good idea to explore exercises involving similar elements from a variety of chapters in order to compare their use in different styles of music. This will further your understanding of the subtleties that define each style.

The accompanying CD provides examples from the text that serve to demonstrate beginning ideas and how to formulate the exercises presented. These are seeds that will hopefully give readers concrete ideas before beginning their own unique explorations. The recordings were purposefully not rehearsed to provide polished performances, but rather are experiences that are open and creative while capturing the essence of the style under discussion. Each player and therapist must find their own way of playing so that they can bring musical authenticity to their work. Just as piano students explore different interpretations and meanings of the same Beethoven sonata, so each exercise can be applied differently according to the therapist's own developing voice. In short, the way in which styles are incorporated in therapy are dependent on the therapist's musical history and maturity of clinical judgment. The listening examples provide only the beginning of the limitless possibilities available in each exercise.

To absorb any idiom takes time and repeated exposure. In order to evoke the feeling of Korean traditional music, for example, it is insufficient to practise the musical elements presented. Extensive listening, along with practising is indispensable, because it is by basing yourself in authentic renditions that you will play it with more credibility. The listening guide (see Appendix A) provides only a beginning. These contain musical examples used to demonstrate techniques and stylistic conventions explored in the exercises. We recommend that you go to a library to borrow the recordings (or find similar titles) and listen to them regularly while studying each chapter.

Although the exercises are often directed toward a particular combination of instruments, many of them are adaptable to different configurations depending on available instruments and therapists' areas of expertise. We acknowledge that the use of the guitar in music therapy is as indispensable as that of the piano and has become central to the development of clinical practice internationally. Since the guitar, however (except with classically trained guitarists), does not lend itself as easily to improvisation as the keyboard, applications in this book have been limited for the most part to specific uses of the instrument. Readers will find that it has more applications in popular styles of music than western classical styles. We hope that in the near future a more specialized book on the use of the guitar in clinical improvisation will be able to complement this present book.

The same would apply to single-line orchestral instruments such as the flute or horn. These instruments are often more limited due to their inability to create harmony. However, there are many possible scenarios where these instruments could be advantageous. With a clarinet or flute, for instance, it is much easier to walk and follow an energetic client who needs to move around the room. Single-line instruments are also ideal for creating musical dialogue. Sometimes the sheer timbre of the instrument might be enough to intrigue and motivate clients to respond musically. We encourage therapists who play these instruments to think about the potential they may contain in therapy by considering their timbre, note range, level of amplitude, and general character, and trying some of the exercises with them when applicable (Schenstead, 2009).

Throughout the book, the use of voice is integral. As with single-line orchestral instruments, voice adds a specific colour and texture. It is also one of the most human of instruments. When using the exercises in this book, always feel free to add your voice. In therapy, the voice is used in two ways. The first is to provide words that are clinically appropriate and that promote the aims of the therapy. The second is to provide an extramusical line through the more nonspecific experience of vocalizes. It is our experience that the second option is used less by therapists. We would encourage the reader to consider this option more extensively in their practising and clinical work. The use of the voice to link the client with the present and to promote the actuality of the experience through words is a valid technique. Using the voice, however, as an extramusical line to enhance the overall aesthetic experience for the client is equally valid and should be used extensively when using this book. Finally, in order to use the voice in a stylistically authentic way (e.g., blues singing), it would be best to listen to recordings and imitate the singers. The exercises do not address the manner in which you should sing in order to give an authentic rendition of a style, as it is impossible to describe in words the subtleties involved in each style. This aspect is beyond the scope of this book.

Individual and Group Work

Although the exercises in this book have been designed for one or two players, they can be also adapted and applied to groups (i.e., more than two players). Since groups are by nature complex systems, each takes on a character with its own specific needs, rules, and tendencies. For this reason, music therapy groups constantly require adaptation of musical resources. We encourage readers to relate the material presented in this book to the current populations they work with and to think about ways of adapting the book for the needs of their groups. Structured musical arrangements of a particular style can often be a good place to start before leading into freer forms of improvising.

Improvising (without any pre-established framework or play rules) tends to work best for individual work or smaller groups. If the group contains more than four members, it is often practical to set up rules or have clear instructions and ways of managing the communication between group members. A structured improvisation may be more suitable for larger groups. Sometimes it is practical and insightful to separate the group in half (those who improvise and those who listen) and then switch roles. It may also be possible to include turn-taking within a larger form where the entire group plays or improvises in one section and single members or duos are focused on in a contrasting section. The role of the therapist can change when supporting a larger group. Although it is possible to contain a number of clients by providing and guiding the form, often the therapist may take on the role of an observer and one who responds to the overall expression of the group, while in individual work, the therapist can take much more space (both intermusically and interpersonally) in improvisations.

In psychoanalytically informed group work such as Group Analytic Music Therapy (GAMT) (Ahonen, 2006) and Analytic Music Therapy (Priestly, 1994), improvisation is at the core of the process. It is the improvisation that provides the platform for the verbal interaction and interpretation. The use of styles and resources in many ways is less important than the overall process that finds its level as a product of the music emanating from the clients. Generally speaking, the therapist takes a more reflective role, although he or she will intervene when necessary to direct and mold the therapeutic process. In music psychotherapy, the therapist often plays an instrument similar to that of the rest of the group. The music then becomes a part of a greater experience and less dictated by the musical skills and interventions of the therapist.

In a music-centered AeMT framework, group improvisations take a different philosophical/musical focus. The therapist normally plays an instrument that is different than that of the rest of the group (e.g., piano, guitar, cello, or other orchestral instruments). The therapist must listen to every strand and provide links between the individual voices, providing musical logic however chaotic the music becomes. In this context, the move from individual work to group work is the same, yet on a more multidimensional level. Listening and responding to an individual and group in an improvisation is the same phenomenon, yet in the group experience the musical strands becomes more complex. In groups, the therapist must listen with even greater attention to detail.

Therapists who work in groups with different theoretical views will find use in exploring this book as it provides the tools to expand musical horizons. Our intent is to share musical ideas and seeds that are not based on theories but instead offer different experiences of music in the therapeutic setting.

Design of the Book

Each chapter begins with a historical overview of the style. This is followed by a discussion on the possible connections with music therapy. Readers can refer to the bibliography for additional reading material dealing with each style. Specific exercises are included on the accompanying CD that serve as starting point and should be developed further as you become more fluent with the musical component being practised.

The exercises have been designed practically and simply so that each step is clear and explicit. Follow them slowly and take time to reflect on each one. The exercises are designed in two formats: *Solo* and *Duet*. Suggested schedules for each are offered in the next section.

Each exercise states the required skill level:

Beginner (B)
Intermediate (I)
Advanced (A)

Every chapter includes different skill levels. We offer exercises that include all musical abilities, although due to the nature of a specific style, some require more advanced playing than others.

Solo

These exercises should be practised alone and give the building blocks to begin using the style. It is recommended that you explore and master each solo exercise before attempting the duets. Solo exercises are mainly for use with piano/keyboard, although single-line orchestral instruments can also be adapted successfully. For the guitar, some exercises — especially those in Part Two — include chord symbols. Guitar players are urged to arrange as many of the piano/keyboard exercises as they can into chord symbols.

Duet

These exercises have been designed to use communicatively and are the next step before incorporating into sessions. We do not advocate a role-play type of experience when practising duets. This is because at first it is important to concentrate on using only the musical elements communicatively. It is possible, however, to think about specific clients when discussing the experience afterwards. It is also advisable when working in teams to record everything for self-reflection and analysis.

The two roles that we advocate and that are delineated throughout the book are *Accompanist (A)*, which reflects the role of therapist, and *Solo (S)*, which reflects the role of client. These terms have been chosen as they suggest the therapist/client roles, but also can refer to two musicians dialoguing with separate roles of supporting *(A)* and being supported *(S)*. The duet exercises offered are from the authors' experience and should be considered as a beginning.

Create your own duet exercises, developing other duet experiences that will be useful in your work.

It is important that at the end of each duet experience that you reflect with your partner on the experience. *S* Consider both your practical and emotional responses to the music. Did your playing change with the stylistic resource? How did your playing change? Did you play louder, softer, faster, or slower? How did your physical relationship to the instrument change? Did you hold your sticks differently as the music progressed? These are what could be considered empirical considerations about the relationship between the music and the actuality of response. How did the music make you feel? What musical components changed your emotional state? At the end of this analysis, do the same exercises and change roles to compare.

Developing an Effective Practice Schedule

It is important to plan and write into your scheduled times to practise. We are aware of the pressures of working as a music therapist in the education and heath care settings. This means that you may need to set a time either before or after work, depending on the empathy of your employer. As a student, on the other hand, you can incorporate times within a planned timetable at the beginning of each term. Try to balance when you practise alone as opposed to working with a fellow therapist or student that incorporates mainly duet work. We advise at least three 1-hour sessions per week. The following plans, for 1-hour sessions, are offered as suggestions and are not prescriptive. Create your own model that is applicable for your own needs and the environment in which you work. The following are suggested methods for solo and duet work.

Solo Practice

Step One: Technical Skill

Begin with a general warm-up of about 5 to 10 minutes. This can take various guises.

> Select one note and systematically play different scales, arpeggios, and modes in different inversions and registers (see Chapter 12: Building a Music-Centered Library of Resources). Play slowly without pedal, systematically listening to every tone and its relationship.

> Choose one of J. S. Bach's preludes and fugues and play through slowly, listening intently to each musical line. Live in every phrase, playing with as much clarity as you can.

> Choose a raga (see Chapter 9) drone and related scale. Play simple phrases, creating an A phrase (repeat until it is a clear statement) and then a B phrase returning to A. Play with clear form and without emotional content.

These exercises serve to clear your musical mind and ears. As you develop your own practice system, you can add to this list of experiences. The purpose of this time is to be precise and listen to every sound as its own life force and creation. If you play and/or use orchestral instruments or voice, take similar ideas to create exercises that will allow you to systematically create sounds and tones for acute and detached listening.

Step Two: Incorporating Styles

This constitutes the main part of your practising, about 45 minutes, and should fall into two categories. These categories can be thought of individually or combined, dependent on your needs and what you are working toward at the time:

1. Creating styles for your general advancement and musical skill-set.

    Try to focus on one chapter/style for at least 1 week if not more. It is not advisable to jump from style to style. Devote yourself to soaking up one style over an extended period. Each time you practise, take one exercise (e.g., a nuevo tango chord sequence or a passacaglia bass line) and play it many times until you become familiar to the point where it becomes a natural part of your improvising in sessions. Play in different keys and become familiar with the exercise so that it becomes second nature. It is not until you have reached this point that you should move on to another exercise, or style; otherwise, your developing improvisational repertoire will be only superficial and not an integral part of your playing in sessions. Always be creative as your learning becomes ingrained in your new musical landscapes.

2. Creating styles for specific clinical scenarios.

    Choose a clinical scenario from a client you are working with or one whom you have worked with in the past. Think of a therapeutic moment and decide upon a style that may be, or may have been useful. Look to that specific chapter and choose one exercise that you think may be of use. As with the previous section, practise diligently over a period so that you can improvise clearly in your chosen style, imagining as you play how the client responds/responded, thus creating new and innovative responses in that style. Once this is mastered, take your ideas into sessions. In order to illustrate, imagine a scenario where you are working with a young, school-age client with cognitive deficits. This client has a tendency to become absorbed into playing quick, steady hits on a drum without any regard for the therapist's music. The client is unable to develop his music by modulating tempo or varying rhythmic patterns. Perhaps containing the regular beating with lively syncopated or accented music (such as that of the tango) would hold the client's attention. In such a case, it may be useful to refer to exercises involving syncopation and bring them into your session, and note how the client responds.

This part should be focussed and clearly planned. Keep a notebook of the exercises, noting their success/failure and how you should focus for the following session. Record some or all of your improvisations once you feel confident with a style and/or exercise. Listen critically and consider how you would incorporate the style in future sessions.

Step Three: Free Improvisation

Take 5 to 10 minutes at the end of your session to freely improvise. Clear your mind from all of the technical skills on which you have focused and play for yourself. Use this as a self-therapy time to explore your feelings of expectancy if the day is beginning or reflections if the day is coming to an end. Enjoy the freedom of being free from all of the rules that have been imposed. In time, you will find that the skills will naturally appear in your personal improvising. This is a sign that you have fully assimilated what you have been practising.

Duet Practice

Practising with a partner takes on a different focus. This time, the purpose is to develop the ability to use music communicatively. For duets to be most effective, the techniques involved must already have been mastered during individual work, for listening and responding to another's music is difficult. Choose a partner who will be able to meet with you regularly. It is best if you and your partner are both music therapists. If your partner is not a music therapist (e.g., another professional with whom you work), be sure that it is someone who is not afraid to be expressive and honest and is able to discuss his or her experience of the styles and idioms you offer.

Step One: Warm-up

Begin your session (5 to 10 minutes) with simple exercises to increase your listening. Here are a few suggestions:

Mirror your partner by imitating as closely as possible his or her expression on another instrument.

Take turns responding to one another in a musical conversation.

Listen to a recording pertaining to the exercises you are working on and share your thoughts about the aesthetics and potential applications in therapy. (This may also be a great way to initiate one another to new music.)

Step Two: Duet Exercises

As with solo practising, this should constitute the main part of your work (about 45 minutes). Choose two or three duet exercises on which to focus. These could be all exercises with similar techniques (e.g., ostinato), exercises that are all applicable to a specific clinical case, or simply different exercises that are part of a single style. Read the instructions carefully and set the instruments at a comfortable angle and distance, where eye contact can be made easily. Create an improvisation (approximately 2 to 5 minutes) based on a duet exercise and then discuss the experience from both perspectives of *S* and *A*. Use this feedback constructively and repeat the exercise if it is necessary to make changes. If both therapists are practising the same exercise, exchange roles and compare the perspectives. Finally, move to a new exercise and repeat the process.

Step Three: Free Improvisation

At the end of the session, improvise freely together. Similar to playing solo, it is important to take the time to enjoy improvising music with another person. The more you do this, the more comfortable you are likely to be with actual clients when the opportunity arises. Discuss the important moments of your musical interaction and, again, try to relate your experiences to your work with clients. This is a time not only to enjoy making music, but also to become more aware of your musical personality.

Commonly Asked Questions

How do I define my personal long-term and short-term learning aims?

It is good to give yourself long-term and short-term aims in order to stay focused and motivated; otherwise, you may risk exploring ideas only on the surface and never gaining a true mastery of one. Long-term aims should relate to your personal vision of where you see yourself ideally in the future as an improvising music therapist. Your long-term aim, for example, may be to learn to apply the classical style, become more fluent with the blues, or begin incorporating a new world style in your improvising.

In order to achieve this long-term aim, one of your short-term aims could be to focus on one or two elements, such as the Alberti bass, cadences, or raga modes, and to repeat these exercises every time you practise for a period of at least a month. Another short-term aim could be to listen to and learn three pieces in the classical style that would inform you about specific exercises to play as outlined in the main text of this book. Give yourself at least two short-term aims in order to prevent boredom or finding that you are too strict in practising a discipline. With at least two aims, it is possible to work on the preferred one if you get tired of the other.

It is important not only to think practically (what could be applied directly to your sessions) but also to choose aims that inspire you. Perhaps there is a style of music that you enjoy but never took the time to learn to play. Finally, it is important not to be too hard on yourself by choosing short-term aims that are too difficult to achieve. For example, if it is too difficult to play jazz sequences, it may be best to adjust your aim by learning basic triadic sequences or simple I-IV-V-I patterns. It is important to recognise your strengths and weaknesses as well as the amount of time you are able to put aside for this work.

How do I adapt stylistic improvising within my clinical philosophy?

While this book comes from an approach that is music-centered, being able to improvise in sessions with clients is a fundamental truth that is applicable to almost all music therapy approaches and theories. This book does not advocate a particular clinical stance, but rather aims to provide musical tools for therapists to be able improvise and think constructively within a musical-therapeutic framework. How you take the ideas presented and infuse them within your own clinical approach is entirely up to you. Because of this, we have tried to avoid making specific theoretical-clinical links.

How do I know what style is appropriate for my work?

This question is at once the simplest yet the most difficult to answer. The straightforward answer is that the style most appropriate for a client is the one that engages them while facilitating therapeutic intent. Garred (2006) addresses this issue:

> But *some* notion as to what kind of idiom to use in different situations is still a part of therapeutic skill and knowledge, based on experience. It is a matter of the way of using these skills and techniques. And this is the clue, *the way of using them,* creatively, dynamically, *not* prescriptively, mechanically, which will not work, because then the dynamics of the creative application of the idioms will be lost, *and* also the *interpersonal* significance of the music made in therapy. (p. 263)

Is there any way to know if a client is engaged by a style or idiom? Aside from musical response, body language is often an indicator. Some clients verbally indicate a preferred style of music, but often therapists have to make that decision on their own. It is important to fully assess a client's musical tendencies and offer music that will fit with their style. This does not guarantee, however, that it will be successful every time. As Garred points out, it is *how* we use the styles, which depends on the interpersonal and intermusical relationship in the moment, that will make the difference. Just because the Nuevo Tango style, for example, engaged the client in playing passionately in one session does not guarantee that the client will react the same way in future sessions. We must consider whether the use of the style was meant for only that particular moment or whether it could become a theme lasting for a series of sessions.

Often we meet clients who continually relate to a particular style or idiom. Musical styles can be thought of as having "personalities" or "characters" and some may match or reflect a client's characteristics. Ask yourself these questions: Is the client passionate and expressive, or more shy and reserved? Is the client bold or passive, angry or happy? Which musical styles are bold? Which ones are more lyrical? Which styles are capable of both? Why do you think your client responds in the way he or she does to the style you offer?

Finally, it is crucial not to forget the intent of the music in the first place. What are the needs of the client? What are the aims and objectives for this client? Does the style of music lend itself to facilitating the intent? Sometimes a style of music that purposely does not match the client's characteristics is needed to help the client work on less developed parts of him- or herself.

It is important to consider how long to use a specific stylistic framework before moving on to a different one. If a stylistic framework does not appear to engage a client, it may be best to transition to a different one or to recombine elements of several styles in order to fit the client's need in the moment. Sometimes it is simply best to abandon a stylistic framework in order to allow the music to flow more naturally. By listening intently and without bias, the client will give you clues and lead you to music that is necessary for his or her therapeutic growth.

How do I move in and out of stylistic frameworks?

Once you have mastered a repertoire of styles, you must then decide how you will amalgamate them within your improvising and general clinical musicianship. How strictly do you adhere to a style? When do you change a style? Which styles complement another? How do you move from away from a style into freer improvising and then back again? How do you develop styles within the ongoing therapeutic process? All of these questions and many more do not have specific answers or formulas. Knowing when and how to use a style is dependent on experience, musical familiarity, and knowledge of the therapeutic process.

Moving in and out of stylistic frameworks comes with years of experience using explicit resources. It is about successes and failures; about knowing the structure of each style musically and emotionally; about listening to the client, then knowing which style will be best suited for each therapeutic encounter; about being in synchronicity with each style and how it develops into new, uncharted territories of freer improvising; about trusting the musical relationship and your part within the overall process.

As with the previous exercises, try combining similar and opposing styles in your playing (see a detailed discussion in Chapter 12). Create symphonies and tone poems that include combinations of different and opposing styles. Practise developing a style and then merging it with another style to create a balanced form that at the same time is able to move freely into other areas. Experiment with combining different styles that you may at first think would not be similar — for example, a classical slow movement combined with a blues song, or a raga combined with a baroque harmonic progression. You may be surprised at and inspired by how opposing styles can provide a dialogue that is fresh and clinically appropriate.

Moving in and out of stylistic frameworks is about knowledge balanced with intuition and passion for the creative essence of music. Without passion and an understanding of the client's needs, styles will only serve to colour at a surface level. Used with insight and dedication, the right style can move the process into deeper areas that are the hallmark of true music-cenetred practice. Styles only serve the needs of the client and the overall aims if the music therapist is able to change and develop them with precision and creativity.

How do I approach and begin a session?

One of the things we often forget to do is to "check in" with ourselves and become aware of our own feelings. Prior to a session, it is important to take the time to meditate or simply take a few breaths, in order to let go of our own thoughts or distractions. Improvisation requires focus, energy, and creativity, none of which function well when we are distracted. Playing music in the moment could be viewed as a form of meditation. If we as therapists cannot find our balance or our own centre, how can we expect to help clients to do the same? Try to create simple musical exercises that will help you to focus before a session begins. This could include quietly humming or playing open intervals on the piano or long tones on an orchestral instrument.

At the beginning of a session, as a client or group of clients enters the therapeutic space, listen intently to the sounds being created. For instance, the client may be making quiet vocal sounds or tapping an instrument as they enter the room. These musical utterances should be taken seriously and are the beginning of the session. Do they give us any musical hints that could be used as a seed for the musical growth and development of the session? Is there a tonality to the sounds? In AeMT, we believe that the session starts when the first sounds are created and heard, wherever the source. Before the musical dialogue begins, consider whether anything should be said (instructions, verbal discussion) or whether it is best to greet the client directly with music.

Other considerations are to decide how the therapeutic space should be arranged (how the instruments should be placed, where the chairs should be, how the therapist places himself in relation to the clients, what sort of lighting the room should have, etc.). All of these can affect the outcome of sessions. It is not always the music we play but the surrounding factors that determine the results of an experience.

Finally, it is the therapist's level of listening that will make a significant impact on the music. Do not begin playing too soon. Often, from sheer panic, we begin to play from a preconceived standpoint and forget to listen carefully to the client's expression. Take time to let the client play, assess the expressive intent and characteristics of their music, and then respond. Through our experience, it seems that the most powerful clinical improvisations are those when the therapist listens carefully and does not try to impose form too soon.

Improvisation Practice Journal

Keeping a journal is important, as it will help to document and reflect on your practice efforts, reflective practice on such topics as achievements and obstacles and connections and disconnections between the practice room and clinical work. This can reveal how you work with obstacles and inspirations. Satisfying learning experiences in improvisation seem contingent on the transferability from theory to practice. Journaling also allows for personal levels of learning that interweave with the advancement of clinical improvisation skills.

Journaling can effect changes in perception and understanding, thus clarifying improvisational attitude. The journal records how your learning moves you or affects your thinking and feeling. The process might bring a question to a perception or a current attitude. Journals are an old form of writing and typically are appreciated for their authenticity, quality of insight, regularity of entries, and as a source of personal knowledge.

Some questions you may ask are: What is musicianship in the therapeutic contexts? What does the musical self mean to you? How have you worked to develop your own style as an improviser? Is this something that you wish to do? How does your practising directly affect your ongoing sessions?

It is highly recommended that your journal include recordings of sessions and notation of musical ideas. Listening back to recorded improvised music and making notations of your ideas are valuable forms of self-assessment and musical refreshment. The recording of improvisations is essential for an exploration of your musical transparency. Aspects of musical transparency that may be explored include changing beliefs about musical expertise, the importance of staying in touch with feelings, or a commitment to exercising the resources of the musical imagination.

If you include an entry about a concert experience or music that is meaningful to you, take the next step. What aspect of this experience did you practise? How did you do this? What happened? What clinical application might this experience have for your work as a music therapist?

Your journal can include music compositions and parts thereof. The compilation of these "sound resources" is an ongoing process, based on your own musical context and experience. Keep a repertoire of learned pieces to which you can refer. They will refresh your spirit as a performer and inspire further your ideas and musical innovations when improvising for and with clients.

CONCLUSION

We hope that this book will provide ample inspiration for developing creative ideas to help expand on possibilities for clinical improvisation in your work both individually and in groups. We cannot separate ourselves from the therapeutic process; therefore, it is important to be genuine and offer music we feel comfortable playing. It is important that you make your own links to clinical practice throughout the book. Creativity in sessions is only hampered by the therapist's lack of skills. Learning to play in more and varied styles will allow the therapeutic process to find new levels, whatever your clinical orientation. By developing a solid musical voice as a music therapist, our clients will be able to appreciate who we are, and through our consistency and uniformity, they themselves will become more aware of themselves. This is one of the highest aims of therapy.

> Wonderful creative freedom. That is what we must have in therapy — creative freedom — but tailored to the child, suited to the child, challenging the child, stimulating, arousing, supporting. We must have this beautiful creative freedom. And it's nothing that's given. You have to work for it. You won't be able to do more than you are able to do. You won't be able to bring more to the child than you have in your heart, in your mind, in your fingers, in your whole body as *living music* with which to transmit the experiences the child must have. (Robbins & Robbins, 1998, p. 79).

PART TWO

CLASSICAL

CHAPTER 2

Baroque

The baroque era (1600–1750) changed many of the musical conventions established in the Renaissance (1450–1600). Modal inferences were replaced by a tonal system that was more grounded (Benward & Saker, 2003). Because of the shift to more secular possibilities of performing, instrumental music for the first time became more important than vocal music. Improvisation developed both in terms of figured bass accompaniments and singers' embellishments of recitatives and arias. The use of dissonance and resolution was another characteristic that defined the baroque era. In the Renaissance, dissonance was used mainly in passing, whereas in the baroque it became more established and a fundamental part of the harmonic experience, albeit within a strong tonal framework. The invention of the continuo, another defining factor of the style, changed how melody, harmony, and counterpoint where perceived and expressed (Bukofzer, 1975). The use of rhythm was also developed to include more syncopation and off beats, especially in dance music. The essence of the baroque style, then, is clarity of form and design, alongside freedom of expressive elements that provides the freshness always associated with this period.

Baroque music evokes feelings of security, lightness, joy, and excitement, balanced with expressions that can be introverted, poignant, and directly spiritual. It is often devoid of harmonic ambiguity and is clean and direct in expression. Its musical formula, however, never seems to be at the expense of its creativity and originality. In baroque music, there is a sense of predictability balanced with ideas that can also be free from formal design. It is this duality that makes it one of the most engaging and powerful periods in the history of western music.

What is it about baroque music that is so exciting and captivating? We believe it to be a combination of various factors:

Orchestra embedded with the sounds of the continuo, most notably the harpsichord
Grandeur of orchestration
Transparency of chamber music
Counterpoint and the art of musical conversation and voicing
Clarity of compositional design, e.g., overtures, dances, arias, and recitatives
Compact nature of movements
Single movements/pieces that, for the most part, remain in the same key
Florid nature of ornaments and melodic development
Consonant rhythms balanced with overt syncopation
Driving energy of fast movements
Spirituality of slow movements
Setting of words and embellishment of melodic phrases in singing

These elements combine to produce music that is powerful and instantly recognizable.

Baroque music is also a product of the social systems in which it grew. Professional composers were normally employed by the state and/or church. Composers had to write commissions continuously and could not always wait for divine inspiration. The huge output of baroque music therefore reflects this professional approach and stress on composers to produce regularly and for different occasions. The baroque era was also one of flamboyance and extravagance, a time of ornamentation and florid decoration. Balanced with this was a predominance of the church in society and its strong influence on all aspects of life. The division between the secular and sacred was complex and at the core of societal growth. Music was not mere recreation but a part of the fabric of life and was used by all for both amusement and spiritual growth.

BAROQUE MUSIC AND MUSIC THERAPY

Baroque music can be highly effective in music therapy. Because of its emphasis on structure that often led into improvisation (most notably in organ music), it can be an important style for music therapists to understand and link directly to clinical work. It can be used as a core resource for improvisations and also as a basis for writing and designing more structured interventions. If we look at the list of musical characteristics, we can immediately relate them to clinical improvisation. Clarity of form, development of melody, and stability of tonal centre are all aspects of musical structure that are needed in music therapy. The question then becomes, How can we harness and understand baroque music and its potential for use in clinical work? Wigram (2004) provides an audio example of "Twinkle, Twinkle, Little Star" in the baroque style, and Nordoff-Robbins (2007) describe how an improvisation "became Handelian in character" (p. 262). What neither example gives us is the musical elements that constitute the baroque style, and how we can extract and use these elements clinically. To understand how baroque music may be used in music therapy, we must first know and understand the historical background and context. Second, it is crucial to experience, through playing and listening, the emotional makeup and potential responses that baroque music has for us; knowing this will affect how we use and offer this style for our clients. Third, through the distillation of musical components, the therapist can begin to explore slowly and securely the musical science of baroque music in sessions.

Not all forms of baroque music are covered in this chapter, as this would be an impossible task. Some important forms and compositional devices have been omitted: figured bass, fugue, ornaments, dotted rhythms, and recitatives. It is not that we consider these components to be unimportant; indeed, each of these areas could be addressed in separate chapters. Instead, we have chosen those components that are hopefully accessible and will give therapists an essence of the music that can be taken directly into sessions. Once having soaked yourself in the resources offered, we hope that you will also adapt the exercises to consider further aspects of baroque music not covered.

This chapter will focus on one composer: J. S. Bach. The reason for this choice is that in our opinion J. S. Bach's music contains perhaps the purest and most precise view of baroque music. It has not only a sheer beauty of form and design, but also an insightful spiritual focus that makes it a perfect balance between the musical and emotional polarities necessary for therapy. Indeed, it would take a lifetime's work to fully explore and extract the genius of his music for clinical purposes. Finally, what of J. S. Bach as a music therapist? How might he have used his music for direct therapeutic purposes, and indeed, could all of his music, secular and sacred, be classed as music therapy? Perhaps J. S. Bach was a great music therapist as well as a great composer, and one day, after studying his music in great depth and applying it clinically, we will be able call ourselves *Bach Music Therapists*.

EXERCISES

COMPONENTS

HARMONIC PROGRESSIONS

Bach's harmonic progressions have a unique sound that forms the core of his style. They speak directly in finding the essence of his music. The combination of stepwise progressions with the use of diminished chords gives a sense of spiritual clarity that is the hallmark of his music. Bach's harmonic progressions are predictable but never boring and allow a myriad of expressions to be contained within small yet secure boundaries. It is these multilayered possibilities that make his music so valuable for music therapists.

Chaconne. Partita No. 2 in D Minor for Solo Violin (BWV 1004)

This piece has an emotional density and impact that is at once reflective and could be used to great effect with clients when a more introvert experience is needed. Transposed to the major, it is immediately reversed and allows for an expression that contains hope and stability. Busoni's arrangement of this piece for piano provides the opening harmonies that will allow us to explore these inspirational chords.[1]

Solo (B)

> Play the chord progression slowly, lyrically and legato. Create two clear phrases. Try not to use too much pedal. Listen to every chord and its emotional content. Live the experience and note any impressions and/or feelings that come to mind.

Example 2.1

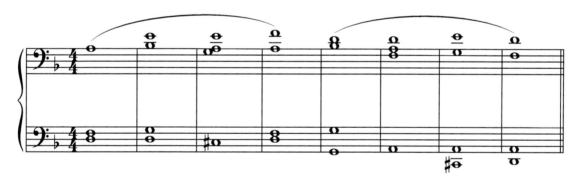

> Play the progression again and play and/or sing a melody over the harmonies. Improvise in and out of tempo. Explore different time signatures and tempi while keeping the slow, lyrical and legato mood.

> Now create a more formalized melody in the right hand, e.g.,

---

[1]Busoni arranged the *Chaconne* in 1893. It is one of the most popular and most played of Bach's arrangements for piano.

Example 2.2

Repeat the melody vocally, then use your voice as a countermelody.

Play the progression in different registers, interweaving melodies with your right hand and voice.

Play the progression in a fast and detached manner in 2/4, 3/4, or 4/4. Experiment using dotted rhythms.

Note the different quality of the chords and the progression as you explore.

Finally, go back over all of the above exercises and play the chords in D major as opposed to D minor. To do this, change the key signature to D major by playing F# instead of F naturals and by playing B naturals instead of Bb. Take careful note of how differently the music is perceived and felt as you play.

Imagine a specific clinical situation where this progression may have been appropriate, e.g., as a possible greeting, good-bye, or more general intervention. Develop with the scenario in mind using the theme as a structural A section. Improvise away from the theme, creating a freer B section that is different in style but that retains an essence of the baroque idiom, returning to complete your formed improvisation. Repeat this exercise, creating a B section that is in opposition to A (i.e., in a jazz or blues style), noting the difference between music that is similar and music that is in opposition.

Duet (B)

Play slowly, freely, and lyrically on a tuned percussion. *A,* listen to the sounds and reflect first with sustained chords based on the form of the *Chaconne*. As the improvisation develops, play the progression more freely, creating themes and melodies. Listen closely to the quality of the music for both players. Replace the B flat with a B natural and then add an F sharp instead of the F natural. Repeat the above, now transposing the progression into D major. Note the difference in musical dialogue.

S, play a steady regular tempo on a drum. **A,** match **S**'s playing with staccato and detached chords. Explore themes using accelerandos, decelerandos, and different textures. Sing words and vocalize. Transpose to the major, then return to the minor, creating an ABA form for your improvisation. Improvise a balance of clearly created melodies as well as freer, less defined musical ideas.

S and **A,** sit together at the piano. **S,** listen to the chord progression as **A** plays. **A,** vocalize, trying to entice **S** to sing with you. Ask **S** to sing when only they feel invited by the music. Create free melodies as well as clearly defined ones with your voice. Try singing words such as a "greeting" or "good-bye" or reflect your partner with simple words that you are feeling. Use the minor progression as an A section, then transpose into the major and use as a B section returning to the minor to conclude your improvisation.

SUSPENSIONS

Suspensions are a hallmark of baroque music. Suspensions in harmonic sequences are used as a means to push forward the direction as well as add a sense of uncertainty and distinct colour. Corelli's use of continued suspensions is so strong that you can almost physically taste them.[2] The sense of musical "bite" that suspensions create can be useful in therapy. Suspensions can be used to push forward the direction of music and add an emotional/tense quality that can cut through when a session becomes dull, lifeless, and without direction. Suspensions are normally followed by a harmonic/melodic release. Tension and release can be crucial in the developing therapeutic relationship. Suspensions can be used clinically to create ambivalence, ambiguity, and a sense of tension. It is how the therapist creates tension and its release that determines the intricate nature of this powerful musical device

Solo (I)

Practise the following principles to create suspensions.

For a typical Sus4–3 suspension, play the melody note a 4th (or compound 4th) above the bass note and resolve it to either the major or minor 3rd, depending on which chord you wish to resolve to.

Example 2.3

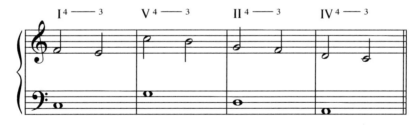

---

[2] Corelli's (1653–1713) use of suspensions and dissonance are a hallmark of his style. The composer Walter Piston calls his use of dissonance the "Corelli Clash." Listen to the Concerti Grossi No. 8 in G Minor, (Op. 8), commonly known as the "Christmas Concerto," to hear how he incorporates suspensions and dissonance as part of his compositional design.

Suspensions are often used to evoke a "sighing" gesture; they are usually prepared by repeating the note from the previous chord on the strong beat of the following.

Example 2.4

In this case, the 4–3 suspensions have been harmonized in 3rds. They can just as easily be harmonized in 6ths.[3]

Example 2.5

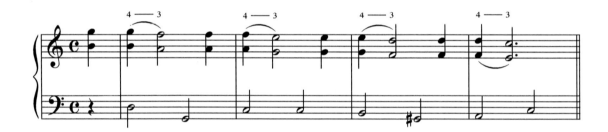

Continue to explore the possibilities of suspensions following the above guidelines. As you become more confident, use your voice to add melodies and phrases in your improvisations that come directly from the nature and sound of the suspensions.

Sarabande. English Suite No. 6 in D Minor (BWV 811)

Solo (I)

Play slowly the harmonic outline of the opening bars, noting their reflective and improvisatory spirit. No clear tempo has been provided. It is suggested that the player experience the suspensions out of tempo or choose a simple 3/4 or 4/4 tempo to begin.

---

[3]Bach's prelude in F minor from *Well-Tempered Clavier Book 2* (BWV 881) is an excellent example demonstrating the use of harmonized suspensions.

Example 2.6

Follow carefully the suspensions, making sure that you hold over the notes indicated by phrase marks and the notes that move, indicted by brackets.

Rest on the pauses, live in the sounds of the dissonances, hold onto them, and then feel the relief when the suspension is resolved.

Play repeated times. Get to know and feel the tension and resolution concretely and then improvise away from the score. Play until you know it from memory. Begin creating improvisations based on the extract.

Duet (I)

 S, play freely and quietly on either wind chimes or a small cymbal. **A,** listen to the quality of playing and respond with suspensions from the above exercise. Rest on the pauses and highlight the quality of tension before you release. For the purposes of this exercise, it is important to exaggerate the time spent on the suspension and dissonance. Only allow the music to be released with a resolution when you feel that the dissonance can be held no longer.

MELODIC DEVELOPMENT

Improvising and developing melodies in music therapy is a difficult technique that requires practice. It is important to be able to improvise and repeat melodic motifs, patterns, and phrases that can be repeated and used to add form. To be able to improvise a simple melodic theme A, repeat it, then add a contrasting B phrase, repeat that, then return to A. This is a technique that should be mastered carefully. After this skill has been acquired, the therapist should look to learning how to extend melodies into longer, more complex phrases. This will allow for the therapeutic/musical direction to be extended as an improvisation develops. Bach's use of melody is masterful and its analysis can aid a therapist in learning how to construct melodic extensions. His melodies often contain a continuous similar rhythmic direction, although if played with a sense of phrasing and rubato, they can feel open and improvised in content. When exploring the following exercises, sing the melody first, then play and sing together with the keyboard.

Jesu, Joy of Man's Desiring. Chorale from Cantata *Her und Mund und Tat und Leben* (BWV 147)

Solo (B)

Play and sing slowly without accompaniment the opening melody. Experience the rise and fall of the melody and the continuous movement until the end of the section. Note how a seemingly simple melodic idea based on steps and small movements can be effective and create a calm and stable ambience.

Example 2.7

Note how the melody is composed of shorter phrases balanced with longer ones. Even though the melody is continuous, there is a sense of arch and shape. The brackets denote both the smaller and longer phrase of the melody.

Consider Bach's use of stepwise intervals as opposed to leaps and phrases built around triads.

Examine how Bach pushes the melody forward with ascending phrases that reach a peak and then descend.

Play and sing the melody A again, with the simple accompaniment leading to an improvisation. Create a contrasting melody B and then return to A.

Example 2.8

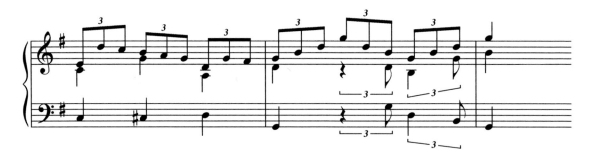

Duet (B)

S, improvise a simple, slow melody on tuned percussion in G major. *A,* listen to the melody and accompany *S*'s playing, using the melody with the simple harmony provided. Match and extend the melody of *S.*

Continue the improvisation, bringing in your voice to add another melodic line.

Consider developing this exercise to include words: a greeting or good-bye song or possibly a song with a nonmusical or musical theme that you might use for children. Write down your ideas and develop them into more structured interventions.

Andante. *Italian Concerto for Keyboard* (BWV 971)

Solo (I)

Play first the melody, considering Bach's use of contrast and melodic extension.

Analyze how the melody is balanced between shorter and longer phrases and how the longer phrases serve to keep the momentum of the melody.

Note the use of longer single tones that are followed by faster, more decorated ones.

Play the melody A again, now with the accompaniment, this time continuing to an improvisation. Create a contrasting melody B and then return to A.

Develop this piece further into a songlike intervention, e.g., a greeting, good-bye, or other clinically appropriate song. Use this simple line in contrast to the more complex lines of Bach's melody. Keep your vocal line as simple as possible.

Example 2.9

Duet (1)

> *A,* use the melodic exercise from above and try to encourage *S* to vocally dialogue with you, either using words or vocalize. Let the intensity of the music grow as you create an improvisation of four voices, two from Bach and two from *A* and *S*. Improvise away from and back to the music.

Create and write down further melodic ideas from J. S. Bach and other composers from the baroque era. Develop a catalogue of baroque melodic inventions and extensions that can be taken into clinical work.

TONIC PEDAL

There are many examples of the use of tonic pedal in J. S. Bach's music. It seems that in almost all of his compositions there is some reference to this technique. Some of the greatest sources to study are the preludes from the 48 Preludes and Fugues (BWV 846–893). Many of these preludes contain examples that can be distilled and used directly in sessions as harmonic progressions for a myriad of different interventions and experiences. The tonic pedal as a compositional technique can be used for:

> Harmonic grounding and stability
> Clarity for the direction and development of ideas
> Base for chromatic harmonies that move away from the tonic, but which still keep a sense of the home key
> Time to rest and give the listener a sense of stability before the music moves forward

Similarly, the tonic pedal and pedal point as a clinical technique can be used for:

> Providing emotional/musical security
> Allowing the therapist to improvise within the bounds of a tonic pedal structure; to pause within the ongoing openness of an improvisation
> Providing music for the client that will allow him or her to know and experience the fundamental tone of the music

Prelude. *Cello Suite No. 1* (BWV 1007)

Solo (1)

> Play the harmonic distillation of the opening section. Measures 29–38 have been simplified from the original to provide clarity from which to improvise.

Example 2.10

Consider how the chords move away from the tonic, providing rich 2nd and 7th intervals. At the 6th measure experience, note how the harmonies move away from the G tonic pedal, returning at measure 16 to conclude this section.

Duet (I)

CD1 **S,** play a tuned percussion instrument to G major, playing simply in steplike fashion. **A,** 2 play the above chord progression as written with rubato and no fixed meter, listening to the connection between instruments.

Play the progression again, this time providing the chord as a simple accompaniment for an instrumental melody and/or vocalize.

Example 2.11

Take the G pedal point and write down a series of chords over G major. Create an improvisation, exploring different textures, melodies, rhythms, and phrases. Play legato and staccato, fast and slow. Explore all aspects of playing and be as free and creative as you can over the G tonic pedal. End your section by resolving onto the dominant and then return to G to continue the improvisation. Try creating songs and vocalize as well as instrumental improvisations with other melodic instruments and keyboard.

Example 2.12

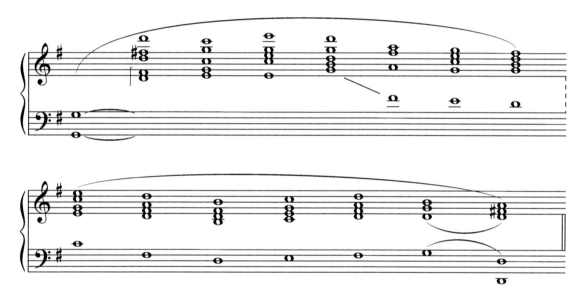

Sarabande. Suite No. 3, The Six English Suites (BWV 807)

Solo (I)

Try improvising in a similar way but now in G minor.

Example 2.13

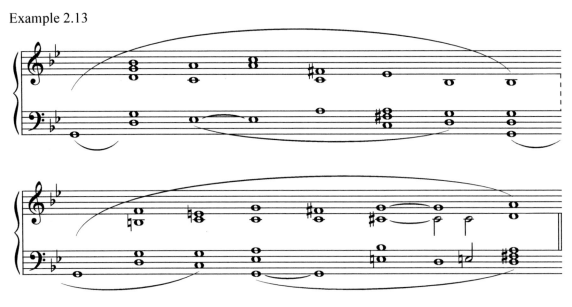

Duet (I)

Arrange the notes on a tuned percussion instrument (xylophone or metalophone) in either G major or G minor. *S,* play freely. *A,* respond, creating an improvisation based on the tonic pedal. Use the pedal as an A section, then improvise a B section in a contrasting style but in the same key. Remember to make your B section distinctly different in style. Return to A, using the tonic pedal to conclude.

Use the G major tonic pedal progression as an A theme for a nontuned percussion intervention such as drum or bongos. Use the tonic pedal to provide rhythmic stability and energy. Create an easily definable melody and add words with your voice to produce a song. Improvise a B section in the minor as a contrast, returning to the more structured A section to complete. Try this the opposite way around, minor–major–minor.

Use the G minor tonic pedal progression as the basis for a song with or without words for section A. Experience the harmonies in relation to the tonic pedal and sing lines that reflect the emotional environment of the music. Now improvise from the G major tonic pedal progression as a distinct contrasting section B, then return to the minor, A. Try this the opposite way around, major–minor–major.

DIMINISHED CHORDS

The use of the diminished chord is a trademark in much of Bach's music and baroque music in general. It gives an emotional quality that is used to great effect, especially in his sacred music. The diminished chord is used to heighten the drama in the story of the Passions and allows the listener to feel music that is austere and emotionally tense. Diminished chords in Bach's music constantly remind us of the power of music to propel and bring tension. As with suspensions, the diminished chord can be held and played for long periods, thus making a final release to more consonant harmonies like a kind of "blessed release." The use of tension inherent in diminished chords is therefore very appropriate for clinical improvisation. A diminished chord can accurately portray the uncertainties and insecurities of the client. It can reflect that sense of instability, and not knowing this is often a part of the therapeutic process. Careful use of diminished chords can reflect the tension of therapy. It is important, however, that the therapist consider equally how the diminished chord is then resolved. It is this balance between tension and release that is at the heart of music therapy.

Prelude. Six English Suites (BWV 811)

Solo (I)

> Play the following harmonic distillation. Listen and explore both the diminished chords and the tonic pedal that adds to the intense character of the music.

Example 2.14

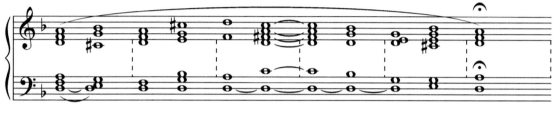

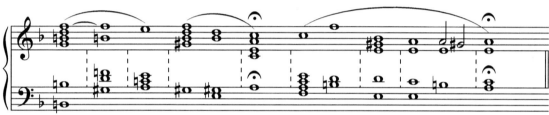

> Improvise freely with the chord progression, creating themes and melodies. Consider clinical situations where this music might be appropriate. Use your voice and improvise with other melodic instruments, creating music focused around the diminished chords. Play in different time signatures and different timbres and experiment in different tempi, staccato and legato.

> Improvise the chord progression as an A theme, then improvise in the dominant major (A major) as a B theme, then return to A.

Duet (I)

> Tuned percussion: D, E, G, A.

> *S*, play the tones slowly and freely. *A,* use the chord progression to colour the tones and develop a clear theme for *S.*

> Take the tones of the above as hand chimes or tone bars. Create a more structured piece, potentially incorporating words. Balance between your composed song A and a second, more free section B, in the relative major, returning to the song A to conclude.

> Experiment using the chord progression for a faster, more detached improvisation. *S,* play a drum. *A,* focus on the diminished chords as the main colour for the improvisation. Experiment using dotted rhythms.

WALKING BASS

Walking bass is a technique used to provide forward steadiness of musical direction. The walking bass provides a calm yet constant sense of movement. It normally contains octave or arpeggio leaps balanced with stepwise motion. For music therapy, this technique can be extremely useful. Cellists, lower string players, and guitarists can utilize this resource to great effect. The walking bass is used not only in baroque music but in many popular styles of today such as country, blues, and jazz. Regardless of the style, walking bass lines provide rhythmic and harmonic stability over which the soloist (or client) is able improvise with autonomy. It therefore functions as a grounding mechanism and emotional container for free expression

Air, on a G String. Orchestral Suite No. 3 in D Major (BWV 1068)

Solo (B–I)

> Play the bass line, listening to the octave leaps and stepwise movements and how the music gently but steadily moves forward.

Example 2.15

> Repeat with the added accompaniment, considering the relationship between the chords and walking bass line.

Now add a vocalize melody with your voice.

Example 2.16

Improvise in the style of a more free-flowing melody based from the original movement. Interweave a more intricate melodic improvised melody in balance with the bass line.

Example 2.17

Continue this example as an A theme moving into a freer section B, and then return to the opening A theme. Consider clinical situations when a walking bass such as this may be appropriate.

Duet (I)

S, play a drum (preferably with one stick) improvising a simple, steady beat. *A,* match the playing with a walking bass line, balanced with a freer, more improvised melody as shown in musical example 2.17. Make note of this duality of expression. Continue the improvisation, creating accelerandos, decelerandos, and different dynamic changes. Begin developing a musical/emotional relationship through the music. *A,* become both familiar and free with the material, always keeping a clear focus in intent and direction.

S, play a single tone chime. *A,* imagine that *S* is a client who needs structure and form. Take the above example and create a song incorporating the child's name, with a pause at the end of each phrase for the child to answer A. After the three lines of the song are known, improvise a contrasting B section. Return and repeat the chorus to conclude. Try creating your own songs in a similar style.

Example 2.18

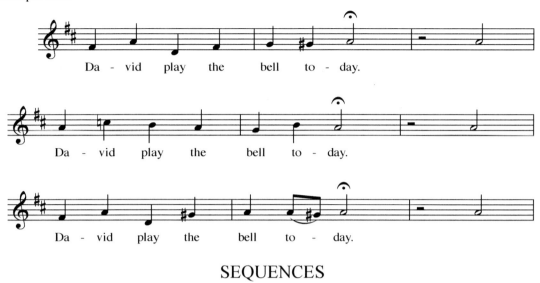

Da - vid play the bell to - day.

Da - vid play the bell to - day.

Da - vid play the bell to - day.

SEQUENCES

A sequence is a series of chords and/or melodic patterns that are repeated in a stepwise motion either ascending or descending. Sequences can also take the music to a new key (Kostka & Payne, 2004). In baroque music, the sequence is a standard compositional device that is used either for a complete composition or as a section to add clarity. Sequences are useful for therapists as they provide clear harmonic content that can be stabilizing. Bach's sequences also can be melodically florid and are one of the main devices that provide a real sense of the baroque style. Sequences can be used to create form and structure. They can be used and then departed from; they can be incorporated as a musical colour or as a more integral part of an improvisation. Once you have mastered the basic technique, you can also add ornamentation and melodic suspensions. As with other sections of this book, build a library of sequences in different keys and styles, noting the different emotional impact of each on the way you play and your own responses to them. Remember that the key and style in which you improvise sequences is as important as the sequence itself. All sequences should be notated for future practice and adapted for structured songs and interventions. It is important to note that sequences can be used either in passing to add colour or as a core that can dictate a complete improvisation.

Adagio. *Keyboard Toccata* in G Major (BWV 916)

Solo (I)

Play the following harmonic sequence.

Example 2.19

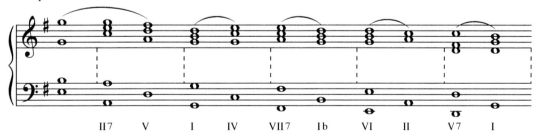

II7   V   I   IV   VII7   Ib   VI   II   V7   I

Play the same sequence but this time with the two-part melody.

Example 2.20

Play again, this time using your voice to add a melodic sequential experience.

Play again, this time creating your own melodic sequence with your right hand on the piano. Once comfortable, add you voice, thus creating a richer musical experience.

Play the harmonic sequence in G minor.

Example 2.21

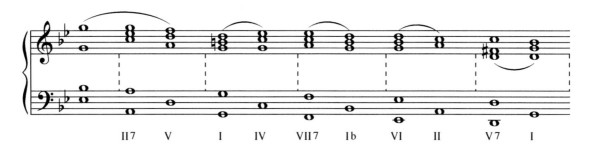

Repeat the above exercises in G minor.

Repeat all of the above exercises, but this time ascending.

Practise both of these groupings in different keys.

Play in different tempi and styles.

Combine all of the above to create an improvisation based on sequences.

Now try embellishing the right hand with baroque configurations that will give the essence of a trio sonata.

Duet (I)

S, improvise on a tuned percussion instrument tuned to G major (one stick) or with one hand on piano, creating a simple melody. *A,* play the sequence (Example 14) in the bass of the keyboard with the simple harmonization as already practised. Relate your playing to *S,* creating a series of sequences that will provide form and direction to the music. If appropriate include your voice. Try the same exercise in G minor. When you have become more confident, introduce more embellished voice parts in the treble.

S, play a drum or other percussion instrument. *A,* improvise an energetic and detached piece based on the above G minor sequence. Create a strong and rhythmic response. Experiment with introducing a more structured intervention (e.g., drum song), possibly incorporating words.

Explore other such sequences in different styles and keys, looking to examples from J. S. Bach and his contemporaries. Let sequences become a natural extension of your improvising so that they instinctively become a part of your resources.

COUNTERPOINT

Fundamental to baroque music is counterpoint. J. S. Bach's music is based on the essential elements of counterpoint, and it is counterpoint that creates some of his most sublime and spiritual compositions (Lee, 2003). To gain a clear understanding of how counterpoint structurally affects his music, you have only to look to his church music: *St. Matthew* and *St. John Passions, Mass in B Minor, Christmas Oratorio,* and the *Cantatas.* Contained in this music are some of the greatest examples of counterpoint ever written. Study this music with scores. Look and marvel at how Bach interweaves voices as dialogue and communication. Notate and build a volume of counterpoint devices for use in therapy. Use these counterpoint seeds as a regular basis for your practising. There is much for music therapists to learn from Bach's use of counterpoint. Listen to the communication between two violins in the trio sonata genre of Bach and his contemporaries Corelli and Handel, studying how this might be if each voice were client and therapist. Imagine the voices as a conversation between two people and consider this dynamic in terms of the music therapy relationship. The following extracts serve only to touch the surface of this most profound compositional device.

Two-part Invention No. 8, in F Major (BMV 779)

Solo (I–A)

Play this piece as accurately as you can. Play slowly and without pedal.

Example 2.22

Note how Bach balances his thematic, melodic, and rhythmic ideas between voices. Play slowly and listen carefully to each part. Think about when this music may be appropriate clinically and how you might bring an essence of two-part/counterpoint writing into your work with clients.

Play the harmonic outline sketch of the complete movement freely and in a similar style.

Example 2.23

Duet (I–A)

> **S,** play a single line melody on either keyboard with one hand or on a single-line melodic instrument tuned to F major. **A,** listen to the melodic line of **S** and develop a single-line counterpoint response based on the two-part invention (Example 2.23). Listen to how **S**'s melodic line is structured and respond with counter themes. If the melody ascends, answer with a phrase that descends. Play long notes if **S** plays faster. Balance the music, forming a clear relationship between the two lines of music.

Baroque counterpoint is based on the consonant intervals of 3rds and 6ths (or 10ths). While examining the above invention, note the intervals between the two voices on the strong beats (or strong parts of the beat). Note the use of parallel 6ths in measure 5.

Solo (B–I)

> Practise the following warm-up exercise in the key of C based on parallel 3rds (10ths).

Example 2.24

> Improvise a simple melody, including step motion and leaps using parallel 3rds.

Example 2.25

> Practise moving up and down the keyboard in parallel 6ths.

Example 2.26

Improvise a melody based on parallel 6ths, as in the following example:

Example 2.27

Once comfortable using parallel 3rds and 6ths (or compound 3rds and 6ths), improvise a melody using a combination of both.

Example 2.28

Occasional octaves and 5ths are also common intervals, as they are consonant triad notes. They can be used along with parallel 3rds and 6ths, forming endless possibilities for counterpoint.

Once you have gained a sufficient mastery of these exercises in the key of C, repeat the process in other keys, starting with F major and G major.

Improvise a two-part counterpoint piece using a rhythmic motif such as the following suggestions:

Example 2.29

Base yourself on a simple but logical harmonic scheme using the chords of I, IV (or II), and V in the key of C major.

Create your own counterpoint ideas in different keys and repeat the above exercise. Refer back to sequences earlier in this chapter as your harmonic foundations.

Duet (I–A)

> Create a three-part counterpoint. *A,* improvise two voices on the keyboard in response to single line of *S,* thus forming a trio sonata.
>
> Create a two-part invention. *A,* use your voice as vocalize with *S* on a melodic instrument.
>
> *S,* use your voice alone, asking *A* to respond vocally, thus creating an a cappella vocal counterpoint improvisation.

Think of other combinations of melodic lines that will create more counterpoint exercises and resources. Always think melodically and thematically about each individual line and its relationship to the other. Improvise slowly and analytically, being aware of every note and phrase you play.

FORM

PASSACAGLIA

A passacaglia is a repeated bass line, similar to a walking bass, with harmonic and melodic variations above. The harmonic realization and time signature of a passacaglia normally remains constant, although it is possible to add colours that will define each variation as its own emotional force (Overduin, 1998). The stability of the passacaglia is ideal for music therapy as it provides a consistency of musical ideas alongside the creative freedom to decorate and embellish. This duality can be powerful for the developing improvisational dialogue. A passacaglia can be created in two ways: first, as a prethought idea brought to a session through the therapist's development musical resources, and second, as a bass line created in the moment from either the client's improvising and/or as a product of the musical relationship.

Passacaglia and Fugue in C Minor, for Organ (BWV 582)

Listen to this complete piece from a recording. Marvel at Bach's inventiveness, use of syncopations, melodic decoration, and emotional, driving intensity. Consider how he turns a simple bass line into expressions of grandeur and genius. Think of the possible therapeutic outcome if we could offer our clients the experience of being part of such musical energy and inventiveness. This music is a colossal improvisation based on a simple ground bass.

Solo (B–I)

> Play the ground bass line from this passacaglia. Experience and live in the intervals and tones and the overall architecture of the phrase as it rises and descends, using predictable and unpredictable intervals.

Example 2.30

Create a simple harmonization.

Example 2.31

Create different variations on the ground bass and explore them freely.

Example 2.32 — Variations 1–5

Variation III

Variation IV

Variation V

Experiment with playing this ground bass in different time signatures (4/4, 6/8, etc.), modulating to the relative major, C. Repeat all of the above in different major keys, and then try creating your own variations above the passacaglia.

Duet (B–I)

CD/3 **S,** improvise on nontuned instruments (e.g., drum/cymbal). **A,** use the variations above, building a clear musical dialogue. Return to the opening harmonization at the end of the improvisation. The structure thus becomes A, ground bass with simple harmonization, B six (or more) variations, returning to A to conclude.

Use the ground bass as the foundation for creating a song with words or as vocalize. Explore the variations as a means to add colour and emotional intensity to your singing.

THEME AND VARIATIONS

Variation form can be seen as an extension of the passacaglia. The player is able to embellish and improvise more open-ended ideas while keeping a clear sense of the theme as the musical core. Variations can be as creative as the improviser's ability to be musically open. Transposing to the relative major/minor, changing time signatures and/or tempi, inverting melodies, and decorating are just a few of the ways in which variations can add colour to the musical dialogue. Variation form can add a distinct flavor to the client/therapist relationship, as it allows a sense of freedom and exploration while keeping the bounds of the theme.

Goldberg Variations (BWV 988)

This is perhaps the most famous set of variations written during the baroque era. The aria (theme) and 29 variations are a pinnacle of musical inventiveness and creative genius. The reader is urged to listen this piece both artistically and clinically as possible influences for sessions. Make time to experience the grandeur and compositional architecture of the music. Take note of your emotional and artistic responses. Follow the music with the score — experiencing Bach's use of colour and the genius of his musical thought. Let this piece inspire you at every level.

Solo (I)

Play the skeleton theme of Bach's aria (theme). Notice the way in which the melody is constructed and the simple yet effective construction as the theme develops.

Example 2.33

Improvise variations, writing down motives as you explore the possibilities of developing the theme.

Some suggestions are as follows:

Embellish the melody
Use trills and ornaments
Change the harmony, adding inversions, 7ths, and other rich chords
Transpose to the relative minor
Transpose the melody to the bass, left hand
Change the time signature
Change the tempo

Enjoy exploring the music and look to making richer possibilities from the original theme. After improvising variations, always return to the theme proper to conclude.

Duet (I)

S, improvise freely single-line phrases with either one hand (keyboard) or one stick (tuned percussion) in G major. *A,* play the theme clearly, adapting your playing to *S*'s phrases. Play one or more variations of the theme. Make the style of your variations clear and distinct. Improvise in different styles as listed above. Return to the main theme once you have concluded your exploration of variations.

S, play simple phrases in a regular beat in 3/4 on nontuned percussion (e.g., drum and cymbal). *A,* play in a detached style, creating a strong and defined structure and using words, if appropriate, to create a drum song.

Example 2.34

Untuned

Balance this interpretation of the theme with different variations, e.g., slow and legato, fast and staccato. Return to the main theme once you have concluded your exploration of variations.

A, play the chords of the theme as an accompaniment and create a vocal melody.

Example 2.35

A, think of words that could be developed into a clinical song/intervention (greeting song, drum song). Use the song as the main theme and improvise variations without words as a clear contrast, incorporating possible clinical/musical aims such as rhythmic patterns or question and answer. Return to the main theme (song) once you have concluded your exploration of variations.

TOCCATA

The toccata is a wonderful style for music therapists. Its repeated patterns can provide a forward motion necessary to add energy to an improvisation. As a specific clinical tool, it can add brilliance and aesthetic affirmation at heightened moments in the musical dialogue.

Toccata and Fugue in D Minor for Organ (BWV 538)

Listening to the vast expanse of energy in this piece, we are reminded of the emotional heights that music is able to attain. One wonders how a client might respond to being a part of such an elevated musical experience and how possible it may be to capture the essence of this piece for therapeutic purposes.

Solo (A)

Play the following arrangement of the opening bars of the toccata. Try to capture the musical intensity and brilliance of its style.

Example 2.36

Take this section and try to continue in the same vein as an improvisation, keeping the following harmonic basis as your guide. Once this is mastered, try exploring similarly in the relative major (D).

Example 2.37

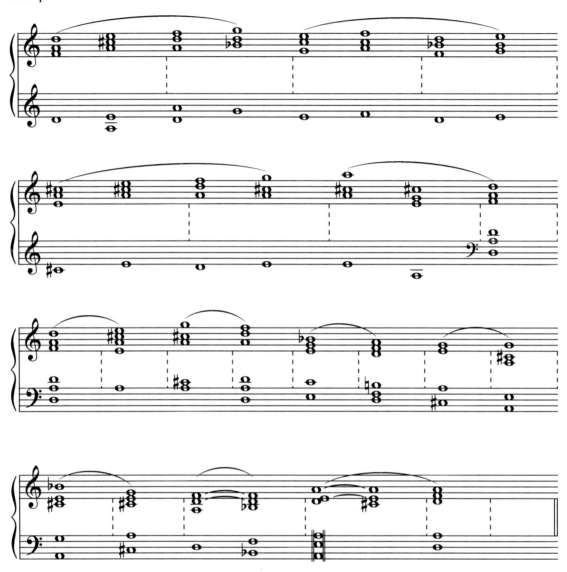

This is a hard exercise. Begin by playing the music slowly and then become faster by degrees. Once you have mastered this example, continue your playing into an improvisation. It is important to be able to play this music solidly and in strict tempo before playing faster. Practise until you can play the music evenly and smoothly.

Duet (A)

CD1 (4)   **S,** play a conga with a regular and steady beat. **A,** use the toccata configuration to meet and develop a lively and rigorous improvisation. Incorporate accelerandos and decelerandos, driving the energy of the improvisation forward using your voice to support if appropriate. Try to offer the experience of energy and vitality. Balance this style of playing with quieter, more reflective, sections, though still using toccata-like configurations. Experiment and make note of the difference when improvising in a major as opposed to a minor key.

Listen to and play as many examples, as you can of toccatas from the baroque era. Once you have mastered toccata sequences in specific keys, try more complex sequences and adapt them for future improvisations. Infuse the progressions with energy and be specific about the configurations you learn. Always start slowly, and never play faster until your mastery of this style is secure. Your toccata improvisations should be crisp, detached, and rhythmically secure. Some wonderful examples come from Bach's collection of the seven toccatas for keyboard (BWV 910–916). These pieces all contain toccata-like preludes as well as beautiful slow sections and masterful fugues. These toccatas are free-flowing and improvisational in structure and character. Careful examination of these pieces can be very fruitful in providing music that is clear in compositional design. Study and practise how Bach writes melodic and contrapuntal lines to produce music that is strong yet delicate and balanced. The energy in Bach's toccatas is infectious and can be harnessed for clinical work to provide music that is directed yet open and therapeutically clear.

CHORALE

Chorales form the foundation of Bach's sacred compositions. Perhaps the strongest use of chorales is when he uses them for dramatic effect in the passions. Here they allow the listener to reflect on the story being told, a time to be still. They also act as a kind of container to which the listener instinctively knows he will always return. Even though in the following explorations we will not use Bach's original words, they were crucial for the musical/spiritual content. This music can have clear links for music therapy. Playing and improvising chorales can provide a resting place in the therapeutic process. If played with a quiet intent, they can call a client into a space that is open and reflective.

The harmonizations and voice leadings in the chorales contain some of Bach's greatest genius. There is stability yet uncertainty, so that you are never quite sure where the harmonies might lead. This provides us with an expression that, it could be argued, is ultimately linked to the human condition. As music therapists, we try to provide music that reflects the emotional state of the client. To provide expressions that will allow a greater sense of the world and allow this nonverbal expression is crucial to the process of music in therapy. Bach's chorales are a gift to us in this regard. If used carefully and with clinical-emotional intent, they can provide an opening necessary for the deepening of the therapeutic relationship.

Bach chorales can also be used for therapists to clear their thoughts before a session begins. Taking time to play slowly and carefully a Bach chorale before sessions, living in every note, phrase, and harmonic turn, can act as a kind of cleanser so that the therapist can be more open to clients and the potential of the therapeutic relationship.

Motet No. 3, *Jesu, Meine Fruede* (BWV 227)

Solo (I)

Play carefully the harmonic outline. Repeat, listening intently to how each chord follows the next, and experience the inner quality of the music. Make special note of the cadences at the end of each phrase.

Example 2.38

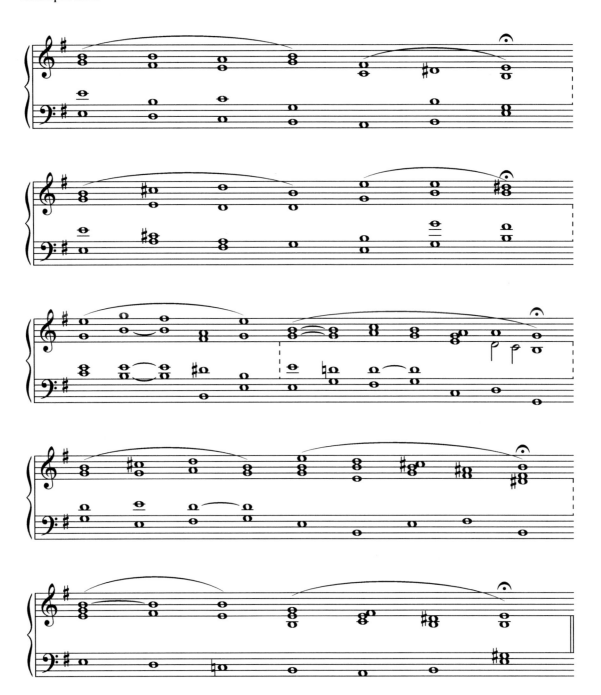

Play again and sing freely over the harmonies. Sing as vocalize, considering words that might be appropriate for sessions.

Duet (I)

CD*1*
(5) *S,* sing single tones freely and quietly. *A,* gently introduce the chorale harmonies. Listen and interweave the music to support and enhance the musical experience.

Use the chorale harmonization as the basis for a "greeting" or "good-bye" song. At first, use one phrase to create a simple melody; then repeat it to create the first phrase of a more formalized song. Create a second phrase to balance the first, and find a second melody that is in contrast to the first. Use more of the sequence, developing it into an improvisation, then return to the first two phrases, recapitulating the original song. Write down the song melody for use in future sessions.

DANCE

Dance was integral to secular music in the baroque era. Dance was used in operas as a means to pause the actions in the ensuing drama. It was used in all forms of secular music and often heralded a lighter, more graceful section, a kind of relief from the main thrust of the composition. Some dances had specific meters, e.g., minuet, 3/4; gigue, 6/8, 9/8, 12/8; gavotte and bourrée, 4/4. Others were developed from their tempo, e.g., sarabande, slow. The main musical construction of the dance, therefore, was the tempo combined with a carefully constructed simple melody that could be easily remembered, with simple yet effective harmonies. Dance was used as the core for J. S. Bach's suites, which contained masterful musical miniatures of the highest order. Dance in music therapy is often something that occurs organically in the therapeutic process. Certain styles of music can elicit the client to begin moving, potentially developing into "free" or structured dance. The therapist should be able to accompany and develop any body movements a client initiates. Dance can develop either from the energy of the music or as an emotional response to the therapeutic process. Incorporating dance, then, in therapy should be treated with caution but also as a product of energy and joy.

There is not the space in this chapter to provide detailed examples of how you can bring all types of dance forms into sessions. For the purposes of practising and bringing in the specific techniques of dance, you should take a harmonic sequence as explored earlier in this chapter and then improvise different dance styles in different meters and tempi. Initially, check back to Bach's original dances to make sure that you are being stylistically accurate. Once you have mastered this, begin moving away so that you can incorporate baroque dance form in your improvisational palette freely and spontaneously. We urge you to listen to and play Bach's dances, specifically the *English Suites* (BWV 806–811), *French Suites* (BWV 812–817), *Cello Suites* (BWV 1007–1012), and *Sonatas and Partitas for Solo Violin* (BWV 1001–1006). These small pieces contain a transparency that could easily be transported into clinical practice. Analyze the delicacy of their composition and make note of how their emotional impact affects your direction and playing. Play with a delicacy of touch and on orchestral instruments practise and develop the use of ornamentation around the basic simplicity of a clear melody.

Bourrée. *Cello Suite No. 3 in C Major* (BWV 1009)

Solo (I–A)

Play the following arrangement of the opening bars:

Example 2.39

Play the extended harmonic distillation and create your own bourrée based on the harmonies provided. Create simple melodies and phrases that you can easily repeat.

Example 2.40

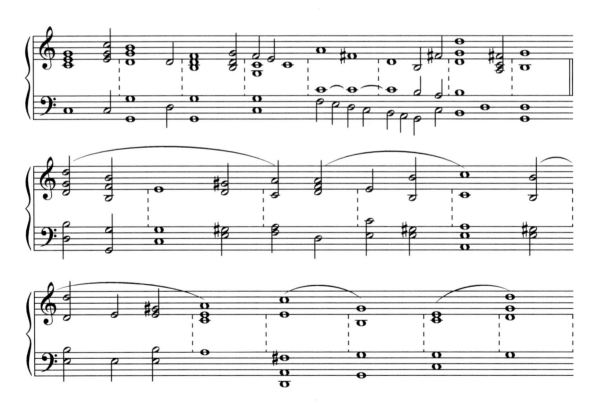

Take other harmonic progressions and create different dances in different tempi and styles. Always keep a detached sense of propriety in your playing that will create a sense of 18th-century movement and dance.

As a guide. try basing your improvisation on one of the two following forms based on Sarnecki (2002; pp. 196–200):

1. Ternary Form: ABA

Section A begins in the tonic and ends with a perfect (V–I) cadence in the tonic key.

Section B explores contrasting material and is usually in a closely related key, such as the relative minor. It may cadence in a new key or in the tonic key.

The final section A repeats the original section A, but may contain variation.

Sections may be repeated.

2. Binary Form: AB

Section A starts in the tonic key and may end with a perfect cadence in the dominant key (e.g., if the home key is C major, the cadence would be D–G or D7–G). The section may also end with an imperfect cadence in the tonic key (e.g., I–V or II–V). For example, if the piece begins in C major, the section ends on a G major chord. If the piece is in a minor key, the section may finish in the relative major (e.g., a minor home key leading to C relative major).

Section B may begin in the key in which A ended or may begin in the tonic key. It usually modulates to closely related keys but must finish with a perfect cadence in the home key.

All sections may be repeated.

Duet (I–A)

> *S,* stand still, then slowly move, swaying your body gently from side to side with your eyes closed. *A,* improvise a bourrée (or other dance), attempting to enhance the body movements and bring them into a more formalized dance.

> *S,* play any nontuned percussion instrument. *A,* match *S*'s playing and bring it into a clear form influenced by dance. Turn into a more structured intervention, possibly with words. Move in and out of the dance form, creating a clear ABA structure.

CONCLUSION

Baroque music is stylistically a gift for music therapists. What has been presented here, as in all aspects of this book, is the potential opening of a Pandora's box of musical treasures. These treasures are ready to be harvested by music therapists, who are fascinated by the life force of music and its potential depth and individuality within the therapeutic process. The baroque era was one of the richest in the history of music. Within the confines of its form and division between the sacred and secular, it produced some wonderful examples of smaller compositions alongside the greater structures of opera and oratorios. It is the clarity of its musical components — accessible harmonic forms, florid extended melodies, and consistent rhythms — that provides the backbone for possible clinical connections. Because of its precision of compositional and emotional intent, baroque music can be readily adapted for the therapeutic arena. Thinking of our clients as a vehicle for baroque expression will add to the richness of the music we bring to therapy. Allowing therapeutic form to develop within a baroque sensibility can provide the inspiration that will allow growth and richness in fulfilling the potential of all of the people we work alongside, whatever their pathology or illness. The baroque style works equally as well with children as it does with adults and the elderly. It is how we adapt and practise the music that makes it ultimately effective in producing therapeutic results.

Bach represents a voice that can be used on many levels, from the simplicity of a structured song to the profound human depths of spiritual oneness available through his scared music. Bach can act as a clinical mentor on different levels. Allowing his music to become a part of your own musical history will in turn affect how you potentially use his musical style in sessions. By listening, playing, and reflecting on the beauty of his compositional intent, you will begin to become more refined in your musicological awareness of clients. Start by using Bach's style for greeting and/or good-bye songs with children. Note how they respond to the introverted and inner yearnings of this music. Keep within the confines of a clear harmonic structure and make sure that you make clear the stylistic components that will make his music effective. Once you become familiar and confident about using his style, allow it to become an integral part and makeup of your improvising. Continue playing/listening and exploring his music and allow yourself to become ever more inspired as you realize the breadth and scope of his contribution to music. To fully embrace Bach in our clinical work could be seen to be a lifetime's work, but it could be one, however, that will pay dividends at every step in our understanding of his music and its implications for music therapy.

CHAPTER 3

Classical

The classical period (1750–1825) is one of clarity, form, and restrained expression. Craftsmanship is the hallmark of this period (Kivy, 1990), producing music that was polished, elegant, and aesthetically pleasing. When listening to music from the classical period, you perceive a feeling of measured elegance that is at once direct but that also portrays a sense of emotional reserve. Many pianists' first experiences come from the classical period, Mozart, Haydn, and Beethoven sonatas nearly always being a part of a young musician's developing repertoire. Although vocal music continued to be written through lieder and opera, this was secondary to the popularity of chamber, orchestral, and other instrumental music. The sonata and symphony became standard, with many composers writing hundreds of opuses for each. The string quartet developed as a replacement for the trio sonata, becoming a medium where composers could show their skills in part writing and beauty of form, especially in slow movements (Benward & Saker, 2003).

In 1709, the modern piano was invented by Christofori. This was perhaps one of the greatest inventions in the history of music as it allowed music into people's homes in a way that had not been previously possible. Thus music-making became less elitist and more a part of people's everyday lives. Everyone could partake in active playing and thus express in a much more direct and personal way. This was also the period in which the orchestra developed and grew in size. The continuo faded from use and the clarinet became a standard woodwind instrument. As the numbers in the orchestra grew, so did its available textures and possibilities for longer and more complex structures. The division between church and state became less noticeable, although composers, in order to live, were still often at the mercy of patrons and benefactors.

The classical period focused on compositional clarity and intellectual freedom. Themes were often composed of short fragments as opposed to the longer melodic phrases of the baroque. Different moods were created in close succession, and chromaticism was introduced to colour the often straightforward underlying and often slowly moving tonic-dominant harmonies and cadential progressions. Modulations became more extensive, often moving to the tonic minor/major. There was also a greater freedom in the use of rhythm, and silence became a vehicle through which composers could rest and consider the ensuing structural form and development. Thus music became much more of a considered and refined practice. There is a sense of intellectualism about the classical period that often betrays its emotional backbone and heartfelt searching.

CLASSICAL MUSIC AND MUSIC THERAPY

What are the musical and emotional characteristics of the classical period that make it useful for music therapy? The classical period was greatly concerned with compositional structure. Its expression was bound by strict parameters, most notably sonata form. The freedom of renaissance and baroque music was replaced with a creativity that was contained within parameters of imposed design. The beauty of the music comes from a sense of detachment that is at once direct yet shrouded behind an emotional curtain. One could argue that because of this, it is perhaps the least useful area of western music for clinical practice. On the other hand, because its musical/emotional environment is once removed, it is potentially more effective in balancing the complex relational components of the therapeutic process. To be unrestrained in the classical style, yet reserved through its form, can provide both musical strengths and freedoms.

The examples in this chapter come from perhaps two of the greatest composers of the classical period, Mozart and Beethoven (the early-middle works). Both composers' lives were fraught with emotional challenges, and both used music to express their personal human journeys. Mozart's creative elegance belies a man fraught with personal insecurities. Beethoven's challenge of physical deterioration toward deafness must have been horrific to one who had lived through sound (Lee, 2003). Both portrayed their inner lives directly in their compositions, albeit from different viewpoints. How would both have considered the field of music therapy? And, had it been a formalized profession in their day, how might they have contributed to the work? This is an interesting debate, particularly in relation to the classical period, not least because there were such distinct musical manners that needed to be adhered to. It was in their final works, however, that we hear the musical-spiritual, musical-psychotherapeutic, and musical-emotional connections. Listen deeply and carefully to Mozart's *Requiem in D Minor* (KV 626). Here we find the relationship between music and the human condition that is at the heart of music therapy.

One area of practice for which the classical style is particularly useful is with children. Its direct structure can be easily adapted to create more formal interventions within a distinct style to which many children relate. The energy and transparent nature of the music make it a wonderful musical tool from which to base energized improvisations. Classical melodies often lend themselves well to words in creating songs for children. Greeting and good-bye songs work particularly well in this style. The therapist can also adapt precomposed pieces to create action songs or write their own music in this style. As always, the chorus (A section) should be the base from which to improvise a B section and then return to A. Rondo form, as will be discussed later in this chapter, is a basic structural component that is at the root of much music-making in therapy.

The classical period had clear stylistic components that constitute its artistic essence as well as its emotional makeup. As a style, it can be effective in therapy if used with focus and intent. The crystal-like quality and clarity can be useful both in individual work and in groups. Songs and instrumental improvisations can be created that have a sense of simplicity yet refined integrity. These can be focusing yet with a quality of freedom contained within a clear harmonic structure. This style can be used to constitute an entire improvisation and/or intervention but can also be used as colour when playing in other styles, e.g., jazz and classical or atonal and classical. We only have to look to the neoclassical composers of the 20th century to see how the classical and baroque periods influenced contemporary composers and were fused to create one of the most exotic musical styles in contemporary music.

EXERCISES

The following exercises contain some fundamental devices that can be useful for the music therapist. All examples are taken from the piano sonatas of Mozart and Beethoven. This chapter, then, perhaps more than any other, is for pianists. Having said this, it is possible to arrange the music for guitar and/or orchestral instruments. The use of voice should be made freely whenever the music dictates. Look to the piano literature of the classical period and play through as much music as you can. Play sonatas by Haydn, Mozart, and Beethoven, and live in the creative genius of this inspirational music. These pieces will inform the potential of using classical music in sessions. Also, embrace orchestral and chamber music from this period. Be inspired by this wonderful yet highly stylized music and imagine how wonderful it would be if you could offer this style as part of your resource palette for your clients.

COMPONENTS

Harmony

Even though the harmonies of the classical period were relatively uncomplicated, chromatic harmonies were beginning to develop. This added to the colour of the music and its emotional content and ongoing, developing form.

Beethoven. *Largo, Con Gran Espressione,* Piano Sonata in E Flat, Op. 7

Solo (I–A)

> Practise and become familiar with the following harmonic sequence. The guide has been chosen as an example that translates a sense of the classical harmonic style. Play following the phrases and try melodic explorations around the pause marks.

Example 3.1

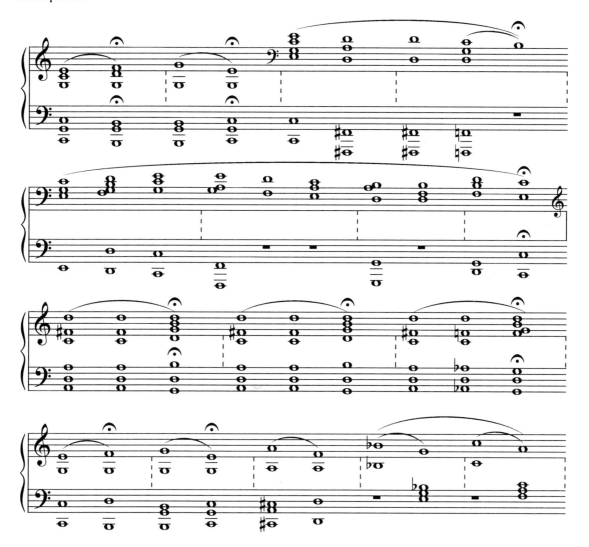

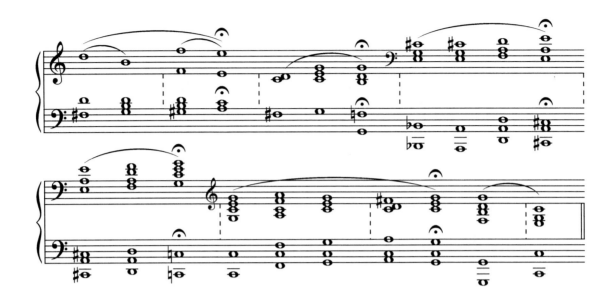

If easier, initially use your voice, then try adding lines on the keyboard with the harmonies. Explore the extract in different time signatures. If need be, simplify this progression to fit your level of playing.

Think of the classical music you know and try to create in that style. It is important that to begin you play the music strictly, although you are also encouraged to experiment with different voicing and positions on the keyboard.

Examine particularly the first two measures: The progression moves from I to V (C to G), then V to I. This sort of question-answer phrase is typical of the period. Experiment with making your own melodies using only the chords I and V.

Once you have become more confident, play the sequence in different keys and transpose to the minor. Live in this progression and play it many times, until it becomes familiar and second nature. Exercises 3.2–3.6 are taken from this same chord progression.

Alberti Bass

The Alberti bass was created by Domenica Alberti (1710–1740). It is an accompaniment formula where chords in the left hand of the keyboard are played as arpeggios or broken chords (notes 1,5,3,5 of the chord), which act as an accompaniment to a melody in the right hand. This kind of configuration can be particularly useful in improvisation as it acts as a constant and repeating figure. Remember, however, not to repeat an Alberti bass too many times and to always include elements of rubato so that it doesn't become rigid. Think of it as adding colour and movement rather than an idiom in itself.

Solo (B–I)

Play the following example and continue in the same style following the harmonic sequence (Example 3.1). Explore further Alberti configurations, adding different melodies and also using your voice. Make note of the dignified nature of the Alberti bass and consider clinical situations when this may be appropriate.

Example 3.2

Duet (B–I–A)

> Piano Duet: **S,** improvise a simple single-line melody on the white notes in the upper register of piano (anywhere above middle C). **A,** use an Alberti bass figure to respond to **S** and take to a more structured theme. Move away from and back to the Alberti bass figure. Remember to keep the harmonic progression simple, emphasizing I and V (C and G major).

Melody and Accompaniment

Apart from broken chords and triadic configurations as just explored, the classical period also used simple harmonic accompaniments to support melody. This next example is a slow movement.

Beethoven. *Adagio,* Piano Sonata in C, Op. 2, No. 3

Solo (I–A)

> Play the opening melody and accompaniment of the piece.

Example 3.3

Explore further on your own, improvising in the same style using this harmonic progression and that of Example 3.1 as an anchor.

Examine Beethoven's use of chord inversions in this piece and try to incorporate them in your own improvisation.

Duet (I–A)

Use the above slow movement as a means to create a musical-emotional environment. *S,* sit quietly and listen. *A,* create a peaceful mood using the voice if appropriate. Try to create a calm musical environment for *S* without expecting him/her to play.

⟨CD/6⟩   *S,* play a tuned percussion instrument in C. *A,* create a lyrical melody and accompaniment based on the progression to create a calm expression. Use your voice if appropriate. Add chord inversions to create variation in your progression.

Play through other examples of slow and fast movements by Mozart, Beethoven, and their contemporaries, making note of different accompaniment figures and how they complement the melody. Play accompaniments and use your voice as the melody. Also play accompaniments in your left hand with melodies in your right hand. Create more structured songs and possible vocal interventions. Create words in the moment and also try creating accompaniments and melodies with a prewritten text. Notate and use your melodies and accompaniments to expand your repertoire of the classical style. As always, transpose into different major and minor keys.

Scales and Arpeggios

Using simple scale passages and arpeggio figures can add direction and movement in the energy of an improvisation. They can also add embellishment to a simply constructed harmony. They should be played with a sense of brilliance. In improvising in the classical style, use them more as colour rather than as the basis for direct form. In this period, scales and arpeggios were often used as a means to add texture and decoration to the often static and simple harmonic structures

Solo (B–I–A)

> Improvise scale-like and passages around the core harmonic progression of the following example. Try to create a sense of lightness in your playing and have fun. Repeat this exercise in the minor and note the difference in the quality and intent of your improvising.

Example 3.4

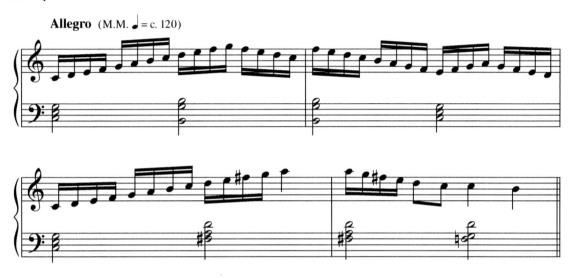

Solo (I–A)

> Repeat this exercise, using instead arpeggio-like figures first in the major and then in the minor as above.

Example 3.5

Duet

> **S,** play a simple, steady rhythm (basic beat) on a drum. **A,** first meet the exact tempo A, then introduce faster scale passages (Example 3.4), thus creating a different texture B. Returning to the original tempo A, complete the experience. Improvise freely and also create a more structured song/activity. Repeat the exercise using arpeggios (Example 3.5).

Octaves

Octaves, without accompaniment or harmony, are a much underused resource in clinical improvisation. In studying *Creative Music Therapy* (Nordoff & Robbins, 2007), we find many references to the use of octaves. Bare octaves are often how Paul Nordoff would begin an improvisation or session. Octaves in themselves do not infer harmony and therefore can lead in any musical direction, tonal centre, or key. Used in a clear key, however, they provide stability and strength. In the classical period, octaves were used for added texture and to give a sense of elaboration. They were normally used to enforce the key of the movement rather than move away from it.

Solo (I–A)

> Play the following octave passage based on the harmonic progression from Example 3.1. If possible, play octaves in each hand; if this is difficult, play one octave between hands.

Example 3.6

> Explore further away from the progression, always keeping a sense of the key you are improvising in.

Duet (I–A)

> **S,** play a steady rhythm (basic beat) on a drum. **A,** create an improvisation using the following form: A octaves as just created in Example 3.6, followed by a B section using a

simple basic beat accompaniment based on the chord sequence. Complete the experience with a return to the octaves of A.

Modulation

Modulating is an important resource for music therapists to master in order to improvise tonally. It consists of a point of transition between two sections of music in different keys. In sonatas and symphonies of the classical period, modulations take place most often in keys closely related to the tonic, the most important being a modulation to the dominant key (V). Other important keys are IV, II, and VI and the tonic minor (or tonic major if the piece is originally in a minor key). In a minor key, one of the most common modulations is to the relative major (III).

The best way to establish a new key centre is to create a cadence. A cadence requires a minimum of two chords: the dominant 7th and tonic. Most cadences are also prepared with a predominant chord such as II, IV, or VI. These make for effective pivot chords as discussed below. Therefore, the strongest modulations are those that emphasize the progression of predominant, dominant 7th, and tonic (e.g., II–V7–I) in the new key.

The following exercises are necessary to master if you intend to improvise in sonata form, as explored at the end of this chapter. Even when keys are closely related, modulations can add variety to your improvisational repertoire and can refresh the tonal palette, bringing a sense of novelty.

Solo (B–I–A)

Major key to tonic minor

One of the easiest ways of modulating is to change from a major key to its tonic minor. This modulation does not require a pivot chord and can therefore be considered a direct modulation. However, to make the transition smoother, the minor IV chord can be borrowed from the tonic minor key, functioning as a predominant chord. Play the following example:

Example 3.7

| C: I | VIb | II | V7b | I | IV | Vb | Cm: I |

As the cadence leads to a C minor chord, it implies that the music continues in the key of C minor from this point forward.

Minor key to tonic major

When going from minor to major, you can simply end on the major tonic and continue in the major key.

Example 3.8

| Cm: I | VIb | II | V7b | I | IVb | Vb | C: I |

Play using an *Alberti bass* in the left hand and improvise a simple melody in the right hand. Remember to use the scale of the new key when in C minor. Become familiar and practise the above examples in different keys. Experiment using different classical styles as previously explored in this chapter and adapt them to the modulation.

Example 3.9

Duet (I–A)

S, improvise on an instrument of your choice. **A,** create a simple piece focusing on the modulations from the tonic major to tonic minor.

Solo (I–A)

Major key to dominant (I–V)

The smoothest way to modulate is by means of a pivot chord, i.e., a chord that belongs in both the key you are playing and the key to which you want to modulate. When improvising, it is safest to think immediately in the new key as soon as you play the pivot chord. *Remember that in order to establish the new key, the cadence must end in the root position.* There are many ways to do this, but the suggestions given here will be the easiest for less advanced pianists. Play the following example in the key of C major:

Example 3.10

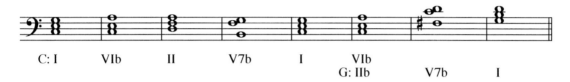

The A minor chord in bar 6 acts as a pivot chord as it belongs to both the tonic and th dominant key. Once familiar with the progression, play the left-hand chords with an Alberti bass pattern and improvise a simple melody. Continue improvising in the new key for a few measures in order to fully establish the new key.

Minor key to dominant (I to V)

The same progression can be used in a minor key. Note that the basic cadence D7 to G is the same as the above progression. It is also possible to cadence in the minor V chord (G minor) in order to keep the music in a minor key.

Example 3.11

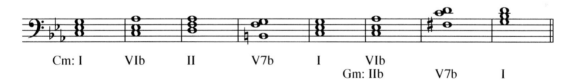

Major key to subdominant (I to IV)

Another common modulation is from the tonic to the subdominant (IV). Here, IV or II may act as the pivot chord. In the following example, we have chosen IV as the pivot chord:

Example 3.12

Minor key to subdominant minor (I to IV)

The same progression can be played in a minor key.

Example 3.13

Cm: I   VIb   II   V7b   I   IV
                                                               Fm: Ic   V7b   I

Now we will consider modulations to relative minor or major. When modulating to the relative minor, VI becomes I in the new key. When modulating to the relative major from a minor key, III becomes the tonic of the new key. Practise the following left hand patterns in all major and minor keys.

Major key to relative minor (I to VI)

Possible pivot chords for this progression include VI (A minor), IV (F major), or II (D minor). The following example uses VI as a pivot chord:

Example 3.14

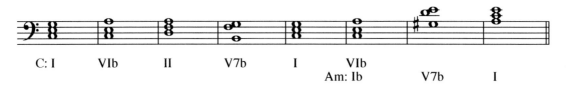

C: I   VIb   II   V7b   I   VIb
                                                               Am: Ib   V7b   I

Try substituting the A minor chord in bar 6 for an F major or D minor chord. These make for stronger predominants.

Minor key to relative major (I to III)

For modulations to the relative major, I, VI, or IV are common pivot chords. In this example, we have chosen the VI chord:

Example 3.15

Cm: I   VIb   II   V7b   I   VIb
                                                               E♭: IVb   V7b   I

Substitute the A♭ major chord in bar 6 with a C minor (I) or F minor chord (IV). Practise these modulations with an Alberti bass pattern, improvising a simple melody in the right hand.

The following exercises are examples of two types of modulation (up one half-step and up one whole-step). After selecting the version that is easier for you, continue each exercise until you have modulated to all 12 major keys. While practising these patterns, note the movement from V to I in the new key and, when applicable, identify the predominant chords.

Half-steps (easier version)

Example 3.16

Half-steps (more difficult version)

Example 3.17

Whole steps (easier version)

Example 3.18

Whole steps (more difficult version)

Example 3.19

The following exercises are examples of two additional modulations (up a minor 3rd and up a major 3rd). After selecting the version that is easier for you, continue each exercise until you have modulated to all 12 major keys.

Up a minor 3rd (easier version)

Example 3.20

Up a minor 3rd (more difficult version)

Example 3.21

In order to play the above exercises in all 12 major keys, you will have to repeat them beginning on D flat and again beginning on D.

Up a major 3rd (easier version)

Example 3.22

Up a major 3rd (more difficult version)

Example 3.23

As before, in order to play the above exercises in all 12 major keys, you will have to repeat it beginning on D flat and again ending on D and E flat.

The following exercises are examples of three additional modulations, up a perfect 4th, an augmented 4th, and a minor 3rd. Again, select the version that is easier for you and continue each exercise until you have modulated in all 12 keys.

Up a perfect 4th (easier version)

Example 3.24

Up a perfect 4th (more difficult version)

Example 3.25

Up an augmented 4th (easier version)

Example 3.26

Up an augmented 4th (more difficult version)

Example 3.27

Down a minor 3rd (easier version)

Example 3.28

Down a minor 3rd (more difficult version)

Example 3.29

The following exercises will complete modulations to all keys.

Down a minor 3rd (easier version)

Example 3.30

Down a minor 3rd (more difficult version)

Example 3.31

You can further expand your improvisational repertoire by modulating between sections. At first, try this only between sections A and B. Initially include the key relationships and modulating patterns already learned. Do not attempt to create four bar phrases or a "theme." Instead, you are creating a bridge, or a detour, on your way to a new B section. Always make sure to arrive in the new key before beginning the B section.

Try two modulations only. If A is a major key, modulate to the dominant between the A and B sections.

Example 3.32

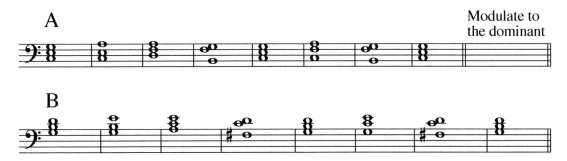

If A is in a minor key, modulate to the relative major between the A and B sections.

Example 3.33

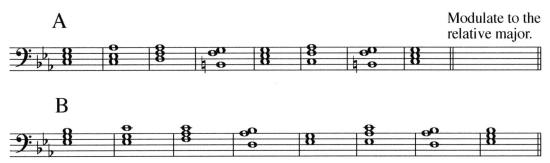

Become conversant by improvising modulations in different keys and styles. Repeat until the modulations become second nature in your playing. It is crucial that you feel and know the chord modulations in a very concrete way. If need be, write down the modulation you are exploring, thus building a volume of modulation styles for future practising. It is only when you are totally conversant that you will be able to use modulations with confidence and clarity in your clinical improvisations. Once you have become fluent with the above modulation exercises, you will be moving toward being able to improvise a short movement in sonata form. In order to do this, you will need to be able to construct bridges between sections without modulating. Continue to modulate between an A and B section as you did previously. Then, return to A (in the tonic) and improvise a bridge that does not modulate but resembles the previous modulating bridge as closely as possible, followed by B in the tonic key.

The new form is: A (bridge) modulation – B – A (bridge) no modulation – B

Examples 3.34

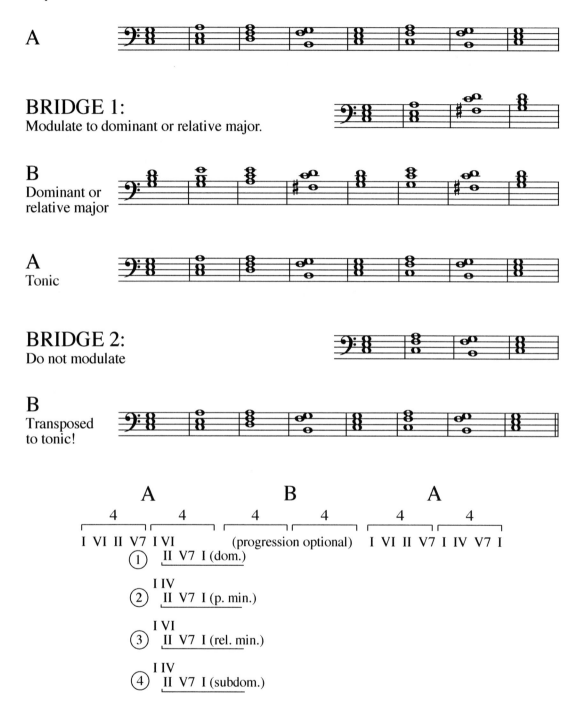

FORM

Sonata Form

Sonata form is perhaps one of the most standard structures in western music. It shaped the development of the classical and romantic periods and continues to influence composers to this day. Linking sonata form to music therapy is a natural association that has gained recent attention. Wigram (2004) explores sonata form as a metaphor for therapy, making connections in terms of: a single improvisation, making a friend, the therapeutic relationship, and the process of therapy. Lee (2003) takes a slightly different approach by structurally linking the sections of sonata form to that of a single session. Its clarity and organic form make it an ideal association with music therapy, whether we decide to make connections from a more therapeutic/psychodynamic stance or a musicological one. This section will take a practical and hands-on approach, with the view to providing a simple yet effective way of using sonata form in improvisations.

Sonata form has the following basic structure (Benward & Saker, 2003):

Section	Key
Exposition	
(1 & 2) Theme 1 or theme group 1	Tonic
(3) Transition	Tonic to dominant (I–V) or tonic to relative major (in minor keys)
(4) Theme 2 or **(5)** theme group 2	Dominant, or relative major (in minor keys)
Theme 3 (optional)	Dominant, or relative major (in minor keys)
(6) Codetta (optional)	Dominant, or relative major (in minor keys)
(7) Development	No standard design, but with one or more keys and themes developed
(8) Recapitulation	
(9) Theme 1 or theme group 1	Tonic
(10) Transition	Tonic (no modulation or return to tonic)
(11) Theme 2 or theme group 2	Tonic
(12) Theme 3 or theme group 3	Tonic
(13) Coda (optional)	Tonic

Having mastered the art of modulation, you are now ready to begin creating simple exercises to improvise in sonata form.

Solo (A)

Use the following analysis of the first movement of Mozart's Sonata in C Major (K. 309) as your initial guide (Benward & Saker, 2003). Study this example carefully: Note how the structure develops and themes are created to provide a clear sonata form. Use this analysis as your guide. Take your time and consider Mozart's subtle and creative use of harmony, modulation, and form.

Example 3.35

Sonata in C Major

W. A Mozart
K. 309

(1) *Measures*   *1–14 Exposition: Theme I, group A (C major)*
(2) *Measures*   *15–20 Theme I, group B (C major)*
(3) *Measures*   *21–32 Transition (C major–G major)*
(4) *Measures*   *33–42 Theme 2, group A (G major)*
(5) *Measures*   *43–53 Theme 2, group B (G major)*
(6) *Measures*   *54–58 Codetta (G major)*
(7) *Measures*   *59–93 Development*
              59–62 Derived from first theme, group A (D minor)
              63–66 Derived from first theme, group A (D minor)
              67–72 Derived from first theme, group A (D minor–A minor)
              73–82 Derived from first theme, group A (A minor)
              83–85 Derived from codetta (A minor)
              86–89 Derived from first theme, group A (A minor)
              90–93 Derived from first theme, group A (A minor–C minor)
(8) *Measures*   *94–109 Recapitulation: Theme I, group A (C major)*
(9) *Measures*   *110–115 Theme I, group B (C major)*
(10) *Measures*   *116–126 Transition (C major)*
(11) *Measures*   *127–136 Theme 2, group A (C major)*
(12) *Measures*   *137–147 Theme 2, group B (C major)*
(13) *Measures*   *148–155 Coda (C major)*

Duet (A)

> **S,** choose a single instrument, e.g., drum, xylophone or cymbal. Improvise a theme. **A,** play in response a simple sonata form improvisation or extemporization based on the themes from the above-analyzed Mozart sonata. Be aware of **S**'s playing and attempt to use the form as a means to allow them to explore further the instrument and their dialogue. Also consider using the exposition as a song form/chorus, potentially adding words that will have a clinical aim. Return to this experience as exactly as possible for the recapitulation.

Once you have mastered the above, begin creating your own sonata themes. It is important that you write down all of your musical ideas and build a volume of sonata themes, developments, and recapitulations. In the development section, improvise and modulate freely to ever more diverse keys, the only stipulation being that you find your way back to the tonic in a musically fluent way without making the experience jarring. Write as detailed music as you need to improvise clear sonata forms that can be taken directly into sessions. Practise from themes you have already developed and return to the Mozart example when needed. As you become more fluent, try improvising sonatas without any previous written themes. To master clear sonata form in a clinical improvisation will take dedication and exact practice techniques. Never be rigid in your use of sonata form clinically, but instead allow it to colour and respond to the emotional/therapeutic needs of the client. Plan carefully how you practise and take time with every theme and every step you take in this process. Once you have mastered sonata form, then your improvising will become ever more formed, creative, and refined.

The above analysis of sonata form and its link as a dialogue in music therapy is a huge undertaking and one that requires dedication and perseverance. We do not pretend that improvising in sonata form is easy; it will take a long period of focused practising. Compare the movement chosen and explore other sonatas of the classical period. Create your own sonatas by keeping a notebook of themes and ideas. To begin, it is important to write down your themes, transitions, and development ideas. Try different duet experiences once you feel confident. Explore hypothetical clinical scenarios in your practising and try little by little to bring this form into your sessions. As you become more confident in the use of sonata form, allow it to become both a foundational resource and one that can be used in part to create specific aims in the development of the musical-therapeutic relationship. To provide clinical sonata form can mean clarity of musical thought alongside the potential for the creative freedom and balance that is necessary for a focused therapeutic relationship.

CD/ (7) *S*, drum/cymbal. *A*, piano.[1]

Theme and Variations

The style of theme and variations in the baroque era, as explored in Chapter 3, is different from that of the classical period. Theme and variations can be a fundamental tool for music therapists. Creating new ways of exploring a theme has clear links between the humanistic and artistic components of music therapy. The relationship between the structure of theme and variations and music therapy has previously been considered. Lisa Summer (1996) relates the form of Mozart's *Theme and Variations* (K 311) to the mother-child relationship. Here, musical and psychological development is discussed hand-in-hand. Structurally, Wigram (2004) describes how the theme "becomes the focus for creative improvisation and exploration" (p. 205). Theme and variations have a clear metaphor with the therapeutic process, the human condition, and development of relationship. The theme is the ground on which new and unchartered paths are explored. A clear sense of the theme, however, must be maintained so that when the theme is reinstated there is a sense of resolution and conclusion.

Listen and play some variations by Beethoven listed below:

> Seven Variations on "God Save the King" (WoO 78)
> Thirty-two Variations (WoO 80)
> Twenty-four Variations on Righini's air *Venni Amore* (WoO 65)
> Piano Sonata in A Flat, first movement, Op. 26

As you become familiar with the music, note how Beethoven develops and plays with the theme. There is often a lighthearted sense and teasing of musical ideas, especially in keyboard music of this period. Note the clarity of ideas and how the simplest decoration of the theme can drastically change the musical/emotional impact of the music.

Solo (I–A)

Mozart. *Theme, Andante, Piano Sonata in D Major* (KV 284, 205b)

> Note how the melody is constructed with a short intervallic opening A, followed by a longer B section. A simple Alberti accompaniment provides as sense of clarity. In the second section, the theme is developed, returning to the opening idea to conclude. Listen, as you play, to the transparency of the music and how effective this theme could be in your own work.

---

[1]This audio example is based on Mozart's *Piano Sonata in D Major* (KV 311), 1st movement.

Example 3.36

Duet (I–A)

S, improvise quietly on a tuned percussion instrument in D major. *A,* play the above theme as written but in an improvisatory style with a sense of rubato. Try to connect your playing, being gentle in your interpretation of the theme. Use the harmonic outline to create other similar themes.

Example 3.37

The following variations have been chosen and adapted from the movement because they highlight different musical variations; plus, if played with different attack and in different tempi, they can be used for various instrumental combinations with piano. Use these examples as a template for complete sets of variations with one instrument.

Variation I — Xylophone (tuned to D major)

A, play the variation as written, continuing in the same style. Adapt to *S*'s playing, creating a dialogue. Note the difference in the musical relationship with the faster repeated triplet figures in the melody.

Example 3.38

Variation II (Mozart's Variation No. III) — Drum

S, play a regular and steady rhythm on a conga. **A,** play the variation as written in a detached and strong manner. Continue the variation, playing and creating energy and moving the music forward as needed.

Example 3.39

Variation III (Mozart's Variation No. V) — Hand Chimes

CD /
11
S, play two hand chimes (A & D). **A,** start the variation as written with 3rds in the left hand and repeated notes in the right hand. Listen to **S**'s playing and create a musical atmosphere between hand chimes and piano.

Example 3.40

Variation IV (Mozart's Variation No. VII) — Voice (Alt. Piano)

CD/ **A,** play the variation as written, using the left hand to create an accompaniment for voice.
(12) Continue in the same style. Sing with or without words, encouraging **S** to sing also in a duet. Alternatively create the variation with piano four hands, **S,** treble, and **A,** bass. Be sensitive to the change in minor key and explore the more melancholy nature of the variation.

Example 3.41

Variation V (Mozarts Variation No. VIII) — Drum and Cymbal

S, play simply, alternating drum and cymbal. **A,** play the variation as written, continuing with a 3/4 variation that is dancelike and full of energy. Play in different tempi and with different dynamics.

Example 3.42

To create your own theme and variations in the classical style, begin by improvising a theme A. Try to make your theme simple but engaging. Use styles and ways of playing that are reminiscent of this style. Repeat your theme and then add variations as desired (A, A1, A2, A3, etc.). If you have trouble remembering what you improvised in the A section, begin by writing your theme down with a simple harmonic outline. Keep a catalogue of themes that you have practised from or that have occurred in sessions. This way, you will create a range of themes that can be used when needed. Each time you practise, go back over the themes you have created, improvising ever more creative variations. Improvise freely, while keeping a clear sense of the theme so that you can return as accurately as possible after your variations are complete. Variations can be as creative as the improviser's ability to be musically open. Here are some suggestions for effective classical style variations:

Transpose to the relative major or minor
Change time signature/meter
Change tempo
Invert melody
Decorate melody
Create rhythmic figure
Use Alberti bass
Change harmony

Variation form can add a distinct flavor as it allows a sense of freedom and exploration while keeping the bounds of the theme. Even though we have only included variation form in the classical and baroque sections, its principles can be adapted for all styles in this book.

Rondo Form

Rondo form during the classical period was often used for the final movement of a sonata or symphony. Rondos are good examples of the principle of repetition and contrast. A rondo can be described as consisting of a basic theme — a melody or whole section — whose repeated appearances, refrains, are separated by periodic occurrences of contrasting material called episodes. A retransition makes the return from an episode to a refrain as even as possible. The most common rondos are in three (ABA), five (ABACA), and seven (ABACABA) parts.

In music therapy, rondo form "provides an opportunity creatively to move away from a theme and then return to it. The 'theme' becomes a grounding element, both in the music and in the relationship" (Wigram, 2004). Aigen (2005) discusses how rondo form reflects a child's explorations away from and their return to their primary caregiver. As the child becomes more confident, they will move away from the theme until tension of the unknown forces them to return to the familiar. This is known as refueling (Mahler, Pine, & Bergman, 2000).

> The healthy development of the child's self requires the ability to learn how to safely manage these rhythms of tension and resolution as seen in contact with the familiar and the unfamiliar. The same pattern of alternating familiar and unfamiliar experiences is at the root of the musical experience of the rondo. And, interestingly, while initially the child must physically return to the caregiver to reestablish contact and effectively refuel, in subsequent stages of development the refueling can take place with eye contact alone and thus can take place at a distance. Musical themes can be similarly referenced at a distance when they are played in altered or embellished forms, yet are close enough to the original to function as the theme. (Aigen, 2005, p. 268).

There are several reasons why learning to improvise in rondo forms can be useful. First, it will help to guide your memory to retain and reuse previously improvised materials within the same improvisation. Second, improvising rondos will give you the experience of constructing longer improvisations without stopping. Last and most important, rondos can provide a balance between stability — *refrain* — and contrast — *episode* — for the client when grounding is needed for the ongoing therapeutic relationship. One idea is that the refrain can become the chorus of a song, with contrasting episodes that can be instrumental or some other balanced idea. There are many other ways of incorporating rondos in either spontaneous improvisations or more structured and ongoing interventions. The one rule to keep in mind is that you must make the refrain musically clear and balanced, in contrast to the episodes and transitions/retransitions that connect.

Beethoven. *Tempo di Menuetto, Piano Sonata in G,* Op. 49, No. 2

Solo (I–A)

Play the refrain (A), noting the balance and construction of the three phrases.

Example 3.43

Play the first episode (B), noting how Beethoven contrasts his music ideas against the refrain (A).

Example 3.44

Now play the transition and note how it seamlessly connects back to the refrain.

Example 3.45

Play the second episode (C).

This episode is in C major, the subdominant of G. This is followed by a short transition modulating back to the tonic and the refrain (A).

Example 3.46

Finally, play the coda, making note of the different musical ideas that are introduced to end the movement.

Example 3.47

Go back over this piece and consider its simple yet sophisticated form. Take Beethoven's refrain and try different ways of stylistically colouring the melody in the classical style. Then create your own episodes and transitions from Beethoven's theme. Find other rondo movements from the classical period and analyze in the same way. Begin to build a library of rondo refrains and episodes.

Duet (I–A)

A, creating your own original refrains and episodes is another way to build to your rondo resources. Start by writing down short, simple ideas that are easily remembered. Create a refrain A and think of an instrument for which this could be useful. For this example, we have chosen the drum. Ask **S** to play with one stick a simple and steady rhythm and **A,** play your refrain to match. As you become more conversant, add more episodes with contrasting musical ideas.

Example 3.48

Now write a simple transition, leading to your first contrasting episode, B.

Example 3.49

Write a second transition, leading to your second episode, C.

Example 3.50

The transition must then lead effortlessly back to your refrain, A.

Example 3.51

REFRAIN A

Once you have become familiar with your above ideas, think of adding a simple coda.

Example 3.52

CODA

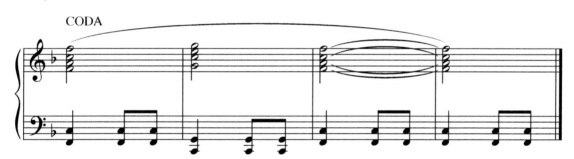

It is important in the beginning to keep your ideas simple. Using a clear harmonic background as offered at the beginning of this chapter (Example 3.1), will give you the confidence to explore further, stylistically creating effective rondos in the classical style. The stability and assurance of the rondo can be useful in therapy on many levels and can be adapted to a multitude of interventions, clinical aims, and combinations for both individual and group work.

Secondary Dominants

Secondary dominant chords will enrich your harmonic vocabulary and add to your knowledge of the harmonic classical style.

Solo (I)

Try the following progression in all major keys.

Example 3.53

Since ii is diminished in minor keys, the V of ii will produce a different effect.

Example 3.54

The following simple exercise in both major and minor keys will help to get you started:

Example 3.55

Slow Movements

Some of the most beautiful and musically satisfying experiences of the classical period are contained within slow movements. We have only to think of the first movement of Beethoven's "Moonlight" piano sonata in C sharp minor, op. 27, no. 2, or the slow movements from Mozart's piano concertos to know and understand the importance of lyricism and melody in the classical era. How can we create these slow movements and lyrical melodies in our work, and what might they bring to the therapeutic process?

Beethoven. *Adagio Cantabile, Piano Sonata in C Minor,* Op. 13, *"Pathetique"*

Solo (I–A)

Play through the opening carefully and slowly, living in each tone and phrase. Make note of how the melody and accompaniment are constructed. There is a precision here, with not one wasted note. Consider the harmonies and how they create music that is searching, full of emotional content and yearning. This is indeed music from the pen of a genius. Imagine the therapeutic effects of being able to offer such a perfectly formed creation.

Example 3.56

In *Healing Heritage* (Robbins & Robbins, 1998), Paul Nordoff takes us through a detailed analysis of the opening bars (pp. 40–41). If we look at an overview of his examination, we can see how carefully constructed the music is in providing balance with unexpected intervals and harmonic directions:

(4) Major 3rd, octave supports the 10th — balance.

(5) The whole picture changes, 5th and a 6th.

(6) Something fantastic has happened. The tritone, minor 3rd, and major 6th … withdrawn, and at the same time there's the possibility of moving out.

(7) The E flat comes and changes everything. It takes away the tritone and leaves a major 2nd and 5th.

(8) The 5th. Another world!

(9) Withdrawn again into the minor 3rd.

(10) The intervals in the right hand open out, chord by chord — major 3rd.

(11) 4th.

(12) Minor 6th.

(13) Minor 13th gives the rising melodic line, while the left hand reinforces this moving out with its stepwise contrary motion.

(14) Only to leap an octave with the climax of the melody.

(15) This last chord in the 3rd measure modulates the dominant on the first beat of the 4th measure, where we can pause.

(16) The interval of a 6th. We have taken a step outside ourselves and now pause, secure in the root position dominant chord — in a 6th supported by the balance of the 3rd beneath.

This kind of detailed analysis is important for music therapists because it acknowledges the importance and potential therapeutic consequence of every musical component we use. In considering these opening four bars, we are privileged to experience an opening into the true microanalysis of music and its possible outcomes in understanding the balance between the "art" and "science" of our practice. If we could understand with such exacting precision all of the music we use in therapy, then how might our outcomes and role as therapists be affected?

Solo (A)

Now use the following outline and begin improvising your own creative responses to the harmonic direction of the music. Find new melodies and melodic phrases. As you become more familiar with the progression, find new textural ways of playing the harmonies and develop your own themes. When appropriate, use your voice. Use this example as a thematic A, improvising to a B section of contrasting ideas and then returning to A. If need be, write these and other ideas down for future practice. Live in this music and allow it to become a natural extension of your playing. Look at other similar slow movements and build your own library of themes, melodies, and harmonic outlines that will further colour your musical creativity.

Example 3.60

Duet (I–A)

S, improvise a simple melody on a tuned percussion instrument tuned to A flat major or, alternatively, on the piano (black notes). **A,** listen to the musical quality and improvise in response, following the harmonic outline. Create melodic themes that will invite; move forward while keeping the calm and fluid nature of a slow movement. Purposefully stay in the precise nature of this mood. Use your voice to add colour as vocalize or create words that are specific to the scenario.

CONCLUSION

The classical period was one of simplicity, grace, and embellishment. Music became a refined art that was sometimes at the expense of emotion. This is both its strength and possible weakness in adapting it for clinical purposes. Mozart's music is exquisite in its creation but is also at times predictable.

The essence of Mozart for music therapists, then, is in our understanding of architectural form and simple harmonic structures. His music is often also aesthetically flawless and as such can bring to our clients the experience of being in perfectly refined dialogue.

In the late works of Beethoven, however, we find music that is about pure spiritual connection rather than sophisticated structure (Lee, 2003). This music is about the human condition and the pain and struggles Beethoven was facing as his health declined. His late music contains some of the most perfect music ever written by man and as such should be fundamental in a music therapist's knowledge of connecting creativity, pain, and expression.

Studying music from the classical period can highlight the clarity of composition that should be at the heart of all clinical work. The exercises in this chapter, if practised carefully and in all keys, will give your improvisations and interventions directness and shape. By also expanding your listening of this period through recordings and concerts, your understanding of this style and its possible clinical implications will begin to become a part of your innate conscious playing in sessions.

Music from the classical period should never be wild or chaotic. It commands attention because of its formality and directness of communicative poignancy. If used carefully, it can provide an opening that will allow clients to find their expressive voice within a form that is clear and contained. It can be a style of transition — that is, moving from one therapeutic position to another — or it can be used as a technique to enhance totality, thus enabling the client to find their own creativity.

Music from the classical period is fresh and commands attention. Its potential expressive elements are those of restrained elegance; it is music that is at once grounded yet unfettered and free. If you allow this music to become at one with your own musical growth and playing, you will find a treasure trove of ideas and creative impulses that will enhance and deepen your improvising in therapy and general musicianship. If you live in this music and allow it to live in you, the dividends it can pay are immeasurable.

CHAPTER 4

Romantic

The romantic era (1825–1900) was one of emotional freedom. Romantic composers, while not discarding the structures of their predecessors, allowed their style to become less constrained and more open to the possibilities of developing chromatic harmony and freer form. There was a sense that the previous formalities were abandoned in favor of more exploratory ways of composing.

Music became more directly emotional, and the gap between artistic creation and human feeling lessened, composers creating music that was more directly representative of all of the range of human feelings. Symphonies and sonatas were freely developed, and the styles of piano pieces and "leider" (song) brought an intimacy through smaller compositions. Opera was crucial in depicting expressions, amongst others, of love, anger, betrayal, and death. Music was highly personal, often translating feelings of being wild, joyous, terrified, and despairing to those filled with deep and profound longing (Schmidt-Jones, 2008).

What is it about music from the romantic era that makes it so directly linked to our emotions and feelings? The following thoughts come from the authors' experiences of listening to and playing romantic music and its subsequent emotional/artistic impact:

Freedom of developing form and structural makeup
Growth and expansion of chromatic harmony
Music directly expressing emotions
Developing link between the human voice and emotions
Expansion of orchestral and instrumental colour
Intensifying conventional structures, i.e., development of symphonic form

Music of the romantic era contains some of the most wonderful and directly expressive tonal music ever written. It connects to the listener and player because it lacks pretence and coercion. It is filled with representations of life and as such can connect us with unpretentious ways of listening.

Becoming attuned with music from the romantic era is not unlike being swathed in pure emotion. Playing romantic music can similarly take us to levels of feeling that will impact our lives as developing musicians.

ROMANTIC MUSIC AND MUSIC THERAPY

The essence of romantic music is a gift for music therapy. Romantic music speaks directly to our emotions and can be used to great effect as a basis for improvisations and as a resource for creating songs and more structures interventions. Embracing romantic music is like embracing a cloth of passion. Admittedly, the music of Chopin is drastically different from that of Wagner, but what both have in common is the desire to express feelings of the human spirit.

In therapy, there are times when we need to allow clients to express themselves more indirectly, to facilitate music that is representative of feelings rather than of an actual direct expression itself. But equally there are times when we want to offer clients musical palettes that are clear in their poignancy. It is these times when romantic music's appeal can serve as an ideal musical/therapeutic intervention.

Embracing romantic music in therapy can yield expressions that are clear but also ones that allow the client to be unfettered in their need for creative freedom. Allowing a client to inhabit a space that is full of romantic warmth is not unlike wrapping them in a cushion of feeling, in the knowledge that it can also depict more intense and raw feelings also. To coexist within a tonal yet potentially chromatic harmonic framework can pay dividends if this is introduced with care and clinical directness. Improvising in a romantic style can be empowering, yet also sensitive and intricate.

Chapter 4 will focus on music by Schumann, Chopin, Brahms, Liszt, Puccini, Wagner, Tchaikovsky, and Richard Strauss. In choosing their music and relevant forms and styles, we hope to give a sense of the possibilities of incorporating romantic music. Rather than concentrate on formal musical theories, this chapter will explore the styles and forms of various composers, suggesting simple ways to bring the essence of their music.

This chapter is oriented toward pieces, mainly from the piano repertoire, looking at specific compositions rather than generalized stylistic musical theories. One of the main difficulties in transferring romantic music into improvisations is finding a simplicity of playing that does not belie the sophistication and complexities of expression.[1] This being said, it is important that you also allow yourself to be inspired by this period that was ultimately about passion and love.

EXERCISES

Chromatic Harmony

The tonic is a fundamental assumption of all western music prior to the romantic period. The tonic was an anchor to which all music returned, and most movements and/or pieces had a single tonic base.

This gave a clear foundational harmonic anchor. Romantic composers started to challenge this assumption by moving, often in fast succession, to related and nonrelated keys while in the same overall key of the movement. This had the effect of diluting the central tonic to give a less directly grounded tonal experience (Benward & Saker, 2003). This important development in musical thinking completely changed the landscape of music. Composers could now create different moods in fast succession, thus adding to the complexities of musical form and expression.

In order to fully embrace the advent of chromatic harmony, music therapists must know and understand the basic theories of nonfunctional harmony. For some, prior knowledge from initial musical education is enough, but for others this will require additional knowledge and practice.

It is essential, as with all other styles represented in this book, that therapists understand some of the formal building blocks and theories of the period they are trying to capture in their work. A basic knowledge of the Neopolitan 6th, augmented 6th, 9th, 11th, 13th, and diminished 7th chords should be understood at a rudimentary level to fully embrace the romantic style.

The development of the 7th chord leading to chromaticism is eloquently described by Paul Nordoff in lectures 11–13 from *Healing Heritage* (Robbins & Robbins, 1998, pp. 98–133). He describes how tonality was extended:

---

[1] The reader is referred to Chapter 18, pp. 194–207, in *Healing Heritage* (Robbins & Robbins, 1998), where you will find explorations of major and minor chords leading to the romantic idiom.

The loosening of tonality is now accepted in music. It's part of the composer's equipment, and he goes on with it. The using of nonchordal tones — of unprepared nonchordal tones — became an absolutely accepted part of music, just as these "old chords" became the chords of our contemporary music. (p. 131)

The reader is urged to read and play through the examples in these lectures, as well as listen fully to the music explored. The time spent reading, listening, and reflecting on these ideas will pay dividends not only in your clinical work, but also in your relationship to music and the subtleties that come with moving away from strict tonality to a more fluid movement of unrelated harmonies that were the hallmark of the romantic era.

It is not the purpose of this section to take the reader through all of the complex theoretical exercises of chromatic harmony needed to fully embrace the romantic style, for indeed knowing comprehensively the development of chromatic harmony is complex. Rather, we hope that by offering examples we will whet your appetite so that you will investigate further and analyze similar components and resources.

Solo (I–A)

Liszt. *Vallée d'Obermann. Années de Pelerinage*

Focus on the beauty of this piece as you play through the opening of this wonderful example of chromatic harmony.

Example 4.1

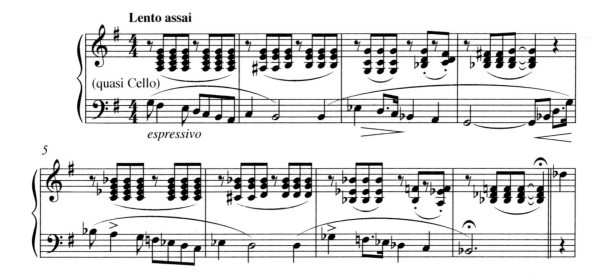

Notice how the harmony and implied tonal centre is always shifting. This is perhaps an extreme example of chromatic harmony but a powerful one nonetheless. The music affords the experience of being in a simple key, but one that is constantly shifting. Experience the balance between melodies in the left and right hands and make sure that you sing them through your playing. Try to play as an orchestra and consider the instruments (e.g., cello, oboe, strings) that would play the melodic lines. Reflect on your emotional response to the harmonic and melodic movement of this passage. The music is warm and contained yet insecure and fragile. Imagine when this style of music may be applicable to your clinical work. Consider a clinical situation when these ever-shifting harmonies might be appropriate. Now play the harmonic outline of this passage and create freer improvisations incorporating your own melodic fragments and ideas.

Example 4.2

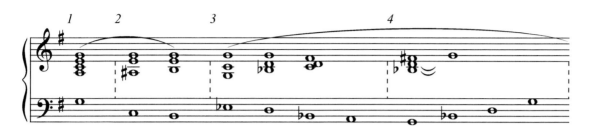

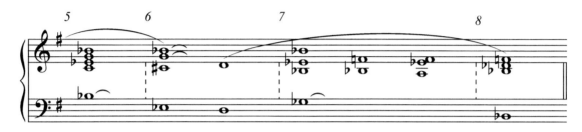

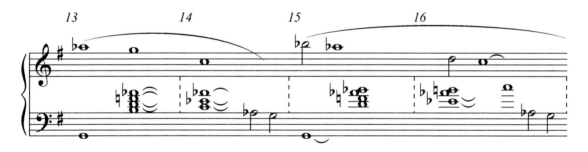

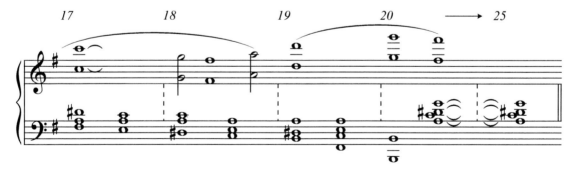

Duet

CD/
(15)   *A,* play with *S,* improvising on a simple reverberating/nonspecific rhythmic instrument such as a cymbal or bell chime. Be free in your rubato, phrasing, and tempo to fit the mood of *S*'s playing. Try to keep the essence of Liszt's chromatic sequences. Compare, and make note of the shifting chromatic harmonies in the roles of *S* and *A.* Reflect on how the chromatic harmonies informed *S*'s playing. Change roles and repeat the experience. Also use the harmonic outline as a basis for a freer improvisation. Move to random and unrelated keys while keeping and returning to the home key of G major. When and if appropriate, use your voice to heighten the experience.

Solo (I–A)

Wagner. *Isoldens Libeestod, Tristan and Isolde*

Play slowly the harmonic outline from this aria.

Example 4.3

Listen as you slowly explore the shifting chromatic harmonies that create a sumptuous and ever-moving harmonic direction. Make note of the three key signatures and how there is no clear cadential ending. When you come to the end of the passage, resting on E major, continue in that key, trying to re-create further ambiguous harmonies in a similar style. Improvise vocally with the harmonies and add some potential words that might be appropriate for a clinical situation. Play the example many times, until you can live in the harmonies and it becomes instinctive. Imagine how this sequence might be used in sessions and how the ambiguous nature of the music might translate to the therapeutic process. What kinds of clients do you think this music may be useful for?

Duet (I–A)

> *S*, sit next to *A* at the piano. *A*, create an improvisation based on the above harmonic progression with piano and voice (using either vocalize or simple words), aiming to entice *S* into the musical dialogue. Improvise accompaniment figures (e.g., broken chords) and simple melodic motives in the piano. *S*, begin singing forming a duet, once you feel comfortable.

A Note on the "Tristan Chord"

> Play the following progression.

Example 4.4

This is the most debated and analyzed harmonic sequence in the music literature and was a turning point in western music (Chailley, 1963; Lee, 2003; Nattiez, 1990; Schoenberg, 1954). It is a passage of genius because of its chromatic direction and lack of key centre. The melodic line moving from leaps (1) to chromatic movement is underpinned with a sophisticated harmonic sense of tension (2) and release (3). Play through this short example and marvel at the simple yet sophisticated progression. There seems to be a lifetime's expression in the three chords. Listen to *Tristan and Isolde* as a complete opera, if possible following with a score, and make note of its emotional impact and feeling of human connectedness. This is music of intense tension/release that could have direct links with the therapeutic relationship, process, and development of improvisational resources.

FORM

Lieder (Song)

Lieder (song) of the romantic period was a defining form that encapsulated the intimacy of a style that was being developed away from the more prescribed music of arias and "art" songs of the baroque era. In lieder, singer and accompanist are united, and both are strongly influenced by the text. Its effectiveness is dependent on both players working together to produce music that is intimate and delicate in relationship. In music therapy terms, we can listen to lieder and imagine the singer as client and accompanist as therapist. Taking this idea in our listening and playing will provide us with many techniques. By analyzing the musical construction from a therapeutic stance alongside the developing musical relationship, we can begin to understand, with more insight, the connection formed between two people in music.

Accompaniment is a crucial aspect of lieder and should be studied as a core component of the style. Accompanying a client in improvisation and song is a crucial technique that all music therapists should master. Accompanying is examined at various stages throughout this book (see Chapter 6) and can be seen as a fundamental clinical/musical technique. Good accompanists often make good clinical improvisers because they know the "art" of sustaining and listening. To accompany well is not only to support but also about breathing and being at one with the singer. This art is clearly transferable to the client/therapist relationship. The therapist's task can also be one of accompanist, both musically and therapeutically. Listening to the sounds of the client as well as the timbre and emotional content will affect how the therapist accompanies musically. Good lieder singers take many years to refine their craft, and it is often said that you cannot perform classical song effectively until you are well into the prime of your career. What this means is that true intimacy in song is not something that can be acquired quickly. Just as music-centered therapists devote their lives to clinical musicianship, so lieder singers devote their lives to being at one with the musical and emotional content of song.

Fauré was a great composer of songs. Nordoff (Robbins & Robbins, 1998) talks of his romantic harmonies as:

> The tenderest, warmest, sweetest, to bring to an adolescent child who needs comfort; who needs the feeling that the music understands her, the music understands him. Understands his turbulent, confused, mixed-up condition, which you get so desperately in the physically handicapped with normal intelligence. When they enter adolescence, they really suffer, and this kind of music can be so meaningful for them. And in this respect, I can recommend to you all, for investigation and further study, the songs of Fauré. (p. 203)

He then goes on to investigate and play "Après un Rêve." The opportunities for experiencing and analyzing Fauré's songs as potential resources are many, and the reader is urged to take time to harness the exquisite sounds and humanistic implications of his songs.

Wigram (2004) describes and outlines accompanying techniques that can be used as a precursor to the examples under examination. There are many different accompanying patterns that can be adopted and used in music therapy when working in the romantic style. Play through as many examples of lieder as you can and make note of how the accompaniment supports the singer and the musical relationship between both parts. Build up a library of accompaniment figures that you could use in sessions, taking their core components and practising them in different configurations and keys. As you study the accompaniments, always improvise vocally and imagine clinical examples where this may have been appropriate.

Downbeat

A word of caution in the use of accompaniments must be highlighted before we turn to the literature. When using accompaniment patterns, the use of the upbeat to the downbeat of the next bar must always be given careful consideration. If the therapist plays the final upbeat of the bar, he will then infer the pulse for the following bar, which could be potentially blocking for the client's creativity. Unless the therapist's intent is to provide music that is ongoing and rigid in tempo, it is better to leave the final beat of the bar silent and as a possible pause/rubato. This then gives the client the role of inferring the first beat of the following bar. As therapists, we must always be open to the fluidity of the developing improvisation and not become fixed. By keeping the final beat open, we are allowing the client the potential of being a truly co-creative partner in the evolving music. This is a delicate balance, however, and at times, depending on the therapeutic aims of the work, it may be necessary to play accompaniment patterns to include every beat of the bar. In the following examples, it is important to experience and work with the accompaniments in both forms.

Solo (I–A)

Schumann. *Dichterliebe,* Op. 48

In considering accompaniments during the classical period, we can find a wealth of material that can be directly applied to improvisation and the development of song. Schubert, Schumann, and Wolf are perhaps three of the greatest figures who devoted a large portion of their compositions to lieder. Living in songs of the romantic era is an intimate and delicate experience. Either by listening or by performing lieder, you sense an openness and vulnerability of relationship between the singer and piano. Nordoff (Robbins & Robbins, 1998), in his teachings, talks of Schumann's song genius:

> How many of you know the *Dichterliebe* (Op. 48) of Schumann? Good! Isn't that lovely. I'm so glad. You should all know them — "The Poet's Love" — some of the most beautiful songs ever written (p. 204).

For this section, we will consider examples from this song cycle.

Aus Meinen Tränen Sprießen

Solo (I)

> Play and sing three times, the first time singing "la" and the second time including the words in German if you can, then in English. Make note of the following components: (a) the clarity of musical expression, (b) how the accompaniment relates to the vocal line, and (c) the difference between singing as vocalize, then using words — what difference does the text make for the song? Also note how the accompaniment follows the meter of the voice exactly. The upbeat is silent, allowing the flow of the music to move freely. Allow the silences to breathe before moving to the next phrase. Live in the simplicity and beauty of this song.

Example 4.5

Play the accompaniment again, this time adding words to create a simple greeting or good-bye song.

Example 4.6

The spaces left for the client are suggestions, and you may find different ways of incorporating their responses. Remember to play and sing with pauses and rubato. Experience the directness and simplicity of the song you have now created.

Duet (I)

S, sit next to *A* at the piano. *A,* play the greeting song from above, creating a chorus A. Improvise a B section in the same style, encouraging *S* to play the piano with you. Keep the three-part voicing simple and clear. Return to the A chorus to complete the experience.

This effective adaptation of this song can create a clinical focus that is simple yet sophisticated and therapeutically beautiful if played with sensitivity and care.

Amleuch Tenden Sommer Morgan

Solo (I)

Play the accompaniment of the song without the vocal line, noticing how Schumann crafts the downward phrases of the right hand and his use and absence of a downbeat to give the music structural freedom. His writing is simple yet beautifully affective in creating music that is calm yet fluid.

Example 4.7

Play again, this time including the vocal line first as vocalize, then with the words. Note the interplay between the accompaniment and the voice, how the accompaniment consists of downward phrases while the vocal lines move upward, and how each part complements the other. Explore how Schumann sets the words, and imagine the kind of music you might use to colour these words. The words depict someone who is in pain when outside the world is beautiful and at peace.

How do these words reflect the clients you work with and how philosophically might you make the link between this song and the broader issues facing people with disabilities and/or living with illness?

Play/sing and become familiar with the harmonic outline of this song.

Example 4.8

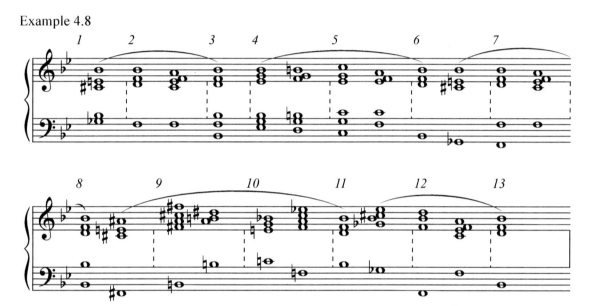

Play the harmonic sequence in different accompanying patterns. Here are a few suggestions.

Example 4.9

Example 4.10

In the first example, play the two versions while noticing the difference between playing the triads in a constant motion as opposed to only the upward phrase ending with a possible pause. Experiment with other accompaniment patterns. Use your voice as you explore the balance between piano as accompaniment and voice as soloist.

Duet (I)

S, improvise a steady and secure rhythm on a nonpitched percussion instrument. *A,* play one of the accompaniment patterns from the above exercise and accompany *S* in his or her playing. Change your accompaniment patterns as the improvisation develops.

Try a second improvisation, with *S* playing a tuned percussion instrument tuned to B flat major. See how differently your improvisation/song develops.

Lieder is an intimate art form and can be an effective style to use in both improvising and more structured song forms. Its strength lies at many levels, both emotionally and musically. Song cycles from the classical period can be very poignant for the listener and performer alike. You have only to hear and experience Schubert's *Die Winterreise* (D. 911) to know the emotional depth that lieder can attain.

Taking the essence of a clear song line and accompaniment into clinical work can be a powerful experience. It can help to define and develop the musical/therapeutic relationship with precision and focus. As with all parts of this book, we urge you to build a library of romantic lieder and lieder accompaniments.

Bagatelle

Short depictive movements commonly known as bagatelles, normally written for piano, were common in the romantic era. They balanced many composers' larger compositions such as sonatas and symphonies. These pieces normally contained one emotion, though musically they could be challenging and harmonically diverse.

This music is excellent for music therapists because it contains a precision of compositional design in a short, defined space. Schumann was perhaps one of the greatest composers of short piano pieces. His music was a central influence on the work of Paul Nordoff, and Schumann's piano pieces are referred to extensively throughout *Healing Heritage* (Robbins & Robbins, 1998).

The pieces under consideration are from one of Paul's favorite sets of pieces: *Davidsbundler,* Op.6.

The piece chosen for distillation highlights Schumann's style of composition and its potential for clinical use.

Solo (I–A)

Schumann. *Innig, Davidsbundler,* Op. 6

Play this piece many times, noting Schumann's use of voicing, melody, and harmonic movement. Revel in its compositional precision and beauty.

Example 4.11

Play the harmonic essence of the movement, this time playing the music with different tempi, dynamics, and with attack. Explore the music freely and creatively.

Example 4.12

Duet

CD/
16 **S,** play nonpitched percussion instrument(s), such as conga or cymbal. Play a simple and steady beat. **A,** improvise, creating patterns from Example 4.12. At first, play the harmonic sequence exactly as written to form section A. When you become more confident, move away and play in a similar style more freely, creating a B section. Return to your original style, A, to complete the improvisation. Try this example with different nonpitched percussion instruments.

Play through as many short piano pieces (bagatelles) as you can from the romantic era. Each time you explore a movement, decide how you will extract the compositional structure. Write out the essence of the music you wish to practise. This may be the harmony, melody, rhythm, or a combination. Once you have mastered the structure of the music and feel comfortable in playing it as written, move away from the original into freer improvised playing. Always return to the original music to conclude.

Mazurka

The piano music of Chopin is a wonderful clinical resource. His compositions contain many original stylistic devices. His mazurkas were written throughout his career. The characteristics of the mazurka are those of a lively dance written in triple meter with accents on the 2nd or 3rd beat of each bar. Chopin's piano music has a distinct style that is simple yet indicative of his home country (Poland) and his personal musical expression. His music is at the heart of the romantic era and his style, if captured successfully, can be a powerful musical tool in therapy. The two mazurkas chosen for distillation come from the earlier part of his career, both being musically and emotionally diverse.

Chopin. *Mazurka in A Minor,* Op. 7, No. 2

Solo (I)

Play the first half of the piece, noting how the melody and accompaniment complement each other. Make special emphasis on the melodic triplets. Chopin purposefully leaves the first beat of each bar in the left hand silent, so that the melody can move forward in a fluid and improvisatory style. Play in different tempi from very slow to very fast, making note of how differently the direction of the music is dependent on the speed.

Example 4.13

Listen especially to the descending chromatic passage of the second half leading back to the theme at bar 25. Here, to help you in your harmonic understanding of this passage, the harmonic essence of bars 17–25 has been notated. This music has a poignant, nostalgic quality. Chopin makes use of the diminish chord to dissolve the sense of harmonic stability in order to modulate back to the home key. This technique can be used in your sessions. Explore this both in relation to the piece but also as a possible sequence that could be used in other improvisations. If possible, practise this example in different keys.

Example 4.14

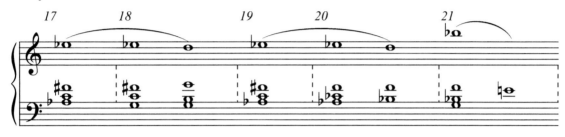

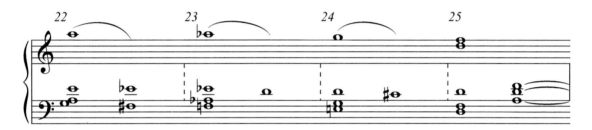

Now play the second half, which is in the relative major. Note how the emotional content of the music changes and how, in contrast to the opening, the piano writing becomes more fluid. The left hand writing is like a cello, allowing a sense of calmness and space.

Example 4.15

Duet (I)

Arrange the following scale on a tuned percussion instrument: F, G, G♯, A, A♯, B, C, C♯, D. Alongside this, place a contrasting nontuned instrument (e.g., tambourine, cymbal).

Example 4.16

S, play the xylophone in a fast and florid manner. *A,* use the opening section of the mazurka, A. Stress the fast and sad style of the music. Contrast this with the second section, B, on a nontuned instrument (cymbal). It is important that you play section B in a way distinctly different to A. Return to section A to complete your improvisation. If appropriate, use your voice and encourage *S* to sing also.

Solo (I)

Chopin. *Mazurka in C,* Op. 7, No. 5

Experience the uplifting quality of this music, considering what instruments might be appropriate for forming a dialogue. Become familiar with the simple harmonic backbone of the piece (I, V, I). Try improvising away from the piece in a contrasting style, creating an original B section in a different related key (e.g., C minor). Return to the theme as written, A, to conclude.

Example 4.17

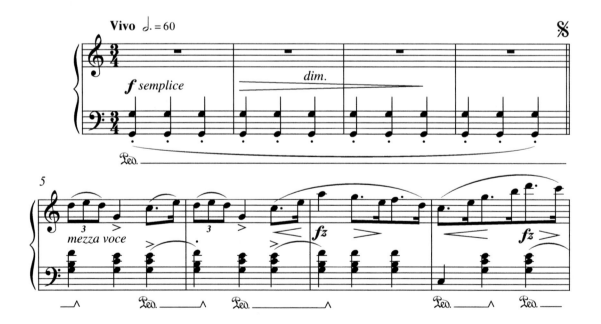

Duet (I)

CD1 (17)   **S,** play a simple, handheld, nontuned percussion instrument such as a tambourine while in a standing position. **A,** improvise by creating energy and direction through the mazurka. Try to entice **S** to move the body as well as play.

S, use your body movement and/or dance when you feel that the music impels you. Try to be free in your movements and take note of how the music affects your body responses as well as your instrumental playing. Keep the simplicity of the melody and accompaniment throughout.

Dance and music are strong allies. Music can initiate movement from clients when played with direction and intent. Examining the dance music of classical composers such as Chopin can add to our palette of triple meter resources.

Intermezzi and Rhapsodies

Brahms was an "absolute composer." His music did not represent anything other than itself and is perhaps the truest representation of the romantic era even though his contemporaries considered him to be old-fashioned.

To know Brahms is to know music of the purest romantic expression. His music is laden with feeling and emotion and is a gift for the music therapist.

Brahms's Op. 118 intermezzi contain much finely placed music. An intermezzo is a middle movement or lighter section of a larger work. The six pieces in Op. 118 include four intermezzi, one ballade, and one romance.

The fact that Brahms placed the intermezzi at the beginning and end of the collection shows that he had an unconventional way of thinking and was not afraid to break rules in the name of artistic expression.

All of the pieces in the collection are tied by neighboring key signatures as well as melodic and rhythmic motifs, which appear in inversions and different keys. The key signatures of the collection are: A minor, A major, G minor, F minor (moving to D major), F major, and E flat minor.

Brahms. *Intermezzo in A Minor,* Op. 118, No. 1

Solo (A)

Play the piece slowly and carefully. There are interesting features that should be highlighted.

First, it is composed in a miniature sonata form: exposition (measures 1–11), development (measures 12–21), recapitulation (measures 22–33), and coda (measures 34–41).

Second, there are elements of opposition and integration. The main theme of the opening is inverted in measure 12, and the tones of the A minor triad are always present even in the diverting tonal development of measures 2, 4, and 6.

These technical compositional techniques add to the overall ever-shifting yet constant feel of the music. The music is not easy and needs care and attention to enable full understanding of Brahms's compositional process.

Notice the ambiguous, ever-shifting tonal base, moving from the implied opening harmonic centre of A minor/C major through to the closing of the piece on an A major 2nd inversion.

Example 4.18

Allegro non assai, ma molto appassionato

Play the harmonic essence of the movement. Explore further and become more confident with the harmonies. Play in different time signatures and textures across the piano. Explore tempo, dynamics, and different emotional intent. Create themes and/or melodic motives and use your voice. Live in the uncertainty and mellifluous direction of the music.

Example 4.19

Duet (A)

S, play a drum with a simple, regular beat. *A,* use the essence of the intermezzo. As the improvisation develops, move in and out of Brahms's harmonic palette, creating music that is constantly and emotionally moving. Try to create a heightened emotional music experience. Use your voice if appropriate.

Repeat this exercise with an instrument that creates a wash of sound, such as a cymbal or chimes.

Brahms. *Intermezzo in A Major,* Op. 118, No. 2

In contrast, this intermezzo in A major is a clear and more directly romantic piece that keeps the grounding of the tonic major throughout the first section and then uses an F# minor as a base for the second section.

This music produces an emotional effect that is at peace and grounded as opposed to the constantly moving sounds of the first intermezzo. Comparison of both pieces proves an interesting exercise for the purposes of taking Brahms's style into sessions.

Solo (A)

Play the first 25 bars. Consider Brahms's use of melody and how he keeps the momentum going through extended phrases that always arch to the end of a phrase. It is the richness of the harmonies that make the music so powerful.

This music should be played with rubato and great feeling. Become lost in the beauty of its sounds and textures.

Example 4.20

Play the harmonic outline of the piece, keeping the calm nature of the music. Improvise in a continued sense of calm and keep the tonality of a major throughout. Use the outline to create specific songs and/or interventions that continue in the same style.

Example 4.21

Duet (A)

S, choose a percussion instrument that can create long, slow phrases (e.g., cymbal). **A,** match the mood, playing to create an improvisation that is slow and calm. Include your voice and/or words if appropriate.

Repeat this exercise using a pitched instrument (xylophone) tuned to A major.

Brahms's music is rich and powerful and while never being overtly poignant is perfectly crafted to produce emotional musical experiences that are strong.

To study Brahms as a therapist is to understand the relationship between craft and emotion that is at the heart of music-making and its relationship to life.

Opera

The connections between opera and music therapy have recently begun to be explored (O'Brien, 2006), specifically in relation to end-of-life care. Drama–music, words–music, and emotional development–music are just some of the areas that could prove fruitful and significant for music-centered practice.

Romantic operas broke the tradition of separating recitative and aria to produce musical drama that is continuous and flowing. In romantic operas, there is often the feeling of a huge and continuous wave of emotion. As the plot develops and the representation of heightened emotions becomes the focus, the listener/audience is transported to extraordinary places that are unrivaled in music.

To be able to translate this experience into therapy could achieve extraordinary results. Balancing words and music is at the core of clinical musicianship, especially for those who use song as their main vehicle of expression.

Learning the art of setting words in opera, alongside that of popular song, could pay dividends in our understanding of the clinical song/arias form. These ideas can be seen firsthand through the groundbreaking work of O'Brien (2006).

Puccini and Audrey

Puccini composed operas at the height of the romantic period. His combination of heightened melody, direct form, held suspensions, harmonic movement, and expression culminate in a powerful musical/dramatic experience.

From the opening moments of his operas, you feel a sense of emotional suspense that continues and becomes ever more reflective and intense as the drama unfolds. Experiencing operas such as *La Bohème,* it is hard not to be affected by the force of the plot and Puccini's depiction of love, pain, and loss (Masden & Geringer, 2008).

The work of Audrey (Aigen, 1998) is a foundational Nordoff-Robbins study. This case is about the marriage between words, music, and drama. Listening to the audio examples of Audrey as the work unfolds in the enactment of *Cinderella,* you can hear many operatic overtones in the style of Puccini in Paul's playing.

Their course of therapy culminated in the final aria, "What shall we do? My stomach hurts" (Audio Excerpt 12).

We can listen to this example on different levels: first, as a product of therapy through Paul and Clive's contextual analysis:

Audrey stood on the piano and sang. She knew we were leaving that next day, and she was troubled and upset. She had greeted us that morning by saying, "My stomach hurts." I began to sing these words, and Audrey's aria followed. We had been improvising for about ten minutes when the audience began to arrive. We continued. Audrey did not stop. She continued to improvise quietly and thoughtfully. The aria you will hear, for aria it truly is, improvised by an 8-year-old child, is an incredible piece of music. (Aigen, 1998, p. 52)

Paul's music reflects and meets Audrey's emotional state with accuracy, thus allowing her to express her feelings of loss. This clinical-emotional-musical accuracy is at the heart of their work.

Listening to this music also from an aesthetic perspective, you are amazed at how Paul is able to capture so accurately the essence of operatic/aria form, offering it to Audrey so precisely. It is the marriage of the "Puccini/Operatic Idiom" and his knowing of her inner world that allows true therapy to happen.

Perhaps the style of Puccini's music — his compositional essence — also becomes a force in the therapeutic process and relationship. The musical partnership thus becomes a triad of roles: Audrey — Paul and Clive — Puccini, Puccini becoming an active part of the therapeutic relationship.

Tchaikovsky. *Eugene Onegin*

Eugene Onegin is a wonderful example of a romantic opera in the Russian tradition. Tchaikovsky's use of connected themes serves to heighten the intensity of the drama and bring musical continuity. The main theme of the opera, which connects the whole score, is stated in the opening notes. This idea of a thematic core is central to romantic operas and was developed later in the musical painting of characters through the operas of Wagner. This example comes from the "Letter Scene," which can be interpreted as the emotional/musical core of the piece.

Solo (A)

Play the opening bars from the opening of Act II. This is the main theme that is developed in different guises throughout the opera. Note the two short melodic phrases, which are then extended.

The sense of urgency and moving forward is further heightened by the harmonies, which provide as sense of relief when returning to the opening chord. This is a wonderful example of calm building to tension and then release.

Example 4.22

Play the harmonic outline of this same passage. Get to know the harmonies and explore other melodic themes and ideas. Sing and create your own aria A, improvising away from this passage B in a contrasting style (if need be, write down a similar harmonic outline so as to keep a musical focus) and returning to the theme of A to recapitulate.

Example 4.23

Duet (A)

Take the passage and create different clinical scenarios.

    a)   A greeting, farewell, or theme-based song
    b)   A drum song
    c)   A group work piece with contrasting instruments
    d)   An instrumental activity without words (but potentially vocalize)

With each scenario create words and then find a suitable melody or theme. Play the example in different tempi and with different attack and textures, depending on the scenario you have chosen. *A,* be dramatic in your use of the music and translate to *S* this sense of operatic form. Allow this music and other operatic extracts to live and become a part of your improvisational vocabulary.

Richard Strauss. *Der Rosenkavalier,* Op. 59

To conclude this chapter, we would like to offer a passage from the closing of Richard Strauss's opera *Der Rosenkavalier.* This example is pertinent for music therapy on many levels and represents a harmonic language that stretches tonality while languishing in the sumptuous sounds of an ever-moving yet constant tonal centre. In *Der Rosenkavalier,* we find some of the most beautiful operatic music ever written. It is not only the simplicity and popularity of melody that constitutes its greatness but rather an overall sense of sumptuousness that envelops the listener for almost the entire duration of the opera. You become swamped with the emotional content of the work.

Solo (A)

Play the piano version (bars 1–25) of the closing trio, singing the melody line wherever possible. Experience the elongation of musical lines with the dissonances and resolutions.

Example 4.24

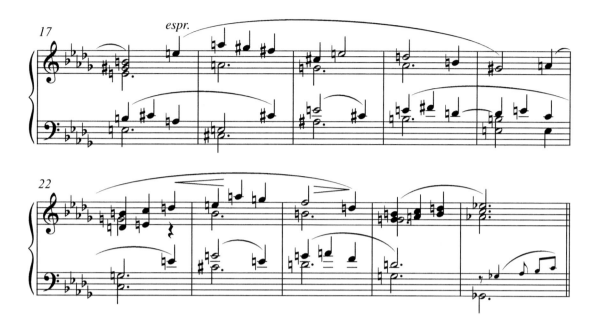

Play the harmonic distillation of this passage and continue bars 26–41 in a similar style, creating your own operatic aria with words or vocalize. As you become more familiar with the harmonies and sounds, improvise in a similar style singing, using your voice intertwined with the piano.

Example 4.25

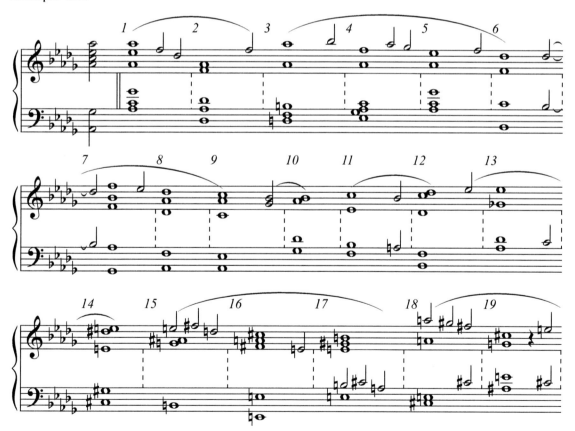

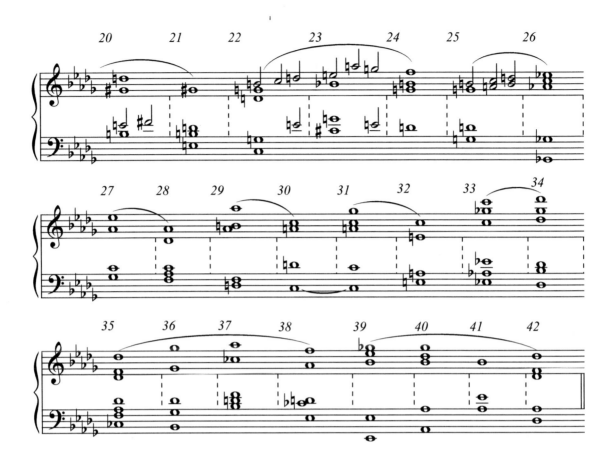

Duet (A)

A, play the opening chord of the progression slowly and with a sense of rubato. *S,* begin to sing simply and quietly on "la." As the music develops, *A,* sing also, creating a vocal duet with the piano accompaniment. Use words, if appropriate, to create a Strauss-like aria.

Opera of the romantic era can be a wonderful resource for improvising music that is brimming with heightened emotion and intensity. It can also act as a backdrop and picture painting for many different therapeutic encounters. Embracing opera as a musician and therapist can be an extremely rewarding experience. It brings together elements of music, emotional depiction, drama, and dance, all of which are potentially crucial aspects in the therapeutic process.

CONCLUSION

What, then, of romantic music as an expressive, creative guide? How can we utilize this music, extract its essence, and offer it to our clients in a way that will embrace their needs and enable a musical/therapeutic path necessary for growth? The answer to these questions lies not in the notes themselves, although indeed the musical-structural makeup of romantic music is a fascinating study, but rather in the emotional impact that is inherent in the music. Romantic composers, perhaps more than those of any other era, opened their hearts to the connection between intense inner feelings and expression. It is this spirit of musical communication that can affect the therapeutic process and move it forward, often with dramatic effects. Because many romantic composers were in tune with their feelings, their music is direct and devoid of formality and emotional distance.

Harnessing the musical components of the romantic style is not an easy task. Each composer, as with all parts of this book, could be a lifetime's study. The composers and exercises represented in this chapter are just a small example of the broad scope of romantic music that is available. Musically, this era is perhaps one of the most difficult from which to extract because of its adherence to theories of tonality. At the same time, through developing theories of chromaticism, the music moves further and further away from a tonal base. This makes the therapist's task difficult if he is to incorporate an essence of this music into his clinical palette. Thus our musical-theoretical knowledge must be acquired slowly and with intent.

Most of us at some point in our lives will have responded to and been affected by the piano music of Schumann, a Mahler symphony, or a great aria from an opera by Verdi or Puccini. How and why is this music so powerful, and what does it say about the connections between the human condition and living?

More than that from any other period, music from the romantic era is about love — often unrequited, painful, and mostly in connection with loss. The idea of love and the therapeutic process is and will always be an area of contention. How can we love our clients, and can our clients love us, while keep the therapeutic boundaries safe for both client and therapist? If we bring music from the romantic era directly into our work, could this be potentially damaging with regard to this dynamic?

Music and love are longtime allies and as such should be integral to our musical/clinical thinking. Our counter-transferential responses to clients are many and complex, and if the course of therapy is successful, there can be intense feelings of compassion and love. This is both healthy and a natural part of the process and relationship between two people. It is how we understand these phenomena and utilize them in a healthy way for the therapeutic alliance that makes it an important force. The exact same consideration could be made for the use of music from the romantic era in therapy and the translation of love. This truly is music of love and as such is a rich and profound resource.

CHAPTER 5

20th Century

As romantic music developed and pushed forward the bounds of functional harmony with a potential absence of resolution, music became freer and less constrained. Harmonic complexity developed to the point where it could not continue without entering the world of atonality. At the end of the romantic era, composers such as Richard Wagner (1813–1883), Gustav Mahler (1860–1911), and Alexander Scriabin (1872–1915) began to stretch and suspend tonality to produce music that was ambiguous and less strongly related to a tonal centre (Roig-Francoli, 2007). You have only to listen to the later works of Richard Strauss (1864–1949) or the early works of Arnold Schoenberg (1874–1951) and Alban Berg (1885–1935) to hear firsthand these phenomena. This weakening of functional tonality was to herald one of the greatest and most dramatic changes in the direction of western music. Musical syntax — that is, how musical elements are connected to each other — also made great strides forward at the beginning of the 20th century (Turek, 2007). This freeing of compositional thought and design brought about some wonderful new innovations and creative, nontheoretical, distinctive music from composers such as Charles Ives (1874–1954), Béla Bartók (1881–1945), and Igor Stravinsky (1882–1971).

Compositional thinking became free and open to whatever sources the composer desired. The advent of the neoclassical movement, popular between the two World Wars, with its influence back to the baroque and classical periods, provided music that was fresh and new. Neoclassicism returned to a sense of tonality that could at any moment move into the strident, less consonant style of atonality. Serial music, as developed by Arnold Schoenberg, became influential in providing a strict set of compositional rules that culminated in music that sounds simultaneously free from tonality and consonance and yet is highly developed and structured.

Moving into the mid-20th century, what is called the "avant-garde" took music into new experimental territories. John Cage (1932–1992) developed his ideas of chance, using new and nonstandard ways of playing instruments (Lee, 2003). Other influential composers were Karl Stockhausen (1928–2007), who further broke the bounds of formality through electronic and stage works; Pierre Boulez (b. 1925), whose music is defined through mathematics and integral serialism; and Luciano Berio (1925–2003), whose most influential music is based on compositions for voice (sinfonia) and solo instruments (sequenzas).

Music also began to be influenced by trends in popular music. Leonard Bernstein (1918–1990) composed Broadway musicals as well as more formal works, creating music that is accessible yet at times intricate. Philip Glass (b. 1937) and Steve Reich (b. 1936) were at the forefront of the minimalism movement, composing music that is repetitive and based on music as a gradual process. Living in minimalism is akin to stepping into music that is slow-moving and static yet highly charged and original. Another area of note is that of sacred minimalism. Composers such as Arvo Pärt (b. 1935) and Henryk Gorecki (b. 1933) have returned to a more static harmonic base both in sacred and secular compositions, creating music that is full of ongoing tension and deep spiritual content. This music needs to be listened to with the space and profound grandeur it portrays.

Contemporary music, then, is the result of perhaps one of the richest and most diverse periods in western music. To be influenced by atonality and the freedoms of form as well as the overt return to tonality and more popular styles is to live in a musical world that is unconstrained and free. Here is music that is full of inspiration and possibilities for the future. We do not know how much of this music and which of its composers will still be heard in the next 100 years. This is not for us to decide. What practising musicians should know and experience, however, is the unfettered joy and freedom of contemporary music. This is music of our time and as such should be treated with our greatest respect and understanding.

20th CENTURY MUSIC AND MUSIC THERAPY

Music therapists misunderstand contemporary music perhaps more than that of any other period. There is often the assumption that bitonality and atonality are not relevant for clinical practice because they are too removed from the cultural and emotional context of our clients. This rather misguided assumption comes from the fact, we believe, that contemporary music is not immediately accessible and is often outside the experience of the music therapist. Atonality, then, has come to represent a style of music that is lacking in form and devoid of melodic content. Unfortunately, these assumptions are untrue, for indeed contemporary music contains all of these elements albeit in a different context. If music therapists are to embrace modern classical styles in their clinical work, they need to open themselves to a style of music that may not be immediately familiar to and comfortable for them. For music therapists who are inspired by and involved in contemporary music, this link into clinical musicianship is natural and inspiring.

Along with the developments of the post-romantic period leading into extended chromaticism and atonality, divisions appeared between popular and art music (Turek, 2007).

> Although music in the 20th century represents, in many important respects, the continuation of past practices, much of it reflects an unprecedented reassessment of the nature and function of melody, harmony, rhythm, form, sound, and even the meaning of music. This reassessment led to a schism between art music and popular music that grew into a chasm. It lasted for the better part of the century, but recently, musicians from both sides (art and popular) have been approaching the cleft and looking across. (p. 663)

It was during this schism that music therapy was born as a profession. Does this fact answer the question as to why the music used in music therapy is so predominantly based on popular tonal music? That clinical practice came from this base because art music became marginalized and less accepted in society? Perhaps the answer to these questions is more complex and cannot be obtained by simply acknowledging the social tastes of the time.

As music is now bridging this ravine, it is ever more urgent that music therapists embrace all aspects of present-day trends. We can now access music that has elements of dance and world fused with jazz, classical, and others. This new music has no imposed boundaries and could be influential in the musical development of contemporary clinical practice.

What, then, of the role of atonality in improvisation in present-day music therapy? How can we balance the polarities between tonality and atonality to produce music that contains a true essence necessary for our clients' needs? It is impossible here to cover all aspects of contemporary music. What we have done, however, is to attempt to give a taste of the diverse music that came out of the 20th century and how that led us into the next millennium.

Hopefully, this chapter will dispel the myth that contemporary and atonal music is awkward and not relevant for music therapy.

EXERCISES

NATIONALISM

One of the most important aspects in the development of contemporary music was the move toward nationalism and the influence of folk music. Composers began to look to their cultural identity as a basis for their developing style. Vaughan Williams (1872–1958) and Aaron Copland (1900–1990) used nationalism as their main compositional style, while others, such as Benjamin Britten (1913–1976) and Dimitri Schostakovitch (1906–1975), allowed folk music to colour but not become their main musical voice.

The first part of this chapter is devoted to covering some of the main nationalistic trends and their implications for distillation into the music therapist's palette of developing resources. Some styles are lyrical and tonal creating the neo-classical and neo-romantic movements while some are strident and more indicative of the atonal parameters of contemporary music. The one country we do not cover is Spain, due to the fact that this distinct style is covered extensively in other publications (Nordoff & Robbins, 2007; Robbins & Robbins, 1998; Wigram, 2004).

Creating a distinct nationalistic style in music therapy not only can add colour to improvisations but also can be important in working with clients who originate from the countries in question.[1]

Paul Nordoff: USA

Paul Nordoff (1909–1977) is unique in music therapy because he is the only established historical contemporary composer who was also a music therapist. Because of this fact, it is critical that we include examples of his art compositions here for investigation.

Much is written and documented about his contribution to music therapy in the development of the Nordoff-Robbins approach (Robbins, 2005). Very little, however, is documented about his compositions before entering music therapy and the importance of his music within the contemporary developments of America.

Paul Nordoff's art compositions spanned from 1923–1962. His music is eclectic and contains many different styles and influences. In addition to his serious and intense orchestral music and neoclassical chamber compositions, he also composed a Broadway musical *(The Masterpiece)* and a vast output of art songs.

As with so many other American composers, in his music you can also hear the links with jazz and developing popular music. There are also a small number of compositions that could be classed as post–music therapy *(Prayers from the Ark, Seeker of Truth)*, bridging his artistic and clinical expression.

Clive Robbins writes in his historical exploration of creative music therapy (2005):

> Alongside his clinical work as a creative therapist, and for as long as I had known him, Paul understandably carried the regret that his compositions from the 25 years prior to music therapy were not being performed, and that he was not known as the composer he knew himself to be. (p. 20)

---

[1]This idea will be further explored in Part Four when we look to the world styles of India, Korea, and Argentina as our musical and clinical guides.

It is clear from studying his scores and listening to the few available recordings that Paul Nordoff was potentially a leading figure in contemporary American music. In 1933, his Piano Concerto was awarded the Bearns Prize. He also received two Guggenheim Fellowships. Martha Graham commissioned from him three ballets: *Every Soul Is a Circus, Salem Shore,* and *In Search of Folly.* His music is uncompromising in its American influences but also has an originality and freshness that makes it unique and inspiring.

In presenting extracts from three compositions, a question arises that is unique in this book, namely: What can a musicological and humanistic investigation of Nordoff's compositional craft — moving from being a composer to being a music therapist — teach us about the balance between artistic and clinical musicianship? Further: By comparatively investigating his compositions alongside his clinical improvisations, what can we learn about the links between using music clinically and artistically?

These fundamental questions cannot be fully answered here, but we hope that by analyzing some extracts of his music for distillation into therapy, we will see the potential for looking further into his art music as a guide for developing clinical musicianship. All of the examples are instrumental and lyrical in content.

Hill Song for Piano

Solo (I)

> Play this lyrical piano piece, noting its craftsmanship and beautifully measured emotional content.

Example 5.1

The folk mood of this expressive music is enhanced by the constant use of secondary 7th and 9th chords in the harmony.

Example 5.2

At letter A, the tonal centre C is skillfully hidden by a series of modulations until it finally emerges at letter B. The form of the piece is unusual, beginning and ending with the material of the introduction (Freed, 1958).

5 Measures — Introduction
8 Measures — 1st theme
9 Measures — Development
4 Measures — Fragment of 1st theme
6 Measures — Introduction

Play the harmonic distillation, noting carefully how the secondary 7ths and 9ths are used to keep the momentum of the music moving. There is a sense of harmonic floating that is the core expression of this piece.

Example 5.3

Duet (I)

CD 1
(19) Piano – four hands. **S,** treble; **A,** bass. **S,** begin playing freely. **A,** create an open improvisation, keeping the calm and gentle mood of the music. Improvise themes and use your voice. Once you have become familiar with the progression, begin to introduce a more structured intervention, such as a greeting or good-bye song, potentially notating it for further use in sessions and as a part of your developing resource library.

Lost Summer, for Mezzo Soprano and Chamber Orchestra

This is a beautiful orchestral song set to a poem by Sylvia Townsend Tuner and is a worthy companion to Barber's *Knoxville.* The song moves with grace and poise, taking us to the broad landscapes of America. The harmonic writing is static yet wonderfully measured, with exquisite orchestration and stunning writing between woodwind, strings, and voice. Emotionally, you feel caught and suspended by a sense of delicacy yet profound longing and pain.

Duet (A)

> **S,** play the opening (in E natural minor) on the treble of the piano, with **A** on the bass, piano four hands.[2] Note how the similar moving accompaniment contrasts with the melodic arches of the oboe. Play slowly, experiencing the simple and elegant beauty of the harmonies.

Example 5.4

---

[2] It also possible to experience this example by playing the oboe line on other orchestral instruments **S,** with **A** on the piano.

Repeat, creating a greeting song as indicated. Try again without the melody line taking the roles of *S* and *A* at the piano. With both examples, use rubato and pauses as you might do with a child in a session. Continue improvising in the same fluid style, creating a B section returning to the opening to conclude with the song.

It is important to note here comparisons between Nordoff's art music and his songs for children in therapy. You can see here how easily he adapted his compositional gifts for sessions and how similar his music was artistically and clinically.

Concerto for Piano, Violin, and Orchestra

This concerto is direct and appealing in style and has a strong neoclassical feel. The first movement *(The Children)* reminds you of an English country dance; the second *(The Lovers)* is lyrical and full of sumptuous melodies; and the final movement *(The Dancers)* is an unashamed American "hoedown."

The Lovers, Largo, 2nd Movement

Solo (I–A)

Play the piano reduction of the opening music for strings. The music is gentle yet full of emotion and intensity of expression. Experience the free-flowing melody with its arches and soaring intervals. Live in the tension and release of the phrases, making note of how Paul subtly uses suspension to create a musical line that breathes, moves forward, and then rests. Try a continuation of this music, improvising in a similar style.

Example 5.5

Duet (I–A)

> **S,** choose a nonpulsed instrument, e.g., cymbal. Play slowly and quietly. **A,** create a dialogue through the above passage. Use your voice if appropriate (vocalize and/or words), allowing the phrases to build a slow-moving and quiet musical panorama.

Solo (I–A)

> Play the piano section from later in the movement. This melody is simple yet elegant and reminds you of a slow movement from a Mozart piano concerto. Notice how the changing time signatures give the melodic direction a sense of freedom that is improvisatory in style yet highly measured.

Example 5.6

Duet

> Piano four hands: **S,** play the white notes in the treble, softy and quietly. **A,** in the lower register, use the above extract, taking the music into a freer section **B.** Remain in C major or move to the relative minor. Return to section A to complete.

Distilling Nordoff's compositions and taking them into therapy provides us with a musical palette that is unique both in terms of the scope of this book and of how music therapists in the future will develop their resources. His compositions are in many different styles, from the tonal popular style of the American tradition to the serious and more atonal expressions of his music that was influenced by anthroposophy. That Paul did not refer back to his compositions after entering therapy raises questions about the validity of now looking back at his past music to influence the future practice of music therapy. In response and after spending time living with his scores, it is our view that by analyzing Nordoff's compositional process and taking those elements into how he created clinical creations, we can better understand the link between the artistic and clinical divide. Paul Nordoff's role in the development of music therapy is significant and far-reaching, although his contribution to contemporary music is yet to be recognized. The quality and originality of his art music is undeniable. Here is a voice that is overflowing with originality and creative energy. Through investigation of his scores, future live performances, and recordings, we hope that appreciation of his art music will one day equal that of his clinical music.

Gerald Finzi: UK

Gerald Finzi (1901–1956) wrote music in the English romantic tradition. Unlike his better-known contemporaries Britten (1913–1976) and Tippett (1905–1998), whose music is more diverse and international in scope, Finzi kept to a singular and direct romantic style. It is because his music is so emotionally reflective that it can be of great use for music therapists. Listening and playing his music is reminiscent of a huge surge of intense, though often understated, passion. Finzi had a relatively short and difficult life, and this comes across in his music. He would spend many years crafting one piece. When analyzing his music for distillation into therapy, you get a sense that each phrase is concentrated and a pure outpouring of his soul. Finzi's emotional and highly crafted music should be treated with great care in the clinical setting. Like J.S. Bach, Finzi can cut through to a client's musical consciousness.

Dies Natalis, Cantata for Soprano (or Tenor) Solo and String Orchestra, Op. 8

This is perhaps one of the most perfect examples of music in the British lyrical/romantic tradition. It has five movements: Intrada, Rhapsody, Rapture, Wonder, and Salutation. Its beauty and poignant outpouring make it a wonderful piece to know and use as a resource for improvising. It was written and perfected over a period that spanned many years.

   Intrada

Solo (A)

   Play the following extract from the Intrada, slowly and carefully noting the voice leadings of the strings and textures that make this style truly British. This music is stately and dignified.

Example 5.7

Become familiar with the harmonic distillation. Explore the chords in different ways with and without voice, creating improvisations and as well as more structured songs.

Example 5.8

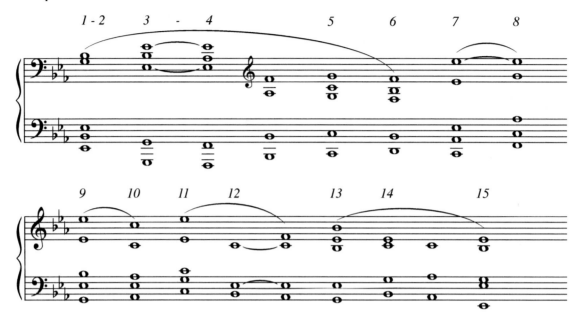

Duet (A)

S, play a cymbal slowly, at a moderate loudness, with slow, broad strokes. *A,* play the above harmonic outline to create an impassioned response. Use your voice to add to the musical intensity, creating words as appropriate. Always keep the dignity of the music.

Rhapsody

Solo (A)

This passage is a series of slow-moving chords. It has been transcribed to include a vocal or instrumental outline from the original voice part. Play the chords and improvise a melody around the tones. Add your voice. Notice the wonderful harmonic shift from A flat major to E major at 4, and how the whole experience lifts in emotional expectancy.

Example 5.9

Duet

> **S,** sit next to **A** at the keyboard. **A,** play and sing, creating a musical-emotional environment for **S**. **S,** sing when you feel encouraged and that it is appropriate to do so. **A,** create a vocal duet with **A** with or without words.

Igor Stravinsky: Russia

Stravinsky (1882–1971) is perhaps one of the greatest and most well-known composers of the 20th century. His music spans different periods, each having its own distinct style: Russian (1905–1913), transitional (1913–1923), neoclassical (1923–1951), and serial (1951–1971). He is perhaps best known for his ballets, most notably *Pterouchka* (1911) and *The Rite of Spring* (1913), which come from the Russian period. These are his most nationalistic compositions and contain some of his strongest colours and flavors.

The Rite of Spring Ballet for Orchestra

This ballet changed the course of musical history. It broke all previous traditions, and on its first performance caused a riot. Its contentiousness derived from Stravinsky's extraordinary use of complex rhythmical structures, unique timbres, and overt use of dissonance. This kind of music had never been heard before by a western audience and thus caused confusion and disregard. Now it is rightly hailed as a masterpiece of contemporary music.

The examples chosen for distillation come from two different points from the first part of the ballet and have been analyzed for their contrasting, forceful, rhythmic drive and calm, textural sounds. They provide textures rather than distinct themes. There are times in the musical/therapeutic alliance when we need strong, uncompromising sounds and/or rich textural landscapes. Utilizing Stravinsky's exotic and powerful music can be a great aid in this aim.

Dance of the Young Girls,

Solo (I–A)

> Play the chord following the rhythmic accents as written by Stravinsky. Play loudly and with force, making each accent strong and clear. Continue on the same chord, playing in a similar off beat and syncopated fashion.

Example 5.10

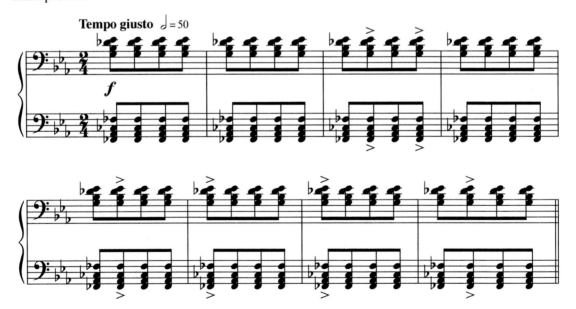

Stravinsky overlays an E flat major 7th chord (1st inversion) with an E major chord. This produces a texture that is strong and uncompromising. Try other chord combinations, noting those that give a distinct sound, and play in a dissonant and syncopated manner The principle of this exercise is to find two chords that don't normally go together and then play them repeatedly with unpredictable accents. Also try different registers on the piano. Build a library of chord combinations from which you can improvise in sessions.

Duet (I–A)

S, play a single drum, at first with one stick only, playing in a style that is perseverative and stuck. *A,* use Stravinsky's chords first to match the speed and tone of *S*'s playing and then to try to break the playing through the strong off beat and accented rhythms. *S,* allow yourself to be influenced by the rhythms and leave your perseveration when you feel that it is appropriate. Try other rhythmic ideas with more than one stick and then more than one drum.

Solo (I–A)

The next examples from the same ballet are in stark contrast: rich, slowly moving chords that are ideal as an accompaniment for the voice.

Example 5.11

A balanced, beautifully arched, small, melodic cell with ornaments.

Example 5.12

Practise each idea separately and then together, exploring and developing each theme, using your voice to create long. arched melodies. Luxuriate in the sounds that Stravinsky creates, and when you feel secure enough, move away into more extended improvisations, always keeping the sounds/themes distinct and clear.

Duet (I–A)

> *S,* sit next to *A* at the piano. *A,* create a calm mood with this music, using your voice, with or without words, to create an inviting atmosphere. When appropriate, *S,* sing or play the piano (or both) in response.

The Rite of Spring is a potential improvisational thesaurus of ideas. Stravinsky's music can be used as a basis both for colourful songs and for improvisational seeds. Through the clinical experience of the authors and other music therapists, Stravinsky's musical contributions have already proved to be a powerful and distinct resource. He often broke the bounds of what was acceptable in music, and perhaps this is why Stravinsky's music works so well in the clinical arena. Music therapy should never be static and stuck musically. Stravinsky and clinical musicianship have strong potential links and beg the question: How might he have adapted his music had he been a therapist?

> Balance both examples to create an improvisation with stark contrasts.

CD*1*
(20)   *S,* drum/cymbal/voice. *A,* piano/voice.

Olivier Messiaen: France

Olivier Messiaen (1908–1992) was one of the leading and unique contemporary French composers of his generation. His music has a distinct style that can be of great use in clinical improvisations. Messiaen wrote extensively for piano and organ, as well as huge orchestral works and perhaps his most famous piece, *Quartet for the End of Time* (1942), which was written while he was in a prisoner of war camp. Messiaen's style is best known for his bitonal harmonies, complex rhythms, and influences from birdsong and the Indonesian gamelan. His music is exotic and multilayered yet always direct, never pretentious, and always appealing.

L'Ascension – Priere du Christ montant vers

Messiaen wrote a vast amount of organ music, his output being second only to that of J.S. Bach. His dedication to exploring the spiritual dimensions of the instrument provides music that is full of mystery and profound theological longing. Messiaen also improvised organ pieces that can be heard as his testament to his own faith and expressions of his belief.

Solo (A)

> Play the piano transcription of the opening. Note how the music moves from harmonies that are layered and bitonal to the end of phrases where a clear sense of atonality appears, thus providing a sense of rest. The musical principles here are the use of parallel 7th chords in diatonic white notes against parallel perfect 4ths using both white and black keys.

Example 5.13

> Break down step-by-step in the harmonic style of Messiaen. 7th chords, right hand only: Keep the same chord inversions.

Example 5.14

Perfect 4ths, left hand only. Note: Perfect 4ths should have at least one black note.

Example 5.15

Hands together and in parallel motion. Note: Try also with (a) left hand starting on a different perfect 4th in the sequence and (b) right hand starting on a different chord of the sequence.

Example 5.16

Hands together in contrary motion.

Example 5.17

Ostinato, remembering to change to a different one from time to time to keep the music interesting. Try longer ostinato, too.

Example 5.18

(In longer ostinati too)

Hands together in chords, using parallel and contrary motion and leaps.

Example 5.19

With rhythmic freedom between hands.

Example 5.20

Repeat the above exercises, using these two different chords and intervals.

Example 5.21

Try the following right hand chord.

Example 5.22

Practise alternating perfect 4ths and major 2nds (each containing at least one black note) in the left hand. Add more rhythmic freedom and independence between hands as you become more confident. Also try adding a low pedal note on the first beat at four-bar intervals.

Example 5.23

Duet

> *S,* choose different instruments, pitched (e.g., xylophone) and nonpitched (e.g., drum), singly and in different combinations. *A,* use Messiaen's style as explored in the above exercises. Explore improvisations in different tempi, dynamics, rhythms, and styles. Play reflectively and then in a more extrovert and dynamic manner. Use your voice when you can to bring an added dimension to the experience.

COMPOSITIONAL TECHNIQUES

DEBUSSY AND IMPRESSIONISM

Using Debussy's impressionistic style in music therapy can be very powerful, as his music contains a sense of reflection to which many clients can relate. It is important to study his music carefully and extract his compositional devices clearly. His extensive catalogue of piano music contains material that will keep a music therapist busy for many years in extracting resources. Alongside this, a study of his orchestral, chamber music, and opera *Pelléas et Mélisande* will further add to an impressionistic style of improvising that could be clinically inspiring and appropriate.

La Cathédrale Engloutie (The Sunken Cathedral), No. 10 (*Preludes,* Bk. 1, No. 10)

> This piece contains passages of intense beauty and expressive groundedness and evokes a sense of "an ancient cathedral submerged under the sea" (Roig-Francoli, 2007). It is divided into eight sections. Play the opening bars of the sections, making note of your responses. How do the musical lines affect the expressive and spiritual content of the music? How could this style of improvising be useful in your own clinical work?

> Practise the style of each section separately. Reassemble them in different combinations to make different improvisations while keeping the sense of the music as Debussy wrote it.

Example 5.24

Profondément calme (Dans une brume doucement sonore - *Gently sounding in a mist*)

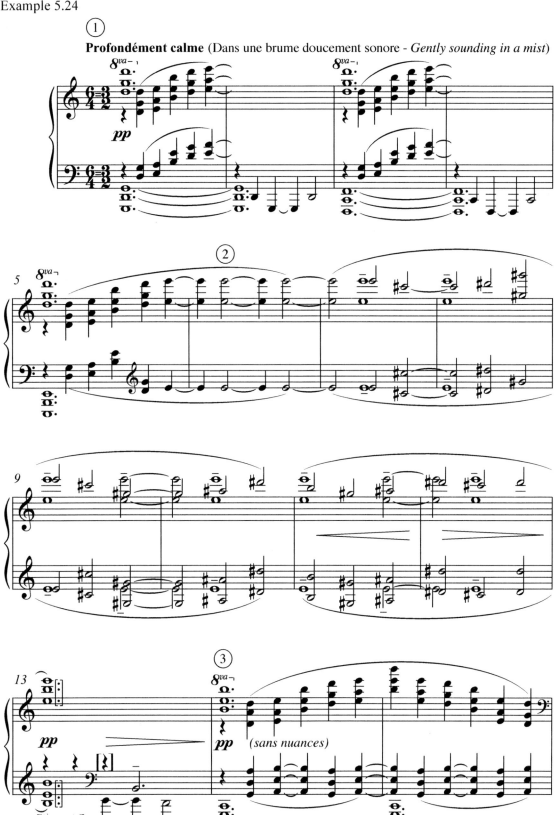

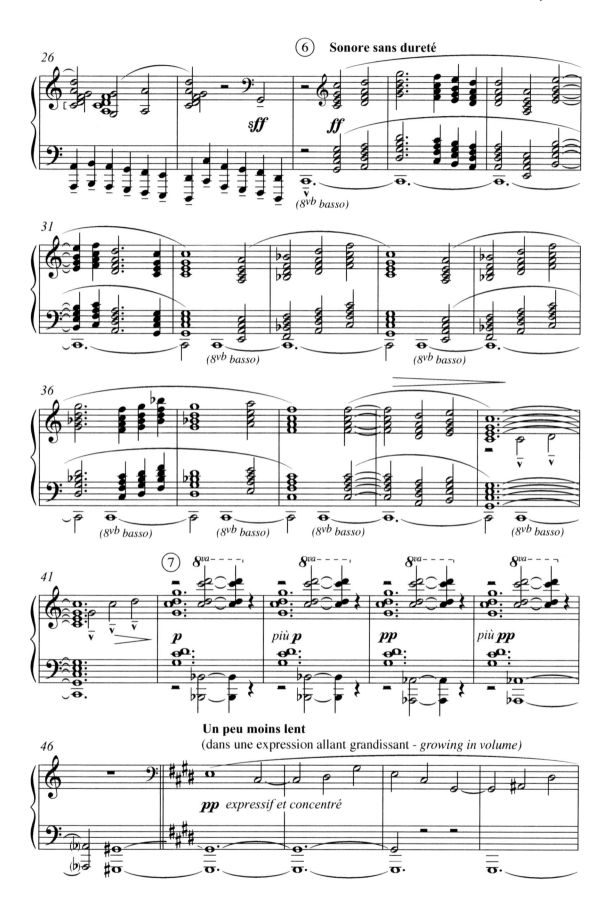

* Comme un écho de la phrase entendue précédemment - *like an echo of the preceding phrase*

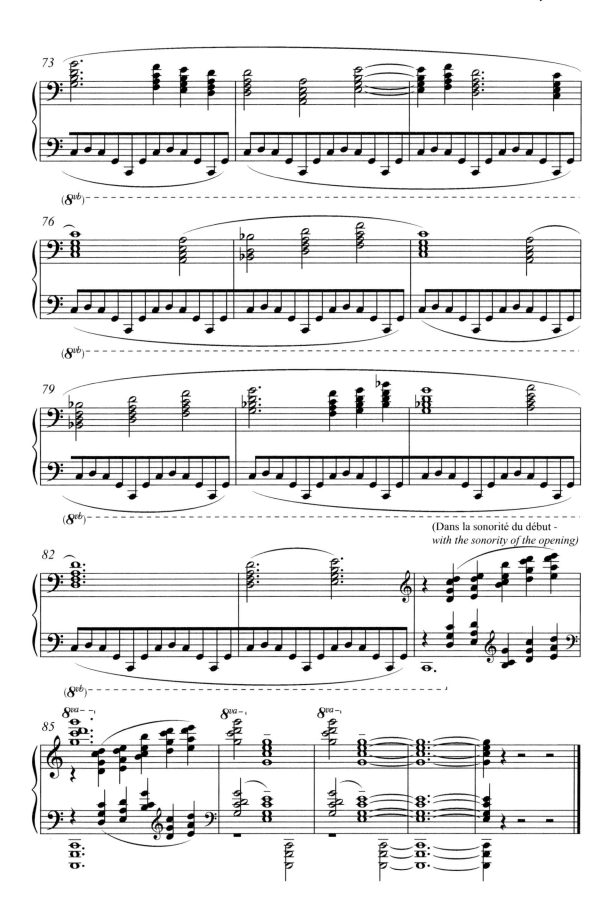

(Dans la sonorité du début -
with the sonority of the opening)

Solo and Duet (I–A)

> Master each section as a solo exploration and then with a partner (*S* and *A*), using different instrumental combinations. Consider also how you might use this music to create a song or vocalize. It is important at first to keep closely to the musical component being studied, e.g., parallel chords. Once you have become familiar with the musical essentials of each section A, you can move away into a freer style B, always returning at the end to the specifics of original idea A.

THE WHOLE-TONE SCALE

The octatonic (an eight-note scale that alternates tones and semitones) and the hexatonic (a six-note scale that alternates semitones and minor thirds) were classed as symmetrical scales. These, as well as the whole-tone scale, were used by composers in the first half of the century (Roig-Francoli, 2007) as a means to move further away from the stability of the grounded tonic. This sense of ambiguity allowed a freedom of harmonic, melodic, and rhythmic creativity that was to change the face of music forever. The whole-tone scale, which divides the octave into six whole tones, is perhaps the most distinctive of these scales and has been used by music therapists to create a sense of suspension, strength, vitality, and neutrality in the therapeutic relationship (Nordoff-Robbins, 2007).[3] The whole-tone scale has a lack of leading tones and also no clearly defined tonic-dominant relationship (Turek, 2007).

> The whole-tone scale can disrupt the tonal logic and remove the possibility of a tonal resolution. Nevertheless, it sits within the tonal framework quite happily, because the whole-tone scale overlaps in part with the diatonic scale (Scruton, 1997).

> The following are the two forms of the whole-tone scale.

Example 5.25

Debussy. *Voiles* (*Preludes,* Bk. 1, No. 2)

Solo (A)

> Play the opening measures (bars 1–10).

---

[3]The reader is urged to explore and play through the exercises set out in *Creative Music Therapy* (Nordoff-Robbins, 2007), pp. 477–480, as well as listen to the clinical examples indicated. These exercises provide an improvisational grounding and fluency in becoming familiar with the whole-tone scale. This in combination with the exercises presented here and, with extensive listening to compositions in and influenced by the whole-tone scale, will give the music therapist an extensive grounding in using the whole-tone scale clinically.

Example 5.26

Modéré (♪ = 88)
(Dans un rythme sans rigeur et caressant - *In a relaxed and gentle manner*)

Note how Debussy creates different lines and textures, providing an overall quality of being suspended. By dissecting the various textural components, we can begin creating an improvisation in a similar style by isolating and then recombining the themes/motives that Debussy uses to create this piece.

Example 5.27

a) Thirds

b) Pedal point

c) Octaves

d) Contrary motion

(a) Thirds
(b) Pedal point
(c) Octaves
(d) Contrary motion rising (and falling) triads

Write your own themes that could be used as the basis for an improvisation. Play them in different combinations, always listening intently to their inflections and how they could be used as both a core musical/clinical idea or as a means to colour an improvisation in a related key. An uplifting section is when Debussy unexpectedly combines a short passage in the pentatonic scale. The music now becomes florid and more improvisational in style.

Example 5.28

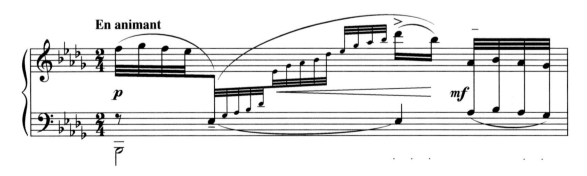

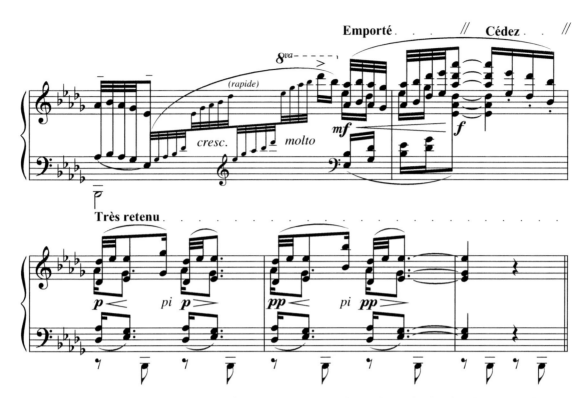

This balances the starkness of the whole-tone scale with music that is without tension, the exact opposite. Try improvising with whole-tone themes balanced with sections in the pentatonic or other modes/scales.

Duet (A)

The following exercises isolate three instrumental uses of the whole-tone scale. It is suggested that all three examples be explored simultaneously, with the same players taking the roles of *S* and *A*. For each example, *A* should isolate and focus on the musical component being explored, listening intently to the sounds and textures of the instrument being supported. Creating a dialogue that has form, direction, and thematic repeatability is essential. Complete the three exercises and then change the roles of *S* and *A*.

S, tuned percussion instrument (xylophone) prepared as a whole-tone scale; improvise freely and gently. *A,* create an improvisation that is floating and ambiguous (use your voice if appropriate).

S, drum, improvising a clear and strong, steady beat. *A,* create an improvisation that is rhythmically directed, creating ritardandos, accelerandos, and passages that are quieter yet still clear in rhythmic content.

S, play a cymbal, improvising clear, slow, strong strokes. *A,* create an improvisation matching the intensity of the cymbal as well as providing contrasting ideas that are quieter and more reflective (use your voice if appropriate).

Solo (I–A)

Practise improvising with hands two octaves apart, using notes of the whole-tone scale, first using octaves and then as a melodic two-part invention. Start with a steady basic beat and then add different note lengths. Vary dynamics, tempo, legato, and staccato, and include rests. Use the whole register of the keyboard. Use your voice if possible.[4]

Play the whole-tone scale in the right hand above a left hand whole-tone ostinato.

Example 5.29

Try other rhythms.

Example 5.30

Using notes of the whole-tone scale, improvise melodically in single notes or octaves in the right hand while playing a strong and constantly moving ostinato in the left hand, A. As you become more confident, move away into a freer, contrasting atonal style B, possibly syncopated, returning to the opening theme to complete A.

Example 5.31

---

[4]Using voice with the whole-tone scale and atonality is a difficult mastery to acquire. You need to think precisely about the notes you are about sing. If practised, however, this style of singing/vocalizing can be a wonderful addition to an improvisation, especially when a heightened emotion is needed.

Melodic line with hands two octaves apart: Start with the whole-tone scale, then begin to add new intervals such as major 7ths and minor 3rds.

Example 5.32

Melodic line in the right hand with an ostinato in the left hand: Add new intervals in the melody and then possibly change the left ostinato as the improvisation develops.

Example 5.33

Lullaby-like ostinato in the right hand with a delicate atonal melody in the left hand.

Example 5.34

Forceful detached ostinato in the right hand with major 7ths in the left hand.

Example 5.35

Duet (I–A)

With all of the above, try different instrumental combinations once you have mastered the exercises individually. When practising, change the roles of **S** and **A**, making note of the move between the whole-tone scale and atonality.

The whole-tone scale has a broad range of stylistic features. It can provide delicate fluidity as well as a sense of strong, granite strength. Used sensitively and with an understanding of its musical-structural makeup, it can provide a musical resource that is clear and direct. As well as being effective in its own right in some clinical situations, the whole-tone scale can also be useful for moving in and out of atonal improvisations. It is particularly compatible to the keyboard and a good starting point for developing a "feel" for playing atonally.

BITONALITY: BARTÓK

Bitonality is a wonderful way for the music therapist to play and understand music differently (Nordoff & Robbins, 2007). Creating music that has two distinct styles while being a part of an overall experience can be clinically liberating. Playing in two individual keys or styles simultaneously can be effective in certain clinical situations. The concept of opposites (Aigen, 1998) is at the heart of bitonality in the music therapy relationship. To play with a client does not always mean that you need to be in the same key or mode. Improvising music that is different from the client's can afford them their individual voice while being a part of joint creative experience. The rather complex art of being able to play in two different keys simultaneously can provide the therapist with a sense of musical freedom and atonal structural knowledge.

Bartók's (1881–1945) music was composed predominantly in the folksong modality. His vast array of piano music is perfect for harvesting ideas and themes for clinical improvisations and songs. The example chosen highlights his use of bitonality and stringent key relationship colouring.

In Russian Style, from *Mikrokosmos*, No. 90, Vol. 3 SZ107

The *Mikrokosmos* are a series of 153 short piano pieces arranged in order of difficulty in five volumes. Many of them are perfect for distillation, allowing music therapists to explore concepts of bitonality and of placing unusual tones and harmonic centres together.

Solo (I–A)

Play the complete piece, noting the strident quality of tones that allow for clear expressions of continued tension. There is a feeling of musical opposites between both hands. The music is tense and tight yet lyrical and beautifully expressed.

Example 5.36

Improvise short pieces for each of the group notes analyzed. Note the type of C Lydian against C minor, which provides a clash between minor 3rd and sharpened 4th against a regular 4th.

Example 5.37

Improvise experimentally at first and then try to introduce a four- or eight-bar structure. Add words if you find it helpful.

Example 5.38

from measures *19 - 22*

Now create your own group of notes (not more than five in each hand) and explore improvisations in a similar style.

Duet (I–A)

Prepare a pitched percussion instrument (e.g., xylophone) to one of the four right hand tone combinations. **S,** explore with these tones, while **A,** support with the tone combination of the left hand. Improvise freely and in more structured forms. Use your voice and develop into more formed interventions such as songs. Explore all of the four combinations and then try your own.

Focus on the use of clashing tones that highlight a distinction between **S** and **A.** Consider this clash in terms of the therapeutic relationship as you improvise.

Also explore these exercises in small groups of five members, each being given a separate tone of the right hand notes. *A,* on either keyboard or guitar use the left hand tones to provide the musical framework and form of the piece. Try both instrumentally without voice and as a more structured piece with words.

Solo (I–A)

For Children Book 1 SZ42

Practise in the following ways.

Example 5.39

Hands two octaves apart, in all major keys.

Right hand in C, and left hand in all major keys.

Left hand in C, and right hand in all major keys.

The tune in perfect 4ths, hands separately and together two octaves apart, in all major keys.

Example 5.40

Right in perfect 4ths in C major, with the left hand in all other major keys playing the tune only, then in perfect 4ths.

Repeat the exercise but with hands reversed.

Repeat all of the above exercises but with a perfect 5th instead of a perfect 4th. Try other intervals, too.

Example 5.41

The tune, right hand in C, (a) tune only, (b) tune in perfect 4ths or 5ths, with your left hand playing an ostinato in another key or mode.

Example 5.42

The tune, right hand in major and minor 7ths (white notes) in C, with your left hand playing an ostinato in another key or mode.

Example 5.43

The tune, right hand in major and minor 2nds (white notes) in C, with your left hand playing single notes in four-bar phrases using the pentatonic (black notes).

Example 5.44

Duet (I–A)

> ***S,*** use various percussion instruments, piano four hands, and voice to work with **A** as your supporter and musical collaborator. Experiment with different tempi, textures, melodic/thematic ideas, rhythms, and intensities of playing. Explore in a detailed and specific manner as well as experience what it is like to play freely in a bitonal framework.

Bartók's collections of folk songs such as "For Children" contain a wealth of tunes that may be found suitable for experimentation in bitonality. His inspired arrangements are of great harmonic and rhythmic interest and deserve study. When improvising bitonally, try different moods, tempi, rhythms, textures, dynamics, etc. Possibly add words and create structured songs and interventions when working with children, such as a drum or tambourine song. Try using the bitonally improvised tune as a rondo theme, improvising out of it in various ways (atonally and in other more tonal idioms and styles). Sometimes a tonal centre at the end of a song or other intervention helps to emphasize the structure.

ATONALITY

Atonality in music therapy is often used but rarely discussed or analyzed in terms of its implications on clinical practice.[5] Atonality has come to imply a stylized approach where there is little or no intervention musically from the therapist. Thus the experience and interpretations are less dependent on the musical infrastructures and more on the extrinsic psychodynamic-analytic interpretations. Atonality is at times treated as a monotone resource rather than one that is intricate and complex, having multilayered components that could potentially affect the therapeutic outcome. This raises a simple note of caution (Wigram, 2004):

> While atonal melodies may feel freer than tonal ones, where there are some expectations in the implied harmonic structure and direction of the melody, they can also sound chaotic and directionless, unless some repeated phrases, figures and patterns are included to give the melody a sense of structure and coherence (perhaps even occasional predictability). (p. 62)

The balance between tonality and atonality is complex and should be considered with great care by the improvising therapist. To be able to play in an atonal framework with dexterity is an essential tool for the music-centered music therapist. After gaining a mastery and understanding of atonality, the balance between this and the polarity of tonality should then be mastered. Moving freely between both extremities will provide music for the client that is clinically focused and appropriate. Our atonal responses to clients should be treated with care and caution just as our tonal responses should be. Music that places itself in a clinically and musically appropriate position, being equally influenced by atonality and tonality, will encompass inspirationally creative music-making that is necessary for our clients' musical and personal growth. In the western world, we are bombarded with tonality; using clinical atonality, then, can bring freshness and a possible new world in which the client can navigate to find his own unique and creative voice.

---

[5]For a discussion on atonality and music therapy, the reader is referred to Chapters 10 ("Atonality: Clinical Intent and Aesthetic Reality") and 11 ("John Cage, Sonatas and Interludes for Prepared Piano: Beauty and Revolution"), *The Architecture of Aesthetic Music Therapy* (Lee, 2003).

Preliminary Exercises

Practise the following.

Solo (I–A)

Augmented 4ths with each hand separately.

Example 5.45

Major 7ths with each hand separately.

Example 5.46

Major 7ths in the right hand and augmented 4ths in the left hand — repeat the held interval as needed.

Example 5.47

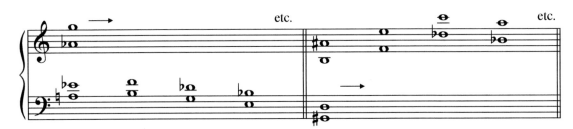

As with the previous exercises, augmented 4ths in the right hand and major 7ths in the left hand.

Example 5.48

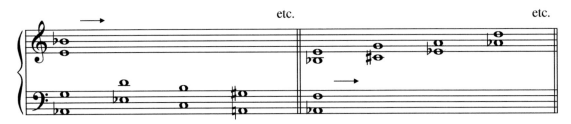

Improvise a slow, regular. atonal melody while holding left hand major 7ths.

Repeat, using more varied rhythms in the right hand and trying different intervals in the left hand.

Repeat, using held chords in the right hand and improvising melodically with the left hand.

Form in Atonal Improvisation

It is important as you begin these exercises that you consider your understanding of musical form. Atonality can contain beautiful melodies and consonance of form equal to that of tonality. When you practise on your own and with a partner, always try to create balanced and formed music. Create themes and repeat them just as you would do with all other aspects of this book. Atonality without form is meaningless and thus will provide a meaningless therapeutic process. Used carefully and with consideration, atonal improvisation can be a wonderful therapeutic/musical tool. Used without thought, it can be unsettling and intimidating.

Combining the Horizontal and Vertical

Solo (A)

Create an atonal melodic line in the bass register, alternating with atonal chords in treble.

Example 5.49

Duet

S, improvise freely on a drum and cymbal. *A,* use the above exercise to respond to both instruments, alternating between the themes. Focus on different textures for the cymbal while creating different textures for the drum, e.g., strong, full, atonal chords for the drum vs. lyrical melodic playing in the upper register for the cymbal. Create a clear form in your thematic playing, extending phrase lengths where necessary.

Solo (A)

Create an atonal melodic line in the middle register, alternating with atonal chords in extreme registers. Experiment with different chord shapes.

Example 5.50

Duet (A)

S, improvise freely on a xylophone and chimes. **A,** use the above exercises, alternating between the two themes to develop **S**'s improvising. Create a clear form in your thematic playing, extending phrases where necessary, and, if possible, use your voice.

Using Sequences to Build Climax and Create Tension

Solo (A)

Play in the left hand octaves, raising a semitone every four bars. In the right hand, play a rising sequence of either augmented 4ths or major 7ths. As the music becomes louder, add octave leaps, increased chromatic movement, and more rhythmic variety in both hands. Begin slowly and in a measured fashion, building toward a climax and continuing your improvisation afterward, bringing your piece to a satisfactory end. At the climax, the music may be changed as appropriate for the clinical situation, e.g., it might become chordal (still atonal) or change to another mode or idiom. Experiment with the various possibilities. When building to a climax, it is sometimes helpful to work towards the dominant of the new style or idiom, in the treble, bass, or both. Outward contrary motion toward extreme registers can be effective, as can chromatic hand clusters.

Example 5.51

Play in the left hand octaves, raising a semitone every two bars. In the right hand, play a rising sequence using an atonal chord. Try using other chords than the ones written. Add octave leaps, chromatic movement, and rhythmic variety.

Example 5.52

Try a similar exercise with a major 7th or atonal chord in the left hand instead of an octave and then with a major 7th or atonal chord in the left hand. Always find chords that are comfortable to play, but keep experimenting and make note of other chords, too.

Duet (A)

S, begin playing a cymbal quietly. *A,* respond by playing slowly, gradually introducing the above ideas to promote and develop a musical climax and tension. After the climax has been held and experienced, allow the music to come down again and return to the quiet spaciousness of the opening.

Creating Atonal Themes

Solo (A)

Octaves alternating with major 2nds in both hands (not necessarily in sequence, although the octaves may rise in semitones at two-bar intervals) — try a variation with minor 2nds instead of major 2nds. Also try major 2nds in each hand, i.e., with hands not moving in octaves.

Example 5.53

Octaves alternating with augmented 4ths — try other notes in the bass instead of always moving up in semitones.

Example 5.54

Octaves alternating with major 2nds and major 7ths.

Example 5.55

Octaves and atonal chords. Note: It may be helpful to practise this hands separately first.

Example 5.56

With the right hand, play broken major 7ths, ascending or descending chromatically. With the left hand, play a pentatonic ostinato (black notes). Change the ostinato periodically when appropriate. Experiment with pedaling, legato, and staccato.

Example 5.57

With the right hand, play broken major 7ths. With the left hand, play freely in the pentatonic (black notes). Introduce rests in both hands as you wish.

Example 5.58

Improvise freely using different textures and moods, combining melodic, rhythmic, and harmonic ideas as appropriate. Try to avoid using octaves. Experiment with different intervals in melodic lines and chords. Include chromatic hand clusters, trills, tremolandi, and glissandi if appropriate.

Improvise arrhythmically as well as atonally, i.e., without a regular pulse. Again try different textures and moods.

Duet (A)

CD / (21)   **S,** use various different percussion instruments, piano four hands, and voice to work with **A** as your supporter and musical collaborator. Experiment with different tempi, textures, melodic/thematic ideas, rhythms, and intensities of playing. Explore in a detailed and specific manner as well as experience what it is like to play freely in an atonal framework.

SPIRITUALITY: ARVO PÄRT

It is important to make special note of the spiritual movement (sacred minimalism), as heralded and developed by the music of Arvo Pärt (b. 1935). Pärt's music is an expression of deep spiritual introspection that is expressed through often simple yet precisely created sounds.

> Pärt uses the simplest of means — a single note, a triad, words — and with them creates an intense inner quietness and an inner exaltation (Hillier, 1997).

His music has a "timeless quality" that makes you feel suspended and "out of time."

> Its simplicity is strictly modern and has appealed to a large audience all over the world, and yet some of the main sources of Pärt's are among the oldest western musical styles: Gregorian and Russian Orthodox chants and medieval and Renaissance vocal polyphony (particularly Notre Dame organum, Machaut, Ockeghem, Obretch, and Josquin). (Roig-Francoli, 2008, p. 335)

> It is interesting that we end this part of the book covering western art music in a vein similar to how we began, that of tonal spiritually informed music.

Cantus in Memory of Benjamin Britten for String Orchestra

This piece is written in the tintinnabuli style — that is, music created around the sound of a bell. The tonic triad and descending diatonic scale is used with no chromaticism or chromatic dissonance. This piece is spiritually intense and is perhaps the most perfect example of a musical expression of loss.

Example 5.59

Cantus in memory of Benjamin Britten

für Streichorchester und eine Glocke
(1980)

Arvo Pärt

(* 1935)

Universal Edition UE 32 469, UE 31 858

2

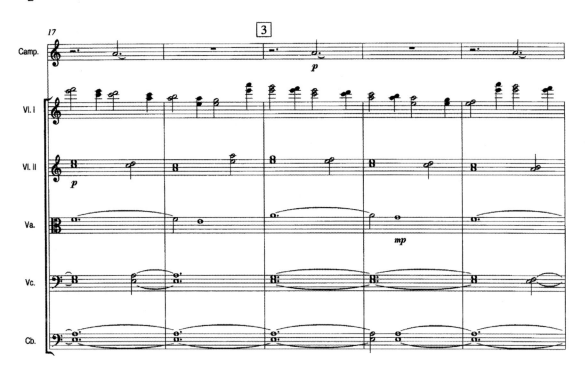

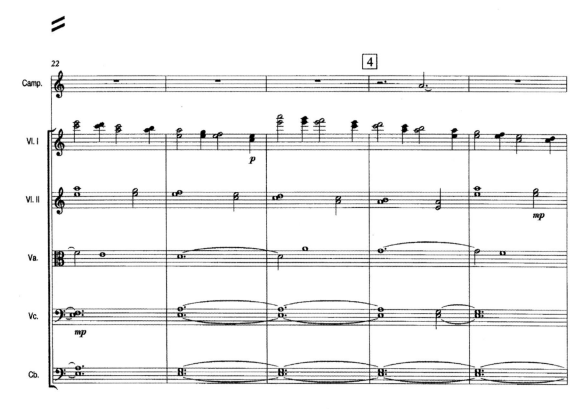

Solo (I–A)

Play the four layers of the music, noting how each is the same descending passage. Play slowly and become immersed in the intervals of the repeated descending scale. Improvise freely, combining the four layers to create an improvisation. Use your voice to heighten the experience. Then try improvising with the five layers simultaneously.

Example 5.60

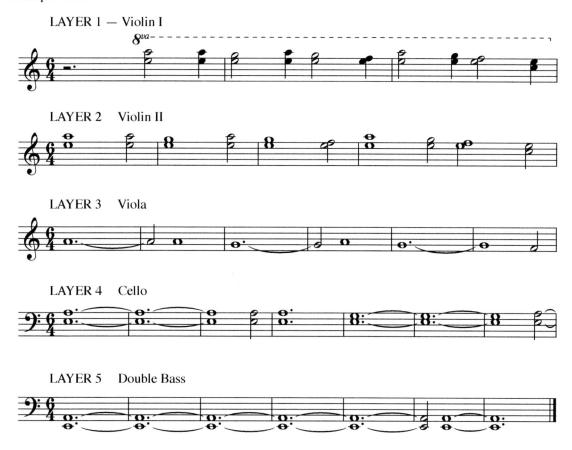

Duet (I–A)

CD/ **S,** improvise on the white notes of a tuned percussion instrument or a series of hand bells.
(22) **A,** use the five layers of the above music to colour and add an intense dimension to the music.

Audio Example 22

Group

A, give four players two bells each: (1) A and E, (2) G and E, 3) F and E, (4) E and C. Direct the four players to play their bells in the rhythm of the four layers. **A,** bind the players together by adding to each level and providing a musical backbone for the whole experience. Ask everyone to sing, thus also creating a vast spiritual emotional landscape.

NEW MOVEMENTS

New ways of composing opened up new and exciting developments in music. Aleotoric, indeterminacy, or chance music allowed sounds to be free from structure or consonance of form. Scores became more graphic in content, and often sections of a piece would have only broad indicators of what to play, leaving performers with the ability to improvise. Electronic and computer music, or *musique concrete* as preferred by French composers, used sounds recorded from the environment (Benward & Saker, 2003).

Sounds were processed or modified in the following ways:

1. Splicing: cutting and rearranging the tape.
2. Playing the tape backward.
3. Varying the speed and pitch of the tape.
4. Tape loops: cutting and splicing the tape in an endless loop.
5. Tape delay: a means of creating artificial echo by rerecording a sound multiple times. (p. 317)

Sound mass was another new contemporary development by which musical textures are layered to produce music that seems to have no definable components such as melody, harmony, and form. The music portrays the sense of a huge wash of sound rather than any specific parts. Perhaps the greatest example *of sound mass, and* a work directly applicable to music therapy, is Penderecki's *Threnody to the Victims of Hiroshima.* This style, while difficult to replicate for music therapy, may be relevant because of its dense musical and emotional content.

Minimalism indicates music that unfolds as a gradual process. Themes and ideas are repeated many times, moving slowly, often imperceptibly, often over the period of a whole piece or composition. The musical content is often simple harmonically and melodically or thematically, although rhythmically it will often include syncopations that are multilayered. Steve Reich and Philip Glass are the two most famous minimalist composers, their works being influenced by different world styles and social themes. Taking minimalism into music therapy is an idea that has fascinated some music-centered music therapists, although because of its ongoing cyclic nature, it should be treated with care in sessions. Because of its repetition, it can become hypnotic, which can be both a positive and possible negative in the music therapy process/relationship.

Other developments in contemporary music are those of New Age and ambient music, which uses smooth, simple, musical phrases to produce music that is calming, without tension, and structurally simple. Its directly pleasing quality has been used to great effect by music therapists as an adjunct technique for relaxation and pain control. Alongside this is the recent explosion of fusion, marrying diverse elements such as jazz, dance, world, and classical to produce music that is ever-changing and dynamically alive.

CONCLUSION

Contemporary music and music therapy is a huge and exciting area to research and analyze. This is music of our time and as such should have a direct influence on the development and future of our clinical practice. This chapter can only hope to scratch the surface of possibilities for distillation, to add to the music therapist's musical palette. By selecting certain critical musical styles, we hope to provide the music therapist with the inspiration and impetus to look further into the rich and diverse world of contemporary music. Music should never exist in a vacuum and thus the boundaries we have included here should be flexible and influenced by other parts of this book. What is surprising is that contemporary music is not only about dissonance. In fact, over half of the exercises developed here are tonal in content and design. Moving into atonality is indeed a complicated step that should be taken with dedication and caution. By opening our ears to the balance between atonality and tonality and actually living in each world, we will begin to see the connections both musically and therapeutically of these polarities. An atonal melody can contain great beauty just as a consonant one can. It is how we know and understand each that creates a far-reaching and insightful experience for our clients.

We hope that through this chapter the myth that modern music is ugly and without melody or harmonic and rhythmic consonance has been dispelled. Examining carefully the building blocks of how contemporary music is composed will give the music therapist a greater understanding of using this style in his sessions. Clinical music should be fresh, alive, and ever-changing. Bringing our own musical passion to sessions will give an authenticity to the process. It is not possible to like all of the music we use clinically, this being very apparent as many therapists struggle to incorporate contemporary art music into their sessions. The music we use should always be therapeutically relevant and used with the greatest of care. There are times when less familiar sounds and textures are needed. Contemporary music can bring, at these times, experiences that are relevant and can aid the process in a way no other styles can.

Music of our time is also about how society has developed and how as human beings we have grown. Music has always represented societal change, and this can be seen no more clearly than in the 20th century and beyond into the new millennium. What is the role of music in everyday life (De Nora, 2000), and how has music therapy developed within the new and developing allied theories of psychology, sociology, sociolinguistics, medicine, and psychotherapy? Music, more than in any other age, has become something that is available to all. As all the straightjacket divisions disappear between musical polarities, so music therapy should be open to all musical worlds. Even if our clients have only a small musical panorama/palette, we should always look to broaden from their preferred choices to offering experiences from totally divergent worlds. If we know these worlds, then we can offer them with assurance and confidence. It is our duty to expand the personal journey of all of our clients. Therefore, knowing the clinical implications of contemporary music should be an imperative and necessary tool for all music therapists.

PART THREE

POPULAR

CHAPTER 6

Song

The popular, or "pop," ballad has a rich history dating back to the times of the troubadours at the end of the medieval period (A.D. 1000–1200). Associated with British and Irish poetry of that time, it most often consisted of a narrative verse based on the theme of romantic love set to music. The terms "pop ballad" and "love song" could be synonymous. We have chosen the former as it is more general and not all contemporary ballads are about romantic love. Although it may not seem relevant to consider the genre's distant roots, Frederick (2004) shows that many of today's hit songs have links into the past:

> Although it may seem strange to link the troubadours of 12th-century France with contemporary songwriters, Jaufre Rudel's "L'Amour de Loin" ("Distant Love") and Paul McCartney's "The Long and Winding Road" have much in common. The story of Layla and Majnun was related by the Persian poet Nizami in the 12th century and later became Eric Clapton's inspiration for his pop hit, "Layla." ("The Troubadours …," par. 3)

The idea of 'remixing' a song or borrowing material (either lyrics or music) from another song has been a trend in popular music since the beginning. The same popular chord schemes are found time and time again in the most recent songs on the radio, and there are love songs in practically any musical genre. However, in the times of the troubadours, to sing about anything else except divine love was considered sinful. Only gradually did it become part of the mainstream: "With the coming of the Renaissance, the Church lost some of its power to control ideas. The notion of courtly love, so distasteful to the clergy, was widely celebrated in the cultural centres of Europe" (Frederick, 2004, "Green Sleeves …," par. 1). One of the earliest well-known ballads is "Green Sleeves," attributed to King Henry VIII. However, the origin of the tune is debatable.

Songwriting as a profession came about only at the dawn of the 1800s. It was during this century that Stephen Foster, one of the greatest songwriters of the United States lived:

> Stephen Collins Foster is considered to be the first professional songwriter in America and one of its greatest. He painstakingly wrote and rewrote his songs until he was satisfied, creating both original lyrics and melodies. Although he garnered wide recognition during his lifetime, due to a combination of personal problems and business deals gone bad, he died in poverty. Among his love songs are such classics as "Jeanie with the Light Brown Hair," "Beautiful Dreamer," and "Wilt Thou Be Gone Love." (Frederick, 2004, "The Rise of …," par. 3)

Songwriting eventually became a major source of economic growth when it became mass-produced through advances in printing and recording technology and the advent of the Top 40 charts in the 1950s (Lamb, n.d.).

Turning to more contemporary songwriters, the 1960s and '70s gave rise to artists such as Paul McCartney, John Lennon, and Elton John, who inspired countless other artists for decades to come. It is in large part on these artists' styles that the pop ballad idiom exercises in this chapter are based.

POPULAR BALLAD AND MUSIC THERAPY

There is no doubt that popular songs have become one of the most widely used tools to facilitate a therapeutic process as they can serve a multitude of purposes (Austin, 2008; Baker & Wigram, 2005; Bruscia, 1998).

As stated by Evan Ruud in Baker and Wigram (2005),

> Popular song continues to capture the hearts and minds of every generation, as well as acting as a mirror in reflecting the cultural, political, and philosophical attitudes at the time. We use them for love and anger, in peace and war, in despair and in hope, to celebrate and to protest. (pp. 12–13)

Bruscia (1998) also articulates the power of songs:

> Songs are ways that human beings explore emotions. They express who we are and how we feel, they bring us closer to others, they keep us company when we are alone. They articulate our beliefs and values. As the years pass, songs bear witness to our lives. They allow us to relive the past, to examine the present, and to voice our dreams for the future. Songs weave tales of our joys and sorrows, they reveal our innermost secrets, and they express our hopes and disappointments, our fears and triumphs. They are our musical diaries, our life stories. They are the sounds of our personal development. (p. 9)

The strength of using popular music in therapy is that it can provide familiarity, predictability, and comfort in what often are times of distress, chaos, and anxiety. In the context of clinical improvisation, a pop song can be a safer way to explore uncertainty by improvising on a song's recognizable chord progression, thus gradually moving away from safety and coming back to it. Braheny (2006) suggests that people long for the familiar not only in therapy but also in everyday life. He believes that although accomplished musicians constantly long for something new to which to listen, there is a need to consider the perceptions and needs of the general public, which doesn't always share the need for novelty (p. 95). Since music therapists are first and foremost musicians, it is important to consider whether our musical choices are for the benefit of our clients or for our own musical satisfaction (Austin & Dvorkin, 1993). This is not to say that musical excellence is a nuisance to the profession. To the contrary, the more musically experienced the therapist, the more sensitive and attuned he will be to the quality of the music offered to the client, and he will be in a position of greater musical freedom and flexibility when making aesthetic choices in sessions (Lee, 2006, personal communication). However, excellent musicians must be especially aware of times when clinical situations demand musical simplicity and familiarity. When offering the pop ballad idiom, well-crafted musicians need to hold back the urge to add complexity, both harmonically and melodically.

Pop ballads in general are associated with romantic love and human relationships and are most appropriate to convey sincere feelings regarding another person. Their musical components are most often designed in a simple way in order to complement and accentuate the message of the lyrics. They are sung at a slower tempo and have simple and repetitive harmonic schemes. Improvised songs have also been used by therapists who employ a psychoanalytic or psychodynamic approach in their work (Austin, 2008; Montello, 2003; Robarts, 2003). Thus the pop idiom may be well suited for such work.

Although songwriting as a therapeutic technique has been shown to be effective for almost all client populations, very little has been said about the value of improvising spontaneous songs in therapy. Is the process different for clients when song content is developed spontaneously rather than premeditated? If so, what are these differences? In her clinical work,

Oldfield (Baker & Wigram, 2005) uses improvised songs to "evaluate how a child interacts verbally as well as nonverbally" (p. 42), thus demonstrating its effectiveness for assessing communication skills. Improvised songs can also provide insight into affect, personality, the ability to handle uncertainty, and creative problem-solving.

It is also possible to compare everyday conversation and improvised song. We believe that the major difference between them is that when words are sung, they are expressed in an enhanced modality. Music by nature is time-bound, which allows for emphasis and repetition (e.g., a repeating chord sequence, a reoccurring rhythmic motif, etc.). Music is also movement, sometimes circular, other times pushing forward, or stopping. When music is combined with words, it greatly enhances a person's verbal expression by providing additional nonverbal meaning. It is for this reason that we believe improvised songs contain strong therapeutic potential.

Austin (2008) specializes in the use of improvised vocalizing and singing in her work. Improvisation in general has been used for the purpose of accessing the unconscious (Ahonen, 2007; Bruscia, 1998; Priestly, 1994). Improvising with words may remind you of the classic Freudian technique of free word association but with an additional element of music. Improvised songs often involve creative negotiation between client and therapist as the therapist may verbally prompt with questions or incomplete sentences during the song in order to stimulate the client's input (Austin, 2008; Baker & Wigram, 2005).

In our own clinical work, we have found that improvising songs, especially greeting songs, brings a more personal dimension into sessions as the music is not based on another artist's creativity. It also allows therapists to be flexible and adapt to events of the here and now, for example, by basing words and melody on something the client said or expressed through body language when entering the room.

This chapter will explore the components of the popular ballad style, starting from a chordal/harmonic approach (the skeletal foundation) and then moving to chord progression embellishment techniques and to accompaniment patterns. The focus will then shift to vocal improvisation and the use of words. The chapter will end with an exploration of song form and a segment on how to incorporate improvisation within precomposed song.

EXERCISES

Most pop songs are based on chord progressions. One of the most important considerations when using a chord progression is to choose between a minor or major one. Despite the popular idea that major chord progressions tend to evoke feelings of joy, hope, and strength, while minor chord progressions reflect sadness, anger, and melancholy, the relationship between chord progressions and emotions is very complex and perhaps contains some mystery. Have we not often heard a song in a major key that had the saddest lyrics? Or a minor song that brought joy when heard on the radio? And what are we to say about songs that blend major and minor progressions? According to the authors' experiences, more often than not, the emotional impact of a song is more strongly dependent on lyric content and the performer's interpretation than on the actual chord progression. A great song, therefore, is one that carefully considers all of these dimensions as a whole. When combining lyrics with chords, there are unlimited possibilities of expression. In the following sections, we encourage readers to explore their own relationship with some of the most typical progressions found in hundreds of songs.

CHORD PROGRESSION (I–IV–V) WARM-UPS

Solo (B)

I, IV, and V are the strongest and most used chords in songs. Play them in sequence in all 12 keys at the beginning of your practice session. This example shows the pattern played in the order of the circle of 5ths (C, F, B♭, E♭, A♭, etc.).

Example 6.1

Play all chords near the middle register of the keyboard and note the common notes between each one.

On the guitar, the I–IV–V pattern is more easily achieved in the keys of D, G, A, and E major. The voice leading is completely different on the guitar, but it does not affect the overall colour.

Practise the same warm-up in minor keys:

Example 6.2

On the guitar, minor I–IV–V progressions are more easily played in the keys of A and E.

Although I, IV, and V are the most used chords in songs, there are innumerable possibilities for chord progressions. Some have more sense of direction, while others are more explorative. Before moving to less common progressions, it is important to develop a solid foundation in harmony in order to understand how to derive strong progressions. The following exercises will explore some of the most typical (strongest) progressions in both major and minor keys.

MAJOR CHORD PROGRESSIONS

The major chord progressions of I–VI–IV–V and one of its variations (I–VI–IV–II–V) are some of the most useful for songs as they give a solid foundation to establish a home key. They work together to help create emotional stability and can be used to harmonize almost any melody in a major key. There are thousands of ballads built on these chords. They are especially useful as they can be played in a variety of orders. Often, only two or three chords will be used for the verse, and a new one is introduced at the chorus for novelty or effect. This section will present a song analysis and series of typical major chord progressions that can be used to create songs.

Solo (B)

Greeting Song Analysis (for work with children)

> Most pop ballads are harmonically simple and are played in a slow 4/4 or 3/4. The following greeting song is based on the chords I–IV–V, with only a few added chords for colour. Play and sing the following excerpt from the verse:

Example 6.3

In the verse, there are only two chords: I and IV (C and F), all in root position. The movement between I and IV gives a sense of warmth and tenderness. Perhaps this is because the progression does not include the stronger V chord. The use of two chords makes the harmonic progression less definite and leaves it open for something more. This creates anticipation during the verse so that gratification comes at the chorus with the new harmonies.

When improvising with a client, whether vocally or instrumentally, I and IV are ideal as they are unambiguous and provide a solid harmonic base. These chords can help clients improvise with ease as they fit well with almost any note of the major scale. Practise improvising your own vocal melody on these two chords.

At the pre-chorus of the song (see "Song Form"), some variation is introduced by adding passing chords, and the V chord appears for the first time. The Am/E acts as a passing chord between IV and II (F to Dm7), finally leading to the V chord (G). Play the bridge, noting the descending bass line and the impact of the G chord:

Example 6.4

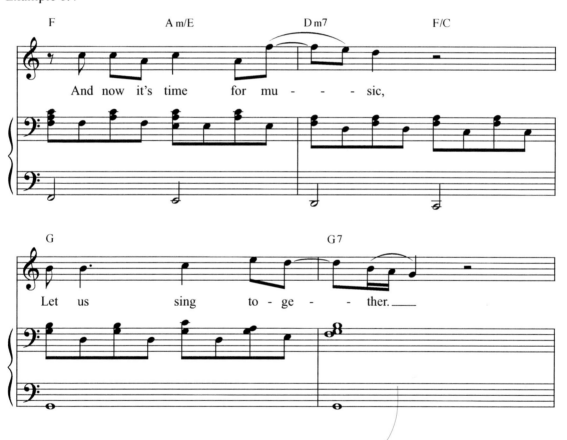

What distinguishes good songwriters from other artists is that they know when to keep harmonies simple and when to add new chords. So far, there are only diatonic chords (chords found only in the key of C major). Finally, at the chorus, an E7 chord is introduced. This leads smoothly to the F chord. The E7 acts as a substitution of the III chord, which is E minor in the key of C:

Example 6.5

The chorus is made up of a basic cadence in the key of C major consisting of predominant (F), dominant (G), and tonic (C), with an added chord (E7) for colour.

Practise using the chords I, VI, IV, V in a variety of orders. Repeat the four chords several times in order to get the feel for it. Here are a few possibilities in the key of C major:

(a) C, F, Am, G
(b) C, G, F, Am
(c) C, Am, G, F
(d) Am, G, F, C

All can be used as the harmonic basis for an improvisation or to create a verse or chorus for a songwriting project.

Practise imitating the above examples by improvising on the I and IV chords at first, while reserving VI and V for further development such as a chorus.

Duet (B)

A, imagine you are greeting a group of school-age children. Following the model below, improvise a greeting ballad using only chords I–VI–IV–V, but reserving the V and VI chords for a B section or chorus. For the verse, greet two children individually while accompanying yourself with chords I and IV as in the verse of the song. Introduce the V chord at the chorus. Keep the melody simple and invite *S* to sing along. After the chorus, greet two new children in the same manner as verse 1.

Verse 1 (Chords I–IV): *A:* "Hello, Rick … How are you today?" (*S* responds, "Good")
　　　　　　　　　　　A: "Hello, Meagan … How are you today?" (*S* responds, "I'm great!")

Chorus (all chords permitted): *A* and *S:* "Welcome to music, its music time"
　　　　　　　　　　　"Welcome, welcome to music"

Verse 2 (Chords I–IV): *A:* "Hello, Jordan … How are you today?" (*S* responds, "Tired")
　　　　　　　　　　　A: "Hello, Michele … How are you today?" (*S* responds, "Good")

Common Major Key Chord Progressions

When improvising pop ballad songs in the clinical setting, it is advantageous to use simple, predictable chord progressions as they allow clients to focus on their expression without worrying about whether they will be able to match the chords of the therapist. The following chord progressions (written with roman numerals and their realization in the key of C major) are based on *The Songwriter's Workshop* from Berkley Press (Feist & Lindsay, 2005, p. 61). They can be repeated indefinitely to form part of a verse or chorus, if not an entire section of a song. The harmonic rhythm is arbitrary (e.g., whole notes can be substituted with half notes or vice versa). Although these progressions are some of the most widely used, there are many other common variations. The following examples are shown with an analysis in terms of movement from tonic (T) to predominant (PD) to dominant (D).

Solo (B)

Play the following progressions and transpose them in the keys of F and G:

Example 6.6 (I–IV)

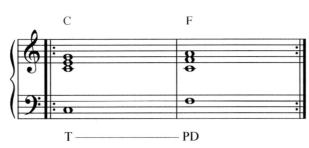

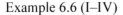

The use of two chords makes this progression ideal for a vocal improvisation or a song verse. Try playing it with different tempi. Vary the chord inversions and sing your own melody over the chord changes.

The next progression is the common three-chord pattern found in the warm-ups at the beginning of the chapter. Thousands of songs are made up of these three chords.

Example 6.7 (I–IV–V)

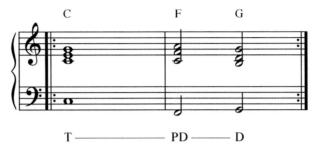

Example 6.8 (I–VI–II–V)

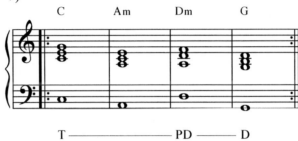

Example 6.9 (I–VI–IV–V, variation of Example 6.8)

This next chord progression features an ascending bass line.

Example 6.10 (I–II–III–IV)

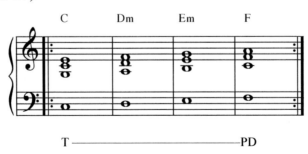

The final progression, used in many pop ballads, such as Mariah Carey's song "Hero," is a typical embellishment of the I–VI–IV–V or I–VI–II–V progression, using passing chords.

Example 6.11 ($I-V^6-VI-I_4^6-IV-I^6-II-V$)

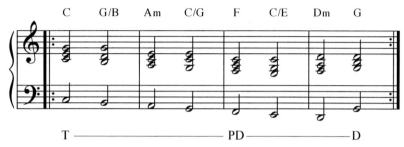

All of the above harmonic progressions have existed in some form or another since the baroque period and are some of the most well established in the western world. The key principle unifying these progressions is that each starts from the tonic (home) chord, moves gradually or directly to a predominant chord (e.g., IV or II), leading to the dominant (V), and a return to the tonic. This creates a cycle of harmonic tension and release.

The harmonic rhythm and choice of chord inversions in these examples are arbitrary. Some songs stay longer on some chords than others but keep the fundamental progression. Variations in tempo, register, accompaniments, and styles of this progression are unlimited.

What makes these progressions useful is that they can be repeated indefinitely without becoming redundant. They can be used for a chorus or verse. Once you are comfortable playing them in the keys of C, F, and G major, memorize them in all keys.

Improvise a vocal melody on a syllable such as "ah" or "oh," accompanying yourself with one of these progressions using solid chords (whole notes) at a slow tempo. Now sing with more movement and more volume in the accompaniment. Note how you feel. What does this progression allow you to express?

Duet (B)

⌒D♪
(1)
A, support *S,* using the progression from (Example 6.11) in a key of your choice. Play the chords in a slow tempo, occasionally pausing if necessary. *S* and *A,* vocalize long tones on the syllable "ah" or "oh," creating a vocal duet. *A,* at first, match *S*'s vocal pitches as closely as possible in order to "join" your voices together. After a moment, sing in between *S*'s vocal phrases, creating a vocal dialogue. End the improvisation on the tonic chord (first chord of the progression).

A, record a vocal improvisation with *S.* Using another progression from above, vocalize a melody on a syllable such as "la" or "na" on the first half or first repetition of the progression. *S,* improvise a phrase ending (on the same syllable). Continue dialoguing in this manner for approximately 1 minute. Listen to the recording together. *S,* choose your favourite melody line. *A* and *S,* sing this melody together. *This exercise can be used as a method of composing a song based on improvised melodies.*

MINOR CHORD PROGRESSIONS

Although major chord progressions can feel emotionally safe and provide solid harmonic grounding, it is important to consider when minor chord progressions are clinically warranted. In this section, we encourage readers to think about clinical reasons to use (or avoid) a minor progression. Again, everyone's experience is different and every circumstance is unique. Therefore, it may be best to negotiate how the music should sound with clients whenever possible.

In our experience, minor progressions can be used to change the mood after a prolonged period of brighter major key sonorities. When is the best time during a session to introduce a minor progression? Can it be used immediately at the beginning of a session to reflect the client's mood, or is it useful to use it in the middle of a session, in between two activities/experiences involving major keys? These are the sort of clinical/musical decisions every therapist should make during the therapeutic process. This section will begin with another song analysis and end with suggestions for typical minor chord progressions.

Solo (B–I)

"Sorry Seems to Be the Hardest Word" by Elton John

Play the following excerpt from the verse:

Example 6.12

This ballad is set in a minor key and uses a typical tonicization to the relative major III chord (E♭) by means of the ♭VII chord (B♭).

Examine the return to the tonic by means of II–V7 (Dm7♭5 to G7) at the end of bar 4. This is a basic cadence for minor keys. The presence of the half diminished chord and raised leading tone (B♮) outline the harmonic minor scale and are perfect for evoking a feeling of sadness (as suggested by the lyrics). Play the following harmonic reduction of the verse:

Example 6.13

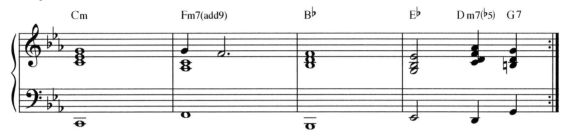

This progression can be repeated indefinitely to make up the verse of a song as Elton John does for this ballad. Play it several times and transpose it to other keys such as A minor and D minor. Become familiar with the minor II–V cadence at the end of bar 4.

Now examine the chorus. Here Elton John makes use of a descending chromatic scale in the bass line, which further enhances the sad feelings of the lyrics:

Example 6.14

This passage, repeated twice (with variation in the lyrics), constitutes the chorus. Apart from an eight-bar musical interlude, these two parts make up the form of the song. Notice the melodic sighs[1] in bar 1 on the word "sad." This, coupled with a chromatically descending line,[2] evokes the feeling of sad lyrical music. The same technique that J.S. Bach employed in the 18th century is therefore still applicable in our modern times (Lee, 2003). The sigh as an embodiment of the expressive (music therapy) dialogue has a subtle yet significant impact on the music. Clients often expel their emotions through the sigh. There can be a sense of "letting go" emotionally and physically (p. 49).

This chord progression featuring a chromatic descending bass line is similar to the one found in the classic rock song "Stairway to Heaven" by Led Zeppelin. Learn the harmonic structure of the chorus and practise it in several minor keys. The following is its harmonic scheme simplified and transposed in the key of A minor:

Example 6.15

This harmonic progression is almost an equivalent to the major progression found in Example 6.11, as it also has a descending bass line (although a chromatic one in this example). When realizing the chord changes, use chord inversions in the right hand that keep close voice-leading; do not keep them all in root position!

Duet (B–I)

A, give *S* the choice between one or two of the tone chimes from the A minor triad (A, C, or E). Indicate when *S* is to play the chime(s) by nodding the head or hand while supporting, using the above chord progression from Elton John's "Sorry Seems to Be the Hardest Word" (Example 6.15). Consider this the A section. As a B section, create a short musical dialogue with *S* where *S* can play freely. Support by matching *S*'s tones or by mirroring *S*'s gestures (intensity, speed, etc.). Use your voice to enhance the dialogue, then repeat the A section chord progression to finish the improvisation.

Common Minor Key Chord Progressions

One of the key features of minor progressions is the use of the ♭VII chord (e.g., G in the key of A minor). This chord can replace or function as a dominant, therefore bringing modal flavors. The following chord progressions can be combined with innumerable other progressions. They have been written in their simplest form (half notes and whole notes) and should be realized by the supporting therapist according to the need of the clinical situation. They can be played at faster or slower tempi, and with a variety of accompaniment styles. They can also be used as harmonic guides for clinical improvisation during sessions. The following progressions are based on *The*

---

[1]See Chapter 1 for further discussion on "sighs."
[2]See Chapter 11 for further discussion on chromatic descending bass lines.

Songwriter's Workshop from Berkley Press (Feist & Lindsay, 2005, p. 64), with some additional ones added by the authors of this book. They are presented with roman numerals and realized in the key of A minor:

Solo (B)

> Play and explore the musical possibilities of each of the following chord progressions by varying the speed, register, and accompaniment style:

Example 6.16 (I–♭VII)

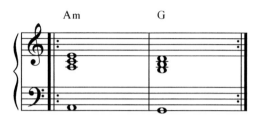

Example 6.17 (I–♭VII–VI–♭VII)

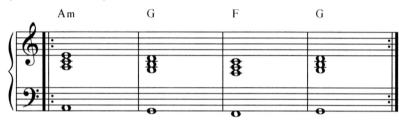

Example 6.18 (I–♭VII–VI–V, variation of Example 6.17)

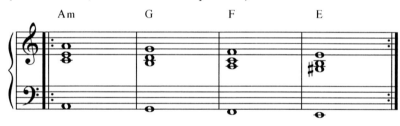

Example 6.19 (I–V minor)

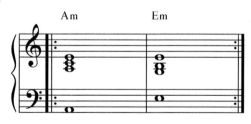

Example 6.20 (I–IV)

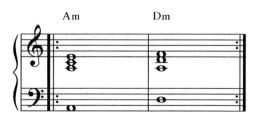

The following two progressions are the minor equivalent of the major I–VI–IV–V progression seen at the beginning of the chapter. Play them and compare them with their major key versions.

Example 6.21

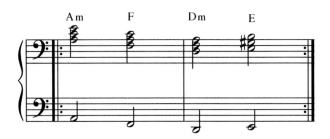

Example 6.22

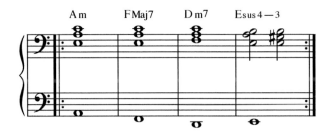

CREATING YOUR OWN CHORD PROGRESSIONS

Although the above progressions are by far some of the most popular and idiomatic, often what makes a song interesting and unique is a less common chord order. Going against the natural order can sometimes add interest and colour, which enhances the meaning of the lyrics.

Solo (B)

Play all of the diatonic triads in the key of C major:

Example 6.23

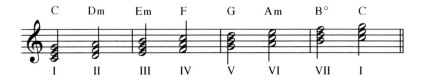

Choose four chords including C major. Play them in different orders and fit them into a four measure phrase.

Hint 1: It is less common to use the VII diminished chord as it is less stable. However, it could make a progression unique.

Hint 2: C major does not have to be the first chord

Here is an example:

Example 6.24

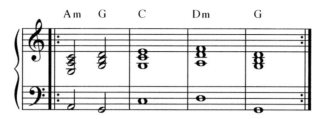

Keep repeating the pattern and improvise a melody over the top with your voice. Sometimes verses contain progressions that are less linear (not following the natural order of chords). These usually include chord progressions that move backward in terms of scale degrees (for example, E minor to D minor, or F to E minor).

These "weaker" progressions allow for less direction, which makes it possible to save the stronger progressions (those which provide clear harmonic direction) for the chorus.

Once you are comfortable in the key of C, create chord progressions in other keys. Practise the same exercise in minor keys. Here are all of the diatonic triads in C minor:

Example 6.25

Note that the G triad has the raised 7th degree of the scale (B♮). It is also common to have a natural minor (G minor) chord instead. The III chord is usually the relative major chord rather than the augmented chord with the raised 7th degree.

Contrary to major keys, the VII degree triad is often used in minor as it is usually a major chord rather than its diminished counterpart. Do not raise the Bb to B natural in this case.

Duet (B–I)

Composition/Improvisation Activity

Step 1: *A,* prepare a visual aid showing triads from the C major (or minor) scale, each on a separate sheet of paper or flash cards. *S,* choose three or four chords from the series and place them in the order of your choice on the floor or a table. *A,* play the chords in the order chosen by *S* (adjust the chord inversions to make the voice-leading smoother). *S,* change the order of the chords until satisfied. *A,* choose your own set of chords to create a contrasting section. Display both chord progressions on a presentation board or wall as in the example below:

S's chords = C, Dm, Em, Am
A's chords = G, Am, C, F

Step 2: *S,* improvise melodies on a tuned percussion, piano, or voice, while *A* accompanies following the chosen chords. *It may be beneficial to record the improvisation in order to review it for significant content later.*

A, listen for significant phrases played by ***S*** and create a melody that fits or matches with ***S***'s melodic and rhythmic tendencies. In the final stages of the improvised song process, ***A,*** guide ***S*** in creating lyrics.

Note: In a real clinical situation, this process can take several sessions to complete.

CHORD PROGRESSION EMBELLISHMENTS

The following exercises are focused on the stylistic embellishments that create the sound of an authentic pop ballad in the contemporary style. The ability of the therapist to create an authentic feel for a song can make a difference in terms of the client's motivation to respond. This is achieved in part by adding slash chords and passing chords.

Slash chords consist of triads or 7th chords that have a note other than the root in the bass. They can represent chord inversions such as C/E (first inversion of C major, E being the bass note) or they can create more interesting sonorities — for example, G/A, which means that the triad of G major is played on top of an A bass. This method of writing chords in pop songs is equivalent to the figured bass in the baroque period.

Passing chords are added chords that create harmonic movement but are not essential to the chord progression. Since most pieces include several of these embellishment techniques, these resources will be presented in an integrated fashion through the analysis of two contrasting pop ballad choruses, each following the same underlying progression, I–VI–IV–II–V.

Solo (I)

Embellished I-VI-IV-II-V Progression

Play and sing the chorus of this song:

Example 6.26

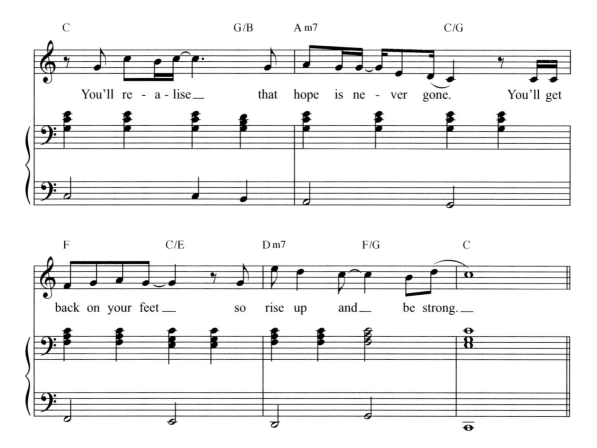

This passage illustrates one of the most typical renditions of a progression based on I–VI–IV–II–V. It contains various embellishments, including passing chords in the form of chord inversions and slash chords.

The progression is predictable and can be repeated indefinitely (as seen from the most typical major chord progressions at the beginning of the chapter). It could be used to form the basis of an improvisation. Sometimes a simple progression in a major key can provide enough safety and predictability for a client to add their own melody. Here is the chord pattern extracted from the first four measures of the chorus:

Example 6.27

Practise the following I–IV–V progression with added slash chords representing the first and second inversion of each chord. Note that the root of each triad is not repeated in front of the slash in order to save space (for example, /E is short for C/E).

Example 6.28

Once you are comfortable with chord inversions, transpose the above progression in various keys. Try a variety of chords, including minor, diminished, and augmented.

Solo (I–A)

Ballad in R&B Style

Play and examine the chorus of the following R&B ballad. If you find the bass line too difficult to play while singing, simply play the harmonic scheme as shown in the chord symbols with the chords in the right hand as written.

Example 6.29

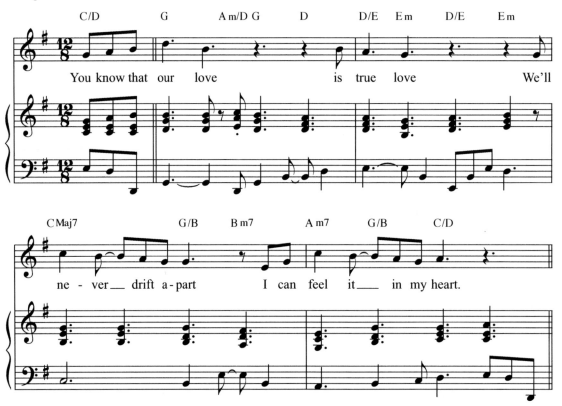

The chord progression is once again derived from the basic form I–VI–IV–II–V, but it is more heavily embellished compared to Example 6.26. Instead of regular triads, many chords include the 7th, which is typical of R&B styles. It also includes more passing chords.

The Amin/G chord in the first measure acts as a neighbor chord, which functions similar to a passing chord.

In the second bar, the listener expects the usual VI chord (Em), but it is delayed with a slash chord (D/E). Slash chords are an excellent way to create harmonic interest in a pop song.

Practise the following embellishment figure in the key of C major. Try it in several other keys:

Example 6.30

Now, examine the harmonic progression in measures 3–4 of the ballad:

Example 6.31

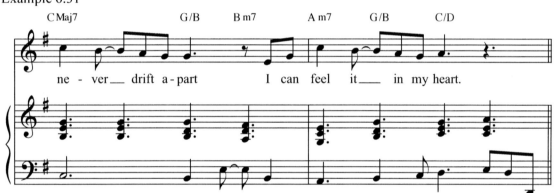

The G/B and Bmi7 chords act as passing chords between the IV and II chords (C–Am).

Examine the slash chord C/D on the word "heart" This is a common slash chord used in many contemporary pop songs, as seen also in Example 6.26 from above (F/G). It replaces a regular V chord. Here is a harmonic extraction of these two measures transposed to the key of C major. It compares and contrasts the same progression with and without embellishments.

Example 6.32

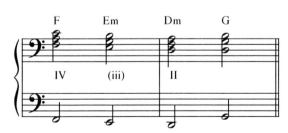

Example 6.33

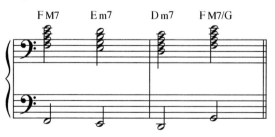

The first example (6.32) shows the raw triads, while the second (6.33) adds a 7th to each chord and includes a slash chord (Fma7/G). The passing chord (Emi) is indicated with brackets. Notice the parallel motion it creates. Parallel motion adds smoothness to a chord progression. Practise playing parallel triads and parallel 7th chords on the white keys of the piano:

Example 6.34

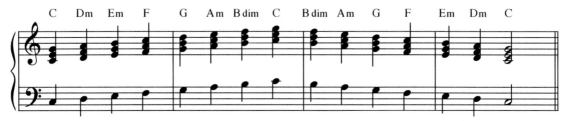

Now, practise parallel 7th chords as shown below:

Example 6.35

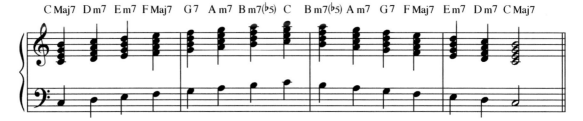

These are all in root position. Once you master this voicing, change the inversion of the first chord and keep the same voicing for all other chords as you move up and down the scale. For example:

Example 6.36

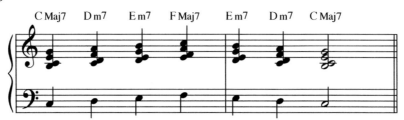

A simple way to voice parallel 7th chords is to play the diatonic triad a 3rd above the bass note (e.g., Emin above C or Cmaj above A). This voicing spaces out the notes of the 7th chord, keeping the root in the left hand and the remaining notes in the right hand:

Example 6.37

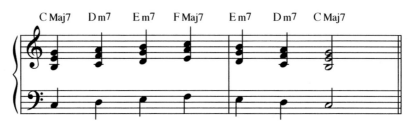

These all make for great passing chords that can be used at any point in a song.

Examine once more Examples 6.32 and 6.33. Instead of a regular V chord (G), the harmony is a slash chord creating a more dense texture (with a suspended 4th and added 13th). It can easily be created by playing a IV or IVma7 chord in the right hand while keeping the V root in the bass. Practise it in its simplest form in the key of C:

Example 6.38

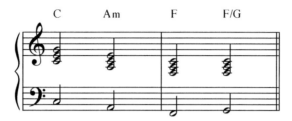

Here are a few possible uses of *slash* chords with their usual resolutions in the key of C or Amin:

Example 6.39

In most cases, slash chords (those other than a chord inversion) consist of a triad a diatonic step lower than the bass note (e.g., G/A). It is also possible to use the diatonic triad a step above the bass note (e.g., G/F) or a 4th below (e.g., G/C).

Practise the major (or minor) I–VI–IV–V progression, embellishing it with slash chords.

Duet (A)

A, play a short repetitive progression (three or four chords) that includes one or two slash chords with a 12/8 time signature similar in style to "End of the Road" by Boyz II Men. *S,* listen to the progression and begin to sing freely. *A,* at the end of the improvisation, play the same progression, this time with simple triads (without embellishment), allowing *S* to experience the contrast in style.

A, Create a "good-bye" song. *S* and *A,* decide on words to include before the song begins. *A,* improvise in an R&B style (based on Example 6.29) by including passing chords and one or two slash chords. *A,* repeat a chorus to create familiarity and predictability.

PIANO ACCOMPANIMENTS

In this section, we will examine two contrasting piano accompaniments, each with a distinct rhythmic feel. These accompaniments are not limited to any specific artist styles. The idea is to consider the differences between syncopated accompaniments with a 3+3+2 feel and those with a straight quarter note pulse.

Wigram (2004) suggests that accompanying is a great method for "joining in with a client's music where the message one is giving is of support and empathy" (p. 106). It is important to play at a lower dynamic level when accompanying clients, thus allowing them be a soloist and the main musical voice. In the clinical setting, it is better in some circumstances not to include syncopated accompaniments for clients who have a poor sense of rhythm and/or pulse, for some clients appear to need a simpler rhythmic structure with which to work. As a general rule, always form accompaniments in a way that invites the client into the music. It is also important for therapists to have a mastery of the chord progression in order to be flexible and concentrate fully on their client's expression. It may be wise to keep the accompaniment simple at first and add a minimum of right hand fillers, which are short rhythmic or melodic passages creating movement in between sung phrases in order to fill the musical space. Wigram outlines the characteristics of a typical accompaniment as:

Simplicity and repetition
A short rhythmic or harmonic sequence that is sustained
Continues in a stable way despite some changes in the client's music
Sensitive to pauses or small developments in the client's music

Solo (I)

Accompaniments with a syncopated 3+3+2 feel

Play the following introduction from Elton John's "Tiny Dancer":

Example 6.40

The piano introduction sets up the 3+3+2 pulse with arpeggios. Note that in this piece each bar consists of two sets of 3+3+2 pulses in 16th notes. Other songs may have an accompaniment in 3+3+2 using 8th notes.

While the right hand creates movement, the bass counters it by keeping a simple half note pulse emphasizing beats 1 and 3.

Practise making your own accompaniment on a C major chord, with a 3+3+2 pulse, using arpeggios (or broken triads) and solid chords, similar to the above example. Keep the bass simple, emphasizing beats 1 and 3. Once you find the groove, play the same rhythmic pattern over the following chord progression:

Example 6.41

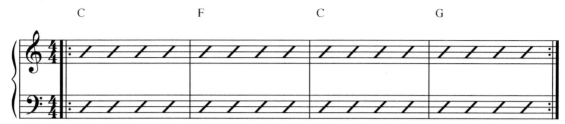

This type of accompaniment is especially suitable for melodic improvisation on a tuned percussion instrument or with the voice. It could be used to motivate a client to create a melody on an instrument or voice. The constant movement could add safety in the case of clients who feel overexposed by the lack of rhythmic support when playing on an instrument.

Practise the same accompaniment pattern, this time with a pedal point tonic (C).

Solo (B-1)

Accompaniments with a quarter note pulse

In contrast, the next accompaniment features a constant quarter note pulse and the use of octaves in the left hand to create harmonic stability.

Example 6.42

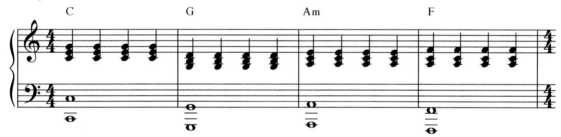

The octaves in the left hand create a strong bass support while the right hand keeps a steady beat with quarter notes. This steady movement allows the voice more freedom to explore syncopation. To create more movement, the following 8th note variation is also a typical accompaniment. This pattern is featured in the Greeting Song Analysis at the beginning of the chapter.

Example 6.43

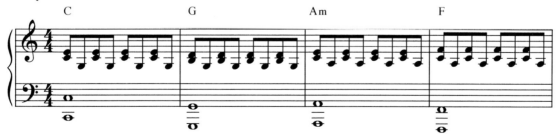

In a clinical situation, the main idea is to find rhythmic and harmonic patterns that are simple enough and meet clients' needs (clinical aims and objectives). For example, if a client tends to get confused by syncopated rhythms, it is probably best to work with straight quarter or 8th notes.

ADDITIONAL ACCOMPANIMENT EMBELLISHMENTS

This section provides ways to create additional stylistic embellishments in a ballad. By making full use of suspensions and added notes, a more authentic rendition of the popular idiom can be evoked. From there, it can be manipulated in order to fit with the particular style that a client is familiar with. Although the I–VI–IV–V progression sounds excellent without embellishment, the use of suspension chords is but one of a few ways to expand on it in order to add harmonic interest and to create movement.

Solo (I–A)

Suspensions and added notes

Play the following original piano accompaniment transcription from Elton John's "Candle in the Wind":

Example 6.44

This accompaniment, although based on a 3+3+2 pulse, leaves much space for the voice. The piano propels the verse with fillers, often with syncopation. These types of accompaniments are usually improvised by the artist. *Indeed, it is easier to listen to a recording and imitate it rather than play each note of a transcription accurately.*

Note the first use of a suspension in mm 8, where the D♮ outlines the A major key, which gives a colourful flavor when embellishing the IV chord.

In mm.10, Elton John uses the sus2 chord in passing, moving from the top note E–F♯–G♯–A.

In mm 12, the A major chord contains an added 2nd (the B), for added texture.

Another suspension is used on the first beat of mm 14, similar to mm 8.

Examine and play the two typical suspensions, often used for pop music:

Example 6.45

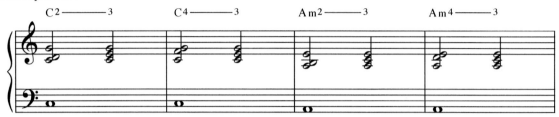

The first two measures feature the sus2 and sus4 on a major chord. Both resolve to the 3rd. The same rule applies to minor chords as seen in the final two measures.

These suspensions can be used continuously without becoming redundant or out of style. By using them, it is easy to create harmonic interest without having to change the chord. However, use them consciously in your work with clients and consider whether the accompaniment should remain simple (using only triads) or embellished.

CD2
(2) Improvise an accompaniment with the use of suspensions on the following progression:

Example 6.46

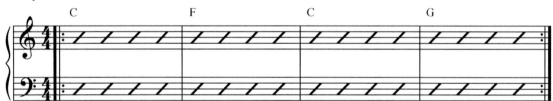

Although many pop ballads use primarily simple triads, in some songs it is common to add notes for texture. The "add 2" chord is a stylistic feature of many pop songs. Again, the purpose of harmonizing chords in this way is to add authentic elements in order to evoke popular music styles. Play the following examples:

Example 6.47

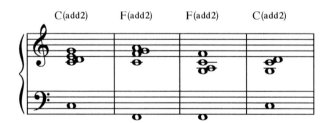

These are used to provide colour and texture and are integral to the modern pop ballad style. They are found in most modern pop and rock tunes. The first example illustrates the use of the added 2nd for the purpose of colour:

Embellished accompaniment patterns

Try the following pop ballad accompaniment patterns. They are simple but contain enough harmonic interest to evoke the pop ballad style.

Example 6.48

The pattern is made up of solid chords using sus2 as an embellishment. The progression uses the same pattern for each chord.

Note the bass rhythm that copies the bass drum. This rhythm helps keep the flow of the pulse and moves the ballad forward.

The following accompaniment pattern is a mixture of 3+3+2 pulse with regular quarter notes. It makes use of both sus4 and sus2 to prolong the chords over two bars.

Example 6.49

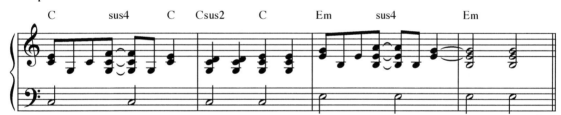

This last accompaniment pattern (Example 6.50) allows the therapist to focus on the client, for the chords in the right hand remain static over a changing bass line. It is an easy pattern to play, while it still evokes the pop idiom. It may be useful especially for beginning pianists.

Example 6.50

When improvising an accompaniment for a client, it is usually best to keep a limit of two or three chords; otherwise, the client may have some difficulty in predicting the sequence. It also makes it more difficult to improvise with a sense of freedom. Practise improvising accompaniments on popular ballads you are familiar with. Explore the various embellishment techniques presented in this chapter.

VOICE AND LYRICS

An essential skill of a music therapist is the ability to help clients find the right words to express their feelings or communicate their life experiences. Some clients, however, may have difficulty or are unable to provide words. In these cases, therapists have the opportunity to improvise lyrics for the client in the moment. We improvise words every day, in our daily conversations with almost everyone we encounter. Improvising lyrics can be seen as an extension of daily conversation set within the conventions and context of a musical form. Lyrics performed in a song are different than normal conversation in several aspects: In a song, words can be elongated, repeated, and set within a larger space as performers can rest in between phrases while the music carries and holds the emotional content. The task of the music therapist is to develop the intuition in order to know when words should be repeated and/or emphasized and when to leave silences creating space to process what is being sung. Although it is possible to study vocal phrasing in songs, therapists must use their clinical awareness in order to find the appropriate words and phrasing when improvising vocally with clients.

Diane Austin specializes in the work of vocal psychotherapy and uses several improvisation-based interventions. Austin (2008) describes her vocal techniques in detail and discusses their clinical purposes. The following exercises are designed for a psychodynamic or psychoanalytic approach to music therapy, based on Austin's techniques.

Vocal Holding

One of Austin's techniques stems from the idea of creating a "holding" space that can contain a client's expression in safety:

> Vocal holding techniques are introduced into the music psychotherapy session in various ways. With clients who are especially anxious about improvising but want to try, I might explain this method in detail. Usually, however, I give a minimal description or simply ask: "Would you like to try singing about this (person, situation, feeling, etc.)?" I then ask clients if they want two or more chords. They sometimes choose the exact chords or give a general description ("something minor"), but if they have little or no knowledge of chord structure or need help finding the sound they want, I might play examples of different chord combinations (major, minor, suspended, etc.) and ask for their preference. (Austin, 2008, p. 151)

It is important to negotiate verbally with the client in order to determine an appropriate chordal framework to support his or her expression. In order to create a true holding musical framework, Austin emphasizes simplicity and predictability, usually consisting in two chords alternating indefinitely:

> Unlike jazz or other forms of clinical improvisation where shifts in harmonic centres are to be expected, this improvisational structure is usually limited to two chords in order to establish a predictable, secure, musical and psychological container that will enable clients to relinquish some of the mind's control, sink down into their bodies, and allow their spontaneous selves to emerge. The simplicity of the music and the hypnotic repetition of the two chords, combined with the rocking rhythmic motion and the singing of single syllables (sounds, not words, initially) can produce a trancelike altered state and easy access to the world of the unconscious. The therapist's singing encourages and supports the client's vocalization. Within this strong yet flexible musical container, the client can explore new ways of being, experience the freedom of play and creative self-expression, and allow feelings and images to emerge. (Austin, 1996, 1998, 1999b)

The client's voice, feelings, and emerging aspects of the self are all held within this musical matrix (Austin, 2008, p. 147).

Solo (B)

Work with two chords at the piano. Explore major, minor, diminished, augmented, and various combinations. When you find two chords that evoke your mood or feelings in the moment, play them, then close your eyes and allow sounds to emerge. The following suggested chords are characteristic of the pop idiom:

Example 6.51

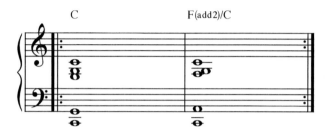

Example 6.52

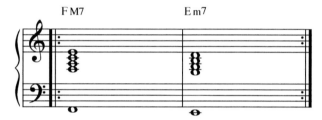

Example 6.53

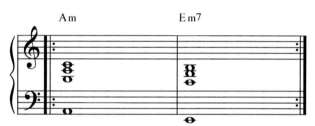

Keep the tempo slow, with a rocking motion that might suggest a lullaby. Let yourself experience the sounds on an emotional level. Improvise vocally, starting from a vowel or syllable. Give yourself permission to express whatever comes in the moment.

Duet (B)

A, ask *S* about his or her preference for a chord progression in terms of major vs. minor or lighter vs. darker. Choose two chords in accordance with *S*'s wish. Play them several times in the manner of a slow lullaby or ballad, based on the exercise from above. *S,* when ready, begin to vocalize freely on *A*'s chords. *A,* decide whether to support *S* vocally in unison, harmony, mirroring (i.e., repeating phrases as played by *S*), or grounding[3] (i.e., a repetitive pattern centred on the tonic, such as a drone).

---

[3]The intimacy of singing together using simple syllables in unison, harmony, mirroring, and grounding can create feelings of early mother-child attunement. This method is therefore especially useful in working through developmental injuries and arrests due to traumatic ruptures in the mother-child relationship or empathic failures at crucial developmental junctures (Austin, 2001, p. 147).

Free Associative Singing

"Free associative singing" is the term used to describe a technique that can be implemented when words enter the "vocal holding" process. Clients are encouraged to sing whatever comes into their heads with the expectation that by doing so, they will come into contact with unconscious images, memories, and associated feelings (Austin, 2008, p. 158) and will be able to work with this material in the music. The accompaniment (two-chord holding pattern or repetitive riff) and the therapist's singing continue to contain the client's process, but the emphasis now is not on "holding" the client's emerging self and psychic contents but on creating momentum through the music and the lyrics that will propel the improvisation and the therapeutic process forward. The role of the "double" is essential to this technique. In addition, the use of "essence statements" and "repetition" are key techniques in facilitating the process of free associative singing. These are explained below.

Technique of "Double"

The therapist sings as the double in the first person, using "I." Drawing on induced countertransference, empathy, and intuition as well as knowledge of the client's history, I give voice to feelings and thoughts the client may be experiencing but is not yet singing, perhaps because the feelings and thoughts are uncomfortable or unconscious, or the client has no words for them or no ability to conceptualize the experience. When the doubling is not accurate, it still moves the process along as clients can change the words to fit their truth. When it is accurate, it provides clients with an experience of being truly seen and understood. It also encourages a bond between client and therapist and over time strengthens the client's sense of self. (p. 160)

Essence Statements

Essence statements — statements that begin with "I feel," "I need," "I want" — are effective in deepening the therapeutic process because they are fundamental expressions of self-awareness and building blocks to identity. Therapists can sing the complete phrase, such as "I feel sad," if they believe this is an accurate observation of the client. If this is true, the client will repeat and/or add to the statement; if not, the client will change the word, usually to the way he or she is feeling. Or the therapist can simply sing "I feel …," leaving space for the client to supply the missing word. (p. 160)

Repetition

Repetition also plays a significant role in free associative singing. What would sound ridiculous in verbal psychotherapy — the client and therapist repeating the same word or sentence over and over again — is filled with meaning in vocal psychotherapy. Each time the word or phrase is repeated by the client and echoed by the therapist, the affect contained in the word is intensified. It is as if the word and the meaning attributed to it have time to sink deeper down into the body-self, where it can be fully experienced. (p. 160)

Solo (B)

Begin with several minutes of deep breathing at the piano. Next, explore and find two chords that express what you are experiencing in the moment. Start singing with only sounds. Then, when a thought enters your mind, sing it. It may feel silly at first. It could be, "I don't want to do this." Give yourself permission to sing anything you desire. Try not to censure or judge yourself. *You have to be comfortable exploring your thoughts and feelings before you can help someone else to do the same.* Continue singing and repeat the same phrase, sentence, or idea if necessary.

If the above exercise is too difficult for you, you may need more structure. You can try beginning with a phrase that orients the lyrics in a certain direction. For example, "I remember." A story also offers more structure and may feel safer because it is a projective technique that uses metaphors. You can try beginning with, "Once upon a time …."

Duet (B)

CD2
3

A, create a simple two-chord accompaniment which as a holding quality. Keep it slow and steady. *S,* begin by singing a statement about your physical self (for example: "My feet are on the ground"). *A,* repeat the phrase as heard in the first person while providing a continuous two-chord holding accompaniment. *S,* continue with a new statement, such as "My breathing is shallow." *A,* repeat each statement. You can also add something they may have observed or intuited about *S,* like: "My throat's a little tight." *S,* if this is accurate, repeat it. Gradually move from physical states to emotional states such as "I'm tired" or "I'm feeling nervous." *S,* repeat statements as necessary and take as long as you wish between statements.

Song Creation Based on Free Associative Singing

As discussed above, free association is a great way to unleash creativity and subconscious feelings. In some cases, it may appeal to some clients to create a song based on free associative singing. The following is a suggestion for a songwriting project in order to achieve a final product.

Duet (B)

A and *S,* record the duet exercise from the previous section on free associative singing. *It may be necessary to record several improvisations before proceeding to creating a song.* Listen to the recordings and note down key words, phrases, or ideas that come from the recordings. *S,* decide which words capture the essence of your feelings and reserve them for the chorus.

SONG FORM

The form of a song is usually simple and contains several repeated sections, such as verses (A section), choruses (B section), and an optional bridge (C section) (Josefs, 1996; Leikin, 2008). Repetition is essential for establishing a stable structure. Think about the clinical purpose of using a simple predictable form of music such as a song. Consider whether your client needs familiarity with a form or style in order to be motivated to participate actively or whether little repetition is needed. Here are the basic components of the song form:

1. Introduction: A short segment of instrumental music (often consisting of two to eight bars).

2. Verse: This is the body of the text, which often contains the equivalent of one or two poetic stanzas. Harmonic progressions are usually more subdued or less adventurous.

3. Pre-Chorus: This is an optional section that prepares for the arrival of the chorus. The lyrics in this section sometimes repeat, similarly to a chorus.

4. Chorus: The main message of the song is contained here. Usually, verses are related to it and inform it. The harmonies and melody are often contrasting. It is useful to save an interesting "catch" phrase (e.g., a metaphor or important word) for this section.

5. Bridge: This is an optional addition to a song. It can consist of another lyrical statement that deepens the meaning of the song. It is usually set to a new chord progression. This creates a renewed interest as it breaks from the predictability of the verse–chorus–verse–chorus form.

5. Coda: A final segment of instrumental music can be used to create an ending or prolong the mood at the end of the song.

The following are typical song forms:

#1	#2	#3	#4	#5
A Verse 1	A Verse	B Chorus	A Verse	A Verse
B Chorus	B Chorus	A Verse	A Verse	B Pre-Chorus
A Verse 2	A Verse	B Chorus	B Chorus	C Chorus
B Chorus	B Chorus	A Verse	A Verse	A Verse
A Verse 3	C Bridge	B Chorus	B Chorus	B Pre-Chorus
B Chorus	B Chorus		B Chorus	C Chorus

Each song form does not have more than three contrasting parts. Some contain only two sections, A and B, while others include a third, C. There are many other possibilities; these represent some of the most typical.

Creating a "Song Without Words"

The following exercise is designed for therapists to enhance their memory of song form. Before attempting to improvise a complete song, practise improvising a tune consisting of two contrasting lyrical sections. Make each section approximately eight measures in length. Practise on form #1 first, ABABAB. The following exercises are designed with a progressively increasing level of difficulty.

Solo (I–A)

> Using only the black notes on the keyboard, create a repeating bass figure consisting of two or three notes in the bass lasting two measures. Create a simple melody for a verse on the black notes on top of the bass figure, lasting four measures. Repeat the verse (four measures). On a new bass figure (using other black notes), create a chorus with a new melody with a contrasting rhythmic figure.
>
> Using only two or three chords (I, IV, V) to support your melody, improvise an eight-measure verse. Repeat the tonic chord often to establish a key. Repeat your verse as exactly as possible. At the chorus (B section), introduce a new chord (VI or II). Vary the chord progression to create contrast. Create a new melody. Remember that melodic patterns such as a sequence may help to create coherence and allow the ear to learn it more quickly. This is the most important part of the improvisation. Return to the verse. Some melodic variation is possible now, but keep the same chord progression. Play the chorus and repeat it. Create an ending by repeating the last two measures of the chorus.
>
> Improvise an eight-measure A section (this could represent either a chorus or a verse), using a simple harmonic scheme (I, IV, V) as a basis for a melody. Repeat the tonic chord often in order to establish a key. Repeat the progression several times until you know it by heart. Add a simple melody to your harmonic scheme. Use a text from a song you are unfamiliar with as lyrics for your own song (the Internet has an unlimited supply). Then create an eight-measure B section that starts on a chord other than the tonic. IV, V, or II are usually good choices as they contrast the tonic chord notes. Return to the A section you created. Again, the simpler your harmonic and melodic scheme, the easier it will be to memorize. Do this every day for a few weeks. Practise creating short A and B sections and alternate between them. Only when you find this process easy should you attempt to improvise a song form with three contrasting sections (e.g., including a bridge or a pre-chorus).

Merging Improvisation with Precomposed Songs

It can be a rewarding experience for a client or a group of clients to create a mood for the beginning or ending of a song that is familiar and meaningful for them. This allows them to create a mental and emotional preparation for the experience of a song. It also allows a more personalized version of their song, thus enabling a sense of empowerment and creative freedom within a more highly structured framework. This technique can work for both rhythmic songs and ballads. The therapist either provides a simple rhythmic pulse on the piano or a drum or allows the music to flow freely out of time. Take, for example, the song "Imagine" by John Lennon.

Duet (B–I–A)

> As in the Greeting Song Analysis at the beginning of this chapter (Examples 6.3-6.5), the verse of "Imagine" revolves around two chords, I and IV. *A,* use these chords as a holding framework for a free instrumental improvisation before singing the first verse of the song. *S,* add percussive sounds or a melody on a tuned percussion over the chord progression. *A,* once the improvisation comes to an end, begin to sing the verse of the song.

A, sing a familiar song of your choice with *S.* Prolong the ending by repeating the final three or four chords indefinitely, remaining in the mood of the song. *S,* add cymbal crashes and improvise on a drum. *A,* reflect the character of *S*'s playing by changing the style of your accompaniment pattern. For example, move from a soft, pedaled, steady accompaniment to a more percussive accompaniment that invites *S* to play more intensively and rhythmically on the instruments.

Instrumental Interludes Based on the Verse or Chorus

What comes naturally within most pop songs is an instrumental solo or musical interlude. Although the therapist can play a solo as clients listen to the music, it is also possible to involve clients in participating by improvising with an instrument. These solos could be as structured or unstructured as the clinical situation requires.

Solo (B)

Choose a song with a verse or chorus that contains few chords or a diatonic chord progression that does not require any accidentals. Many songs contain only two or three chords in the verse. These are ideal for a melodic improvisation. Practise making your own solo based on the verse or chorus of your song (create a new melody or a variation of the original). For example, if the song is in the key of F major, improvise using the notes of the F major scale.

Duet (B–I)

CD2 (4) *A,* take a chord progression from a familiar song. Create a lyrical accompaniment as *S* improvises using any instrument of his or her choice (the piano is also acceptable). Consider the nature of *S*'s playing and change the style of your accompaniment to match and respond with occasional right hand fillers. *A,* finally, return to a lyrical accompaniment in order to perform the verse of the song as a ballad. *A,* begin to sing the verse and invite *S* to join.

Group Activity: *A,* ask each group member to choose a hand bell from among C, D, E, F, G, A. Perform the first verse and chorus of "Imagine" by John Lennon in the key of C major. Instead of singing the second verse, create a musical interlude by accompanying the group with a steady quarter note pulse on the chords from the verse (C and F) and point to each individual or each bell in order to improvise a melody. Allow the group members to play their bells freely in the manner they wish but only during the times they are prompted to do so.

Group Activity: *A,* repeat the previous exercise. This time, invite one of the group members to lead the group as a conductor, pointing to the bells one by one. Continue to accompany and respond to each member's tempo and changes in the music.

Group Activity: *A,* instruct the group members to take turns playing an ocean drum during the musical interlude of a song. Reflect each participant's expressive use of the ocean drum (either reflecting the speed or matching the intensity). Base yourself also on each member's body language. Maintain the structure of the verse or chorus by following the chord progression.

CONCLUSION

Pop music as a whole encompasses a very large number of individual genres and styles. Although this chapter is based mainly on the styles of the 1970s and 80s, such as John Lennon, Mariah Carey and Elton John, it is evident that any number of other artists would have yielded similar results. The pop ballad idiom has a recognizable aesthetic that is familiar to the majority of music therapy clients. The exercises in this chapter were designed not only for clinical improvisation but also for use in song composition projects with clients. Although many embellishment techniques have been provided in order to create authentic performances, these are not always necessary for a successful therapeutic process. A simple two- or three-chord progression can lead to a most inspiring vocal improvisation. On the other hand, a more colourful harmonic scheme such as the progression from Elton John's "Sorry Seems to Be the Hardest Word" can open up an entire emotional world for a client. The harmonic archetypes of pop ballads will forever remain in our consciousness and will undoubtedly time and time again provide inspiration for musicing due to their simplicity and familiarity.

CHAPTER 7

Blues

Whether experienced through the sound of the guitar, voice, drum, or piano, the blues is immediate and emotionally direct. It is a deeply felt music that touches upon something profoundly human. It is genuine, sinful, and sexual. It is raw.

The blues is a form of music associated with African-American culture. Many definitions begin by mentioning the 12-bar form, but there are many other starting points. Some consider it more than a musical form or genre and more as a philosophy or state of mind. People often use the expression "I have the blues" as if it were a symptom referring to depression, loneliness, or general suffering. Brooks, Koda, and Brooks (1998) perceive the blues as a mournful style of music and means of self-expression, providing "the artist and, in turn, the listener with some relief from the pain of life's woes" (p. 8).

The style was developed by a new generation of agricultural workers in the region of the Mississippi delta, in the southern part of the United States, in the second half of the 19th century (Barlow, 1989; Oliver, 1997; Scorsese, 2003; Weissman, 2005). These communities suffered from political oppression, lynching, abuse, and the confines of the lowest economic status in America. The blues, therefore, allowed African-Americans to express their daily concerns and anxieties by literally singing their troubles away. Indeed, many song themes are centred on money, freedom, sex, relationships, and longing for home; these are most basic, everyday, worldly concerns. For this population, these basic needs were met inadequately and often not at all. It is no wonder that the blues contains within it a certain rebellious sentiment.

Many of the style's influences came from West Africa, where most African-American slaves originally lived (Barlow, 1989; Oliver, 1997; Scorsese, 2003; Weissman, 2005). Music in Africa was intimately linked with the divine or spiritual, as well as movement (Mereni, 1996; 1997). One of the primary goals of music-making, for African people was to reach a state of catharsis by singing and dancing to the entrancing rhythms of the drums, which led to the release of tension and the acting out of feelings (Barlow, p. 5). The blues appears to carry this same undertone as it often relies on a repetitive rhythmic groove on which syncopated phrases are superimposed.

By the end of the Depression, toward the 1940s, America had changed and so did its music. Although the blues originated in the South, some of its most prominent developments took place in the North, more specifically in the city of Chicago. There, record companies sought artists who came from the South but who "had the vision to alter their sound to make it more urban and therefore more attractive to black Americans living in northern cities like Chicago, Cleveland, Detroit, and Gary, Indiana" (Scorsese, 2003, p. 25). Memphis also became one of the major blues centres, as the city, just east of the Mississippi delta, thrived on the cotton commerce (Scorsese, 2003, p. 26).

Partly due to the economic exploitation of the genre, the new blues sound became thicker and incorporated jazzier musical accompaniments, which often included drums and piano. This brought more energy and excitement, compared to the music of a solo musician playing an acoustic guitar. The guitar was eventually electrified, which opened new sound possibilities of distortion and volume. As a result, the urban blues became associated with entertainment and stage concerts.

To this day, what remains one of the most important contributions is its characteristic "blue" notes, as Scorsese (2003) describes:

> These notes are usually made by flattening — lowering by a half-step — the third, fifth, or seventh positions of a major scale. Presenting all kinds of emotional possibilities for the musician, blue notes give the blues its special feel, and when they are draped around a blues chord progression, the results can be so rich and *human* that it satisfies the soul in a way no other music can. (p. 16)

Now the blue notes are heard not only in blues records, but also in country, jazz, gospel, soul, rock, hip hop, and even the classical music of George Gershwin.

BLUES AND MUSIC THERAPY

It could be argued that the creators of the blues used their music primarily for therapeutic purposes. As Scorsese (2003) describes, "Music was a real escape; it took black people away from the drudgery of fieldwork, the poverty of their homes, and prejudice that greeted them practically every time they came in contact with a white man or woman" (p. 27). You could draw a parallel between the creators of the blues and clients who have perhaps suffered similar hardships. Many clients have likewise been deprived of accommodation, money, and even the opportunity to be in a loving relationship due to their physical conditions or life circumstances. They lack the same freedom that many blues creators did.

This style may appeal to future generations of adult and elderly clients, as it influenced the development of most modern popular styles of music, such as rock and roll, rhythm and blues, funk, gospel, soul, and even hip hop, which are the styles with which they will most likely be familiar. It could also be an attractive style for clients who have an affinity for the guitar, as the acoustic or electric guitar is usually the featured instrument of the blues.

The simplicity of the blues form allows for the release of tension, as it is designed for endless variation while remaining grounded by the quick return of the tonic. The style is easily accessible to clients of all ages and can be fun and entertaining while offering possibilities for the serious and intense expression of feelings. Turry (2005) describes in detail the process of a group of clients participating in a blues improvisation and examines the specific advantages that the blues form brings along with its implied social conventions. For example, he makes use of the characteristic "breaks" in the form to allow a child to interject vocally into the silence. Aigen (2002) gives a detailed account of the use of the blues idiom along with other popular idioms as interventions in the therapeutic process of a young man with developmental delays and psychosocial difficulties. Baker and Wigram (2005) explore the use of the form for the purpose of clinical songwriting and suggest that it can be of benefit to clients who "have a need to express sadness, frustration, loneliness, pain, regret, or similar emotions" (p. 235). The form is easily approachable and contains a limited number of chords; therefore, it is an ideal resource for the beginning or intermediate clinical improviser.

Indeed, the blues is far-ranging and can be applied to an endless variety of clinical situations with all populations. This is why we believe that it is an important tool for the improvising music therapist.

EXERCISES

We suggest that exercises in this chapter be played with minimum or no pedalling and an unrefined pianistic technique. It is through the rough quality of the blues that clients may be motivated to respond.

MELODY AND PHRASING

The most defining element of the blues is melody. The "blue" notes can add elements of dissonance contained within the regularity of its form. The blues scale contains a wide range of expressive potential. It can motivate clients to play immediately, as its sound is distinct yet familiar to the ear. The following exercises will focus on the creation of melodies, the use of tritons, and phrasing.

Solo (B)

Blues and Pentatonic Scales

Play the following blues scale accompanied by an open 5th drone in the left hand:

Example 7.1

Listen to the sound of the 3rd, 5th, and 7th (E♭, F♯, and B♭) against the bass drone. Create melodic phrases that emphasize these three characteristic tones.

Play the pentatonic scale accompanied by an open 5th drone in the left hand:

Example 7.2

Note how bright this scale sounds when compared to the blues scale (the major 3rd and 6th add brighter intervals against the tonic).

Create short melodic phrases using pitches of both scales while holding a C dominant 7th chord in the left hand. Here are some examples:

Example 7.3

Note the chromaticism that is created by using the notes of both scales in stepwise motion in the final example. The natural 3rd and 5th can be substituted by the blues 3rd and 5th, and the natural 6th and 7th are interchangeable at any time. To create darker or minor melodies, the scale on its own suffices, but for brighter, or more festive melodies, it is useful to borrow pitches from the pentatonic scale.

Here are several suggestions to prepare tuned percussion instruments for blues improvisations based on the pentatonic scale. Other than the blues scale, here are a few alternative possibilities:

Example 7.4

This scale (Example 7.4) outlines the 3rd and 7th. This scale is "safe" and "solid."

Example 7.5

This scale (Example 7.5) outlines the blues 3rd and the major (pentatonic) 6th, creating the possibility of an E♭–A tritone.

Example 7.6

This scale (Example 7.6) offers interplay between major and minor 3rds, creating tonal ambiguity.

Example 7.7

This scale (Example 7.7) includes all notes of the blues scale, without the natural 5th, resulting in more dissonance.

It may be necessary to transpose these scales according to available pitches. One of the most practical transpositions is the key of D, as all the notes of the first two pentatonic scales are white notes on a keyboard (D, F, G, A, C, D, or D, E, F, A, B, D). The other two scales can be achieved with the addition of a single F♯ or A♭/G♯. In this transposition, the accompanying chords are D7, G7, and A7 (see "Additional Resources").

The keys of D, A, and E are also useful transpositions for improvisations using guitar (see "Additional Resources").

Duet (B–I)

CD2 (5) **S,** play a short melodic phrase (three to five notes) on a tuned percussion instrument prepared with the blues scale notes. **A,** mirror **S**'s phrase as accurately as possible. Continue, creating a musical dialogue. Develop **S**'s phrases by extending them (completing them or making them longer), then add a supporting drone 5th in the bass register (in the key of the chosen blues scale).

Tritones

When combined with the pentatonic tones, the blues scale conceals several tritones that can make melodies sound unsettled and tense. They can be used melodically as well as harmonically (solid). Using tritones can accentuate important musical events and can be useful in the clinical setting to attract a client's attention. The blues scale conceals three possible tritones. The following exercises will focus on these intervals.

Solo (I–A)

The following example illustrates the A–E♭ tritone both descending and rising. It is created by joining the A (or major 6th) from the pentatonic scale with the blues 3rd. Play and accentuate the tritone, listening to its effect:

Example 7.8

Both tritones (B♭–E and A–E♭) in Example 7.9 correspond to the 3rd and 7th of the respective chords (C7 and F7). These are transposable tritones and can be used on the 3rd and 7th of any dominant 7th chord.

Example 7.9

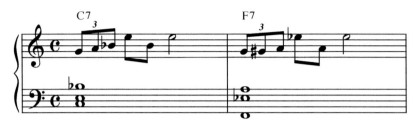

Practise creating melodic phrases using the major 3rd and 7th of the C7, F7, and G7 chords. Transpose the phrase as exactly as possible, creating unity and predictability.

In the next example (Example 7.10), the Cs used to create the F♯–C tritones are mainly ornamental, providing continuous 8th-note movement.

Example 7.10

Practise improvising melodies that feature some of the presented tritones against a C major triad in the left hand. Listen to the clash between the blues 3rd (E♭) or 5th (F♯) in the melody against the notes of a C major chord in the left hand.

Duet (I)

S, play on a nontuned percussion instrument. **A,** support **S** on the piano with a simple pentatonic melody (either C major pentatonic or E♭ pentatonic) accompanied by a drone or ostinato in the key of C. In the middle of the improvisation, introduce a tritone. Accent the "new" pitches loudly and repeat the idea several times. Move back and forth between the pentatonic scale and the melodic tritones.

Phrasing

According to Blumenfeld (1992), there are three general principles underlying the phrasing of blues melodies: (1) syncopation, (2) emphasis on the tonic, and (3) descending motion (pp. 1–3). In order to phrase melodies stylistically, it is important to listen to as many recordings of the blues as you can. Although the three principles mentioned above are useful in the beginning, blues phrases are often based on the performer's feelings and do not always follow conventional rules. To "feel" the blues, you must first listen to the great innovators of the style. By gaining facility in the style of its phrases, you can then gain flexibility and increase the range of expression possible in your improvisations.

Solo (B–I)

> Play the following example (Example 7.11) demonstrating the three principles outlined in Blumenfeld (1992):

Example 7.11

> Repeating the tonic note can give a sense of stability. The harmonic and melodic tensions are resolved quickly.

> Create melodic phrases that adhere to the three principles above (repeated tonic, descending motion, and syncopation). Play them in different keys and registers.

> Create a one- or two-measure melodic phrase in the key of C that outlines the blue notes and repeat it over a steady beat in the left hand, similarly to the above example.

> Try the same phrase over the bass notes of C, F, and G (the root notes corresponding to I, IV, V, in the key of C).

> Play the phrase in several registers. Vary your phrase by changing the placement of the syncopations or by alternating the melody.

Duet (I)

> *S,* improvise syncopated melodies on a tuned percussion instrument prepared with the notes of the blues scale. Choose one of the scale tones to accentuate more than others. (e.g., constantly return to the blues 3rd by repeating the note often). *A,* respond to *S*'s phrases with phrases of your own, supported by the tonic in the bass. Play in between *A*'s phrases as much as possible, being careful not to overplay. Be thoughtful and expressive and play with intent. If *S* appears to focus on a single note such as the blues 3rd, base your phrases around this note and end your phrase on the tonic. When comfortable, vary the bass notes, choosing I, IV, or V (e.g., in the key of C, the bass notes are C, F, and G). Listen carefully and note how each bass note changes the flavor of each pitch of the scale.

GROOVE AND RHYTHM

Popular styles such as blues, jazz, and rock often come with their own terminology. The word "groove" generally refers to a particular feel for the style and includes knowledge of idiomatic rhythmic patterns, tempo, and overall conventions of execution. The rhythm section (bass, drums, piano) of a band is usually responsible for creating the proper groove. In this section, we will examine blues grooves starting from typical bass patterns. In clinical improvisation, the use of bass grooves can bring a sense of excitement while providing a solid harmonic foundation. The groove's simplicity and repetitiveness makes it a wonderful tool for allowing creative expression at all levels of music-making.

According to Blumenfeld (1992), there are three types of bass motions found in the blues: (a) still or static, (b) forward motion, and (c) rocking (back and forth) motion (p. 47). All three can be used in clinical improvisation in the form of ostinatos, which provide safety and a sense of a forward-moving pulse. They may also function as a motivating element for free improvisation. It should be kept in mind, however, that although grooves are often integral to the blues style, they are not a prerequisite in the clinical setting. The following exercises explore various bass patterns

Static Ostinatos

Solo (B)

Play each ostinato (do not use pedal) and notice the density and texture for each one.

Example 7.12

Vary the dynamics from p to ff and listen to the change of mood that each one evokes.

The perfect 5th in a low register played loudly can bring a festive or folkloric sound. Indulge in playing it as crudely as possible, using a heavy percussive touch.

Play the ostinatos in different keys and registers and note the difference in the atmosphere each one creates.

Forward Moving Ostinatos

Play the following walking bass and boogie ostinatos:

Example 7.13

Example 7.14

Experience the use of chromaticism in the walking bass ostinatos (Example 7.13).

Observe the outline of the Mixolydian mode and pentatonic scale in the boogie ostinatos (Example 7.14).

Vary the speed and dynamics of each ostinato and play each in a different key signature, noting the change of atmosphere or mood. Compare and contrast these ostinatos to the static ones from the previous section.

Rocking (Back and Forth) Ostinatos

CD2
(6)   Play and listen to the following ostinatos:

Example 7.15

In order to achieve an authentic shuffle groove, accent the weak 8th notes. This removes the emphasis on strong beats. Eighth notes should not be played straight, but approximately like triplets (this takes practice and much listening exposure).

Contrast shuffle playing with straight 8th-note playing. All grooves using 8th notes can be played in a shuffle (except for faster tempi). For slower tempi (usually in 12/8 time), shuffles are identical to triplets.

Notice the final ostinato from Example 7.15. The presence of the E♭ and B♭ does not necessarily denote that the key is C minor, for the tones are borrowed from the blues scale.

Vary the speed and dynamics of the ostinatos and compare them with those of the previous ostinato exercises

Syncopated Ostinatos

Play the following ostinatos and feel the dotted quarter–8th note syncopation played on the second half of beat 2:

Example 7.16

Example 7.17

Note the presence of the blues 7th in the first two examples and the blues 3rd in the third example (Example 7.16).

Octaves are a common feature. They add power and strength, creating excitement. The final example (Example 7.17) demonstrates a typical New Orleans bass pattern used by Dr. John and Professor Longhair.[1]

Apply the same variation techniques for further ostinatos.

Duets (B)

S, improvise freely on a drum and cymbal in a clear tempo. *A,* wait and listen to the tempo, dynamics, and quality of timbre, then support *S* with an appropriate ostinato. Consider whether the movement should be static, moving forward, or alternating back and forth. Change the ostinato if it is no longer suitable to match *S*'s rhythms.

S, improvise by playing melodically (up and down the scale) on a prepared tuned-percussion instrument with the pitches of the blues scale in the key of C (C, E♭, F, F♯, G, B♭, C). *A,* support by accompanying *S* with ostinatos in the lower register of the keyboard. Experiment with different kinds of ostinatos. *S,* note how each ostinato affects your playing.

FORM AND HARMONY

The strength of the blues form is that it can provide a simple and familiar structure in improvisation. It may be especially useful when a client has difficulty creating form or producing coherent musical ideas. In such cases, the therapist may openly suggest improvising a blues or bring it spontaneously into a free improvisation in order to contain and ground the client's music. Therapists should feel free to change the blues form in order to serve the clinical purpose rather than preserving authenticity for its own sake. The following explorations and exercises will focus on the blues form, 7th chords, extended harmonies, and cadences.

The Blues Form and Basic Chords

Solo (I)

Play the outline of the blues form in the key of C:

Example 7.18

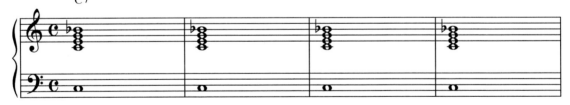

---

[1]For a more elaborate demonstration of the New Orleans piano style, refer to the books *Dr. John Teaches New Orleans Piano,* Vols. 1 and 2.

Observe the voice-leading. These are all dominant 7th triads in various inversions. Note how close in range the chords are. Instead of directly transposing each chord to fit the changes, find inversions that are closest to one another. This will ensure smoother voice leading. Chords sound warmer in the surrounding registers of middle C, while they can have a more piercing effect when played in the upper register.

In order to become familiar with the blues 7th chords, practise various sets of I, IV, V dominant 7th progressions in all 12 keys. Be systematic, playing the same chord pattern in various keys following a strict sequence. Example 7.19 demonstrates the progression transposed according to the circle of 5ths, while Example 7.20 shows the same pattern transposed according to an ascending step sequence:

Example 7.19

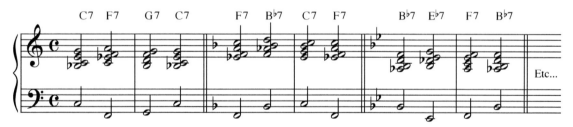

Example 7.20

Keep all chords in the middle register. If the sequence leads the chords in the upper or lower registers, choose a more appropriate octave.

It may be beneficial to write out a complete set of progressions in all 12 keys in order to have a quick reference for practising or for actual clinical sessions.

Although 7th chords form the basis of blues harmony, in many instances chords are reduced to triads or even open 5ths, which is probably due to the fact that the music has a tendency to adhere to its folk roots.

Improvise melodic phrases over the 12-bar form (Example 7.18). At first, use the basic root triads of I, IV, V to support the right hand:

Example 7.21

Note that the blues form consists of three 4-bar phrases, where the second phrase repeats the statement of the first (sometimes with variation) and the final phrase is contrasting, giving an answer to the two first phrases. The form therefore consists of an AAB phrase structure.

When comfortable, use an ostinato pattern instead of chords and transpose it to fit the chord changes.

Create an improvisation at a comfortable tempo using the strict 12 -ar form along with its designated chords. Gradually alter the form using the methods below:

1. Adding dissonance or foreign chords

2. Elongating the form through augmentation (staying on some chords for longer periods of time)

3. Changing the style (e.g., blues in the style of classical music, using an Alberti bass)

4. Adding interjected musical material in between sections of the form (e.g., adding a two-measure atonal passage in between measure 4 and 5 of the blues form)

5. Eliminating the sense of pulse and playing freely and dynamically

As long as roots I, IV, and V are present in the correct order, anything can be changed and the blues form will still be perceived. The idea is to keep the AAB phrase structure, where the B phrase contains the highest amount of tension-release. The above exercise is meant to develop imagination and flexibility in order to adapt the form to the spontaneous events of a session or the needs of individual clients.

Duets (I)

> *S,* improvise on a tuned percussion instrument prepared with the blues scale. *A,* create a supporting framework for *S* using the blues form, playing whole-note chords within a 12-bar structure, keeping a clear steady pulse. Give *S* time to explore the sound palette, responding to the melodic phrases with your own. Repeat the exercise, this time without pulse. Take as much time as necessary between chord changes. Compare both improvisations.

> *S,* improvise freely, alternating between two contrasting instruments such as a drum and cymbal or drum and metallophone. *A,* when *S* plays on instrument 1, support with elements of the blues form, while listening carefully for tempo and dynamic changes. When *S* switches to instrument 2, abandon the blues framework and improvise freely or use a contrasting musical framework, such as atonality or a different style.

Blues for the Black Keys

One of the easiest ways of initiating a client to play the piano is to offer an improvisation on the black keys. The blues form can be adapted to fit the pentatonic scale (black keys only) and can be used as way to develop the therapeutic relationship. It can be played in the key of E♭ major or minor.

Solo (I–A)

Play the following skeleton of the blues form in the key of E♭ major:

Example 7.22

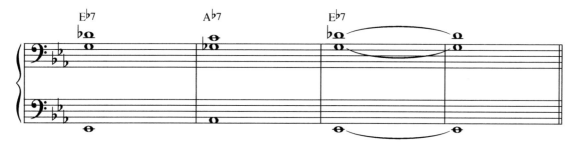

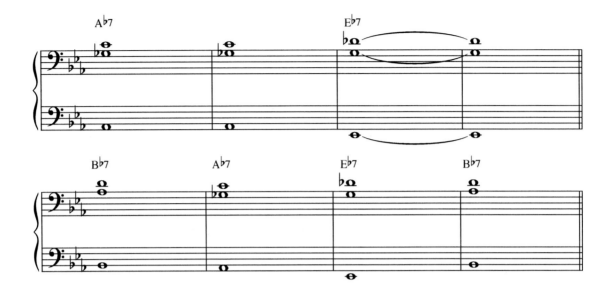

Each chord is composed of the root in the left hand and a tritone including the 3rd and 7th of the chord in the right hand. This is the barest harmonic texture that still results in the appropriate blues sonority. Of course, simply playing the root notes in the bass can suffice. The form can also be played using regular full triads and 7th chords, as shown in the previous exercises.

Once comfortable with the tritone skeleton, add short melodic motives played on the black keys or the full blues scale in E♭, which includes all black keys with the addition of the note A.

Change the texture from lyrical to staccato and dramatically alter the mood. Observe the final B♭7 chord at the end. This chord is useful for creating a turnaround, which propels the form forward and begins the cycle of chords again (see "Turnarounds and Endings" below).

This exercise can also be practised in E♭ minor for a darker sound. The dominant 7th chords would simply be replaced by minor 7th chords (Example 7.23).

Example 7.23

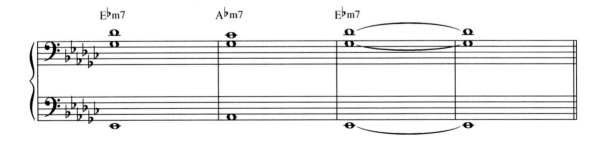

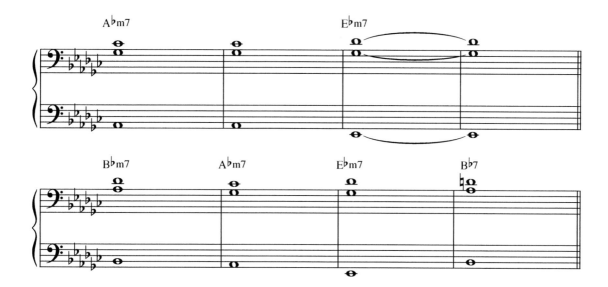

The final chord remains as B♭7 to create a stronger pull toward the tonic

Duet (I–A)

S, improvise only the black notes in the upper register of the piano. **A,** support **S** with a blues accompaniment in the key of E♭ in the bottom and middle registers, similarly to the example provided in the exercises above. The improvisation does not have to be pulsed. **A,** leave musical space in order to allow **S** to feel heard. Alternate between lyrical and detached playing, using whichever matches **S**'s expression.

Breaks

A break consists of an interruption in the regular blues form where — in the context of a band — a soloist plays alone into the silence left by the other musicians. Turry (2005) employs the technique of stop time, described as "a bass line followed by a complete rest, so that no pulse is being produced from the piano" (p. 63). Blumenfeld (1992) refers to it as a musical "break" or "an interruption in the course of the performance of a musical composition during which the normal content and momentum is suspended and new material interjected" (p. 209). This device allows his client's vocalizations to be heard in the foreground, which gives his client a very different experience than when singing with the pulse of the music.

In music therapy, this technique can be useful especially for clients who crave to be seen or heard. It can provide an opportunity to feel validated, which can contribute to the building of confidence and self-esteem. The sudden change in form can also capture a client's attention and provide motivation to play. Therapists must be careful, however, and consider whether it is appropriate or not to single out a client, for some may find the sudden attention unbearable.

Solo (I)

Play the following example:

Example 7.24

This demonstrates the elongation of the first phrase by extending it from four to eight measures. In a typical break, the band leaves rests after accenting the first beat of every bar (or every two bars) as the soloist showcases his or her riffs (melodic patterns). This allows the performer to express himself and display some virtuosity. Sometimes, the 12-bar form is extended at the beginning, as in the example above. After the first eight measures, the break ends and the groove resumes.

Notice the glissando at the end of the first system. Glissandos are useful in signaling the end or beginning of phrases. In a clinical context, they can serve as a musical cue for a change of section or simply to create a festive atmosphere.

Duet (I–A)

CD2
(10)   **S,** play freely on a nontuned percussion instrument. **A,** accompany in the blues form with a regular steady pulse using an ostinato in the left hand. Imagine working with a child. Sing a chorus that fits the blues AAB phrase structure as you accompany **S**'s free improvisation. For example,

"We've got the blues, we've got the blues, Jordan!
We've got the blues, we've got the blues, Jordan!
We're gonna play some music, 'cause we've got the blues."

Then create a break section in order to allow *S* to play into the silence. Return to the chorus at the end of the break. Consider adding the verbal prompt "Let's hear Jordan play his drum!" in order to cue *S* to begin soloing.

Extended Harmonies

Extended harmonies include the 9th, ♯11th and 13th intervals above the root. Borrowed from the jazz tradition, they often serve to increase the level of density in chords or to add colour. They also create clusters, depending on the inversions used. These may be used to support higher levels of tension during louder moments in improvisations.

Solo (A)

Play the following examples (Example 7.25) in order to become familiar with extended harmonies:

Example 7.25

The 9th is equal to the 2nd degree of the diatonic major scale, in this case, the D. The ♯11th, equal to ♯4 or ♭5, is always raised, as otherwise it would conflict harmonically with the 3rd of the chord. The 13th is equal to the major 6th above the root.

Note that all harmonic extensions generally include the 9th. The ♯11th can be substituted by the 13th, or in some cases both can be present in a chord.

Experiment using extended harmonies on each chord as the blues form progresses. Be mindful that consistency and coherence will yield better results. For example, if a ♯11 voicing is used, keep the same voicing when changing chords.[2]

Turnarounds and Endings

The blues form is cyclical and was never intended to have a beginning or end. It is timeless. For practical reasons, however, the music must end at some point. Creating a satisfactory ending when playing the blues can be a cathartic and pleasurable experience for both client and therapist. Letting the sound of the final chord rumble and swell with a tremolo naturally communicates an ending. For clients who enjoy making loud sounds, this can be an opportunity to offer release in a creative and positive experience.

---

[2]See Chapter 8 for a more detailed discussion on extended harmonies.

Solo (I–A)

Here are some typical endings based on Blumenfeld (1992):

Example 7.26

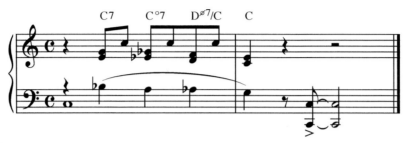

Example 7.27

Note the use of chromaticism (both ascending and descending) in these two examples (7.26, 7.27).

Example 7.27 shows dense chords using extended harmonies, which are typical for blues endings. These are borrowed from jazz. It consists of the ♭II7 chromatic neighbour chord, which resolves immediately back to I in parallel motion.

Here is another idiomatic ending used in both blues and jazz styles:

Example 7.28

The decorations on the final chord can be substituted with other extended harmonies. The idea is to end on a dense chord. The final chord can also be extended by playing it in a tremolo[3] and finishing on an accented punctuation. Many clients are accustomed to this type of cathartic ending, as it is still performed in today's rock styles.

---

[3]See "Ornamental and Stylistic Devices" below for more details on tremolos.

For turnarounds at the end of choruses within the body of the piece, similar techniques as those found in the final ending cadences can be used; however, a V or V7 chord must be inserted at the end of the measure in order to prepare for another chorus.

Example 7.29

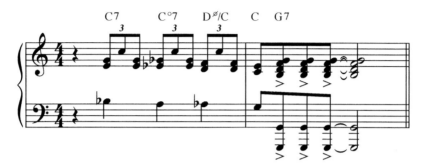

Although the above example is based on an authentic pianistic rendition, a simpler version of the turnaround can be achieved by playing strong repeated octaves in both hands on the dominant V chord on the last measure of the chorus. The idea is to keep the music at a peak of intensity on the final V chord in order to propel it forward.

Duet (I–A)

> *S,* improvise freely on an instrument of your choice (a piano duet is also acceptable). *A,* support *S* using the blues, initiating a groove with a steady pulse. *A,* signal turnarounds and endings by introducing some of the idiomatic figures from the above exercises. Repeat the form several times before creating an ending. Make clear eye contact with *S* as the ending approaches. Rumble the final chord, allowing *S* the time to play, then add a final accented chord to signal the final note.

ORNAMENTAL AND STYLISTIC DEVICES

The following exercises focus on some of the blues' most important ornamental and stylistic devices. These are grace notes, repeated figures, tremolos, octaves, and breaks. In general, these are needed to convey a more authentic rendition of the style. They can also be used to respond to clients' musical gestures in order to facilitate musical dialogue in improvisation. We recommend exploring the basic musical components of the blues discussed in the previous three sections before practising the exercises in this segment, as these require a certain facility with the blues form and scale.

Solo (I–A)

Grace Notes

> Play the following grace note figures:

Example 7.30

Grace notes can be added either in the treble or bass, whether it is a repeating figure or repeating melody. They add a folkloric character to the music and produce a piercing sound at the top register of the piano. This can be effective in supporting loud percussive instruments.

Create your own grace note figures. Note that they are often played on the blue notes or on the semitone below leading to them.

Repeated Figures

Play the following repeated figures:

Example 7.31

These devices add energy and drive to a blues improvisation. They can act as a motivating element or musical response reflecting the spontaneous expression that can arise during an improvisation. Note the accented figure in the top register in the second example (Example 7.31, bar 2), which creates a three-against-two polyrhythm.

Create your own repeated figures based on the examples above. Play them in various registers and keys.

Tremolos

Play the following tremolos:

Example 7.32

Tremolos can consist of octaves (Example 7.32, bar 1) or block chords (bar 2). Sometimes an entire melody is played with the tremolo effect (bar 3), which gives the illusion of sustained pitches. This is particularly useful for crescendos and diminuendos. Finally, this device can be grandiose when executed with two hands (bar 4).

Create your own tremolo effects. Try them in various registers of the piano. Experience placing your hands in the extreme registers of the piano.

Octaves

Play the following octave passages:

Example 7.33

Example 7.34

Example 7.33 outlines the blues scale in octaves. Play it in straight 8ths or a shuffle meter in various registers of the piano.

Example 7.34 demonstrates a festive New Orleans style. The octaves emphasize the pentatonic scale pitches with chromatic embellishment. The strong syncopated bass ostinato is reminiscent of the barrelhouse styles of Dr. John or Professor Longhair. This type of figure can be very arousing when played loudly in the bottom register of the piano.

Create your own octave passages, exploring different keys and registers.

Practise the blues scale in octaves with both hands up and down the range of the keyboard.

Duet (I–A)

S, sing freely, recounting the events of your day in song. *A,* begin a simple bass ostinato and answer the vocal phrases with stylistic devices from the above exercises, matching and mirroring *S*'s tone and energy. *This exercise is designed to prepare therapists for more extrovert clients who demonstrate creative leadership.*

S, play quick, repeated notes on a drum. *A,* support the rhythmic pulse with an appropriate repeating figure and follow *S*'s dynamics and articulations. Establish a clear rhythmic pulse, either in 4/4 or in a triple meter such as 12/8 (with *S* playing 8th-note values). *S,* continue to keep a quick, steady beat in response, creating a three-against-four polyrhythmic repeated figure as in the examples below (7.35, 7.36). Discuss the possible use of polyrhythmic figures in clinical improvisation. See the following examples:

Example 7.35

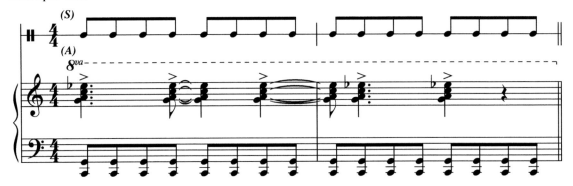

Example 7.36

ADDITIONAL RESOURCES

PREPARED GUITAR

When a client plays on a prepared guitar, it can be a challenge to support with the piano, as both are harmonic instruments. Clients often play it unconventionally because they do not have the ability to finger chords on the fret board. In sessions, it is often more practical to tune the strings to a desired sonority, such as open 5ths. Some of the early blues songs were accompanied with a single stringed homemade instrument that did not have the ability to produce chords. The open 5th sound is reminiscent of the older folk blues of the Mississippi delta. Therefore, tuning the guitar to an open sonority is not only practical but also has an aesthetic significance. Here are four variations on the open string tuning:

Example 7.37

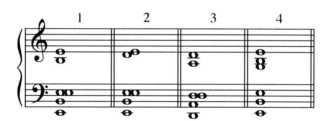

Tuning Instructions

Configuration 1: Roots and 5ths (open 5ths) in the key of E. (1) Leave the first lowest string open, (2) raise the second A string a whole tone to B, (3) raise the third string D a whole tone to E, (4) lower the fourth string G a minor 3rd to E, and (5) leave the last two strings open.

Configuration 2: The same notes except for the fifth string, which instead takes the blues 7th. The D forms a cluster against the E, which is a most welcomed dissonance in the blues. (1) Follow the same procedure as Configuration 1 and (2) raise the fifth string B a minor 3rd to D.

Configuration 3: The same as Configuration 1 (open 5ths) but transposed down a whole tone in the key of D. (1) Lower the first string E down a whole tone to D, (2) leave the second A string and third string D open, and (3) lower the last two strings B, E down a whole tone to A, D.

<u>Configuration 4:</u> E minor chord. In reality, the G note of the fourth string functions as a blues 3rd and can easily be played against an E major or E7 chord on the piano. (1) Leave the first string E open and (2) raise the second and third strings A and D up a whole tone to B and E.

The first three configurations lend themselves well to bar chords (blocking an entire fret with the finger or hand). For capable clients, this allows the opportunity to change chords by taking hold of the frets without using fingers. Individual clients may benefit from learning the blues form and its chords I, IV, V in the key of E.

The electric guitar may be easier to play for some clients, as the volume level can be controlled through an amplifier and chords require less finger strength.

Here are a few tips when supporting the guitar on the piano:

> There is no need to change the harmony using the chords of I, IV, and V. Most of the early folk blues did not contain identifiable chords. These were added later due to the influence of western classical music. Rather, support the rising and falling of the music's intensity level.

> Take more melodic initiative, as the notes on the guitar do not lend themselves well to melodic playing. The voice is also very effective in adding a melodic component. Often clients may be able to improvise using both voice and guitar simultaneously, thus taking on the persona of a true delta blues musician. In such a case, a simple accompaniment at the piano and vocal support may suffice.

> Listen for accents or notes that the client emphasizes when improvising. You can respond to these by using some of the ornamental and stylistic devices discussed previously.

USING SINGLE-PITCH INSTRUMENTS
(REED HORNS, WHISTLES, TONE CHIMES)

For single-pitch instruments, it is useful to choose blue notes (blues 3rd, 5th, or 7th) in order to give the client the experience of the style's most expressive tones. Remember that blue notes are made to fit all blues harmonies; therefore, clients can play their note at any time during the form.

In the event of a group with several clients playing on single-pitch instruments, here are a variety of interesting note combinations for the keys of C, F, and G, starting from the lowest note:

Example 7.38

Key of C	**Key of F**	**Key of G**
A, E♭ (6th, blues 3rd)	D, A♭ (6th, blues 3rd)	E, B♭ (6th, blues 3rd)
C, E♭ (tonic, blues 3rd)	F, A♭ (tonic, blues 3rd)	G, B♭ (tonic, blues 3rd)
G, B♭ (5th, blues 7th)	C, E♭ (5th, blues 7th)	D, F (5th, blues 7th)
C, E♭, F (tonic, blues 3rd, 4th)	F, A♭, Bb (tonic, blues 3rd, 4th)	G, B♭, C (tonic, blues 3rd, 4th)
A, C, E♭ (6th, tonic, blues 3rd)	D, F, A♭ (6th, tonic, blues 3rd)	E, G, B♭ (6th, tonic, blues 3rd)
G, B♭, C (5th, blues 7th, tonic)	C, E♭, F (5th, blues 7th, tonic)	D, F, G (5th, blues 7th, tonic)

THE BLUES FORM IN THE KEYS OF D AND A

The blues in the keys of D and A can accommodate tuned percussion instruments that do not include sharps or flats. Moreover, these keys are comfortable on the guitar. Here is a quick chord reference (for piano or guitar) for each key and suggested pentatonic scales for prepared tuned percussion instruments:

Blues in D (prepared instrument: D, F, G, A, C, D):

D	/D	/D	/D
G	/G	/D	/D
A	/G	/D	/A

Blues in A (prepared instrument: A, C, D, E, G, A):

A	/A	/A	/A
D	/D	/A	/A
E	/D	/A	/E

CONCLUSION

The blues is a versatile form of music that has an unmistakable identity. This makes it ideal for a wide range of musical/clinical interventions. The blue notes are familiar to the majority of western ears. The style is always fresh and never becomes outdated or redundant. There is an appeal for simplicity and sincere primal expression, this being its strength as a therapeutic intervention.

The blues can incorporate a wide range of emotions from joy and playfulness to anger, frustration, and sadness, allowing stylistic variations from bright to dark or major to minor. Music therapists in favour of the more popular entertaining blues styles often disregard the serious blues of the Mississippi delta. We encourage therapists not only to familiarize themselves with contemporary blues styles but also to experience the fathers of the blues such as Robert Johnson, Muddy Waters, Skip James, "Blind" Lemon Jefferson, and other artists originally from the South. These artists are symbols of the music's roots, as they lived by its philosophy. They have indirectly contributed to music therapy not only by leaving us music that expresses and captures human suffering, but also by providing a means for therapeutic relief and acceptance through instinctual expression in the present moment. The more therapists immerse themselves in recordings, the more they will absorb the fullness that the blues has to offer.

CHAPTER 8

Jazz

Excitement, romance, sensuality, soulfulness, and freedom are only few of the many terms that can describe the genre of music known as jazz. Evoking a range of moods, blasting spontaneously from emotion to emotion, jazz musicians never cease to innovate and feel at home in the unexpected. But, most importantly, they seek to unify — with others and with the divine. The music has a strong sense of community and strives for innovation at its core. Shipton (2007) describes the global impact of jazz in the world:

> Of all the musical forms to emerge during the 20th century, jazz was by far the most significant. In the early years of the century, it spread first throughout the United States of America and then quickly to the rest of the world, where its combination of syncopation, unusual pitching, vocal tones, and raw energy touched the hearts and minds of people across the entire spectrum of social and racial backgrounds. Its message was universal, and it stood for something new, something revolutionary, something risqué that overturned the old orders of art music and folk music alike. (p. 1)

Indeed, jazz is an all-American music with a rich history and evolution, with its roots in early 20th century New Orleans, where famous trumpeter Louis Armstrong once lived.

> New Orleans played a great role in the evolution of jazz music in the 20th century. At this time, the people of New Orleans hailed from many different cultures. As new settlers arrived in New Orleans, musical traditions from all over the world began to unite. African-American musicians merged European musical tradition with such music as blues, ragtime, and marching band to create a new style of music — jazz. (A History of Jazz, n.d.)

Although the roots of the music are found in New Orleans, in around the 1920s musicians began to migrate to other major cities. Soon, New York and Chicago became major cultural centres for jazz music; they have produced many of the artists who later created the big band classics we still hear today:

> Already, in Chicago, the Midwest, and New York, larger bands had replaced small groups as jazz's dominant format. A new generation of big band leaders launched the Swing Era in earnest. Born as America emerged from the Depression, big band swing — a music that offered upbeat escape — became a popular phenomenon. (Sutro, 2006, p. 93)

The 1930s and '40s are often referred as the "Golden Age" of jazz or "Swing Era" (Sutro, 2006). These were times of social gatherings where people danced all night to the entrancing, exciting sounds of the orchestra. Such names as Duke Ellington, Count Basie, Tommy Dorsey, Benny Goodman, and Glenn Miller are but a few of the genre's greatest leaders of that time. These orchestras have left us with the most beautiful songs, melodies, and ballroom dance pieces, which will remain classics for years to come.

During World War II, dance halls began to close all over the country due to a "recording ban imposed by the musicians' union in a dispute over artist's royalties" and "a newly imposed entertainment tax" (Sutro, 2006, p. 115). As the culture of America changed, jazz continued to adapt and evolve. The '40s and '50s produced the greatest "bebop" musicians, such as Oscar Peterson, Bud Powell, and Charlie Parker, who helped to raise the status of the music from entertainment to art. With virtuosic solos, relentless energy, and creativity, they took the music to smaller club venues. As the popularity of orchestras faded, smaller ensembles known as combos began to emerge. With only a few musicians, each member assumed an important role; a drummer and bass player served as the rhythm section, which propelled and maintained constant movement to support a soloist. A pianist or guitarist filled the role of harmonies in addition to supporting the rhythm section. The combo, in a sense, was a compact orchestra, but one with more flexibility and individuality, which allowed more spontaneous improvisation on the part of all members. Though the sound of jazz had changed dramatically, musicians still held the same attitude of community and innovation that had shaped the music from its conception.

At the dawn of the 1960s, jazz was further threatened by the increasing popularity of rock and roll. But once more, new creative sounds arose from modal jazz[1] and the avant-garde movements. Miles Davis, one of the style's most influential personalities, had already made his mark in the second half of the 1950s by bringing some of the best musicians together and now was leading the modal jazz scene with musicians such as Bill Evans and John Coltrane (Sutro, 2006, p. 144). Rather than emphasizing relentless soloing over complex harmonic progressions, some jazz tunes had only one or two harmonies onto which endless melodic variations would occur. Modal scales brought new exotic sonorities. The turn by some musicians toward harsher sonorities no doubt reflected the social turmoil that black Americans were facing at the time. Sutro (2006) gives an account of jazz as a social expression:

> From the beginning, jazz had social and political significance. Listening to melting-pot-early-jazz from New Orleans, sweet-Depression-antidote-jazz from the 1930s, or wake-up-bebop from the 1940s, it's easy to see how each type of music reflected those times in America. In the 1960s, jazz's social messages screamed with blatancy, especially in the music of African-American musicians for whom the music became a direct expression of new ideas about being black in America. (p. 159)

Although jazz continued to be present from the 1970s onward, it gradually parted from the mainstream but was prominently featured in media and movies as it is still on occasion today. However, jazz is far from being an extinct form of music. Nowadays, there are vibrant jazz communities in almost all major cities of the world. Despite their being overshadowed by pop culture, the defining sounds of jazz are here to stay. Jazz has brought back the value of improvised music-making in western music, an art form that had been long forgotten over the centuries.

In retrospect, it is a difficult task to define the boundaries of jazz, as the style has branched off in many directions throughout the course of the 20th century. The music evolved in so many distinct individual styles that it can no longer be captured under a single umbrella word. Now we speak of mainstream jazz, cool, hard bop, Latin, fusion, avant-garde, and so forth, and each of these subcategories contains a plethora of individual styles (Sutro, 2006). In this chapter, we will focus on the mainstream jazz styles of the swing and bebop eras and the typical stylistic conventions that have stood the test of time. Upon a general observation and according to most

---

[1]Modal jazz refers to compositions based on fewer harmonic changes, which leaves room for greater melodic freedom in improvisations. These compositions often entail the use of specific modal scales. The theoretical foundations of modal jazz are attributed to George Russell, who introduced these ideas in his book *Lydian Concept* (Sutro, 2006, p. 144).

comprehensive literature, the following musical elements appear to be at the heart of the jazz idiom:

Swing feel and syncopated rhythms
Blue notes (3rd, 5th, and 7th)
Modal scales
Extended harmonies (9th, 11th, 13th)
Typical harmonic patterns involving II–V
Short cyclical forms

Many of these features have commonalities with the blues. This is not surprising, as both styles took their roots in New Orleans and evolved side by side, allowing cross-pollination. The features that are specific to jazz will be the focus of this chapter.[2]

JAZZ AND MUSIC THERAPY

Why is jazz relevant for music therapy? First, improvisation in the clinical setting could be regarded broadly as a form of jazz, since improvisations in both settings are compatible not only in terms of their humanistic ideologies (which put a high value on human connectedness, expression of life in the present moment, creativity, or the search for the divine or higher states of being), but also in their formal aspects. Aigen (2006) compares his experience of listening to a jazz combo versus a clinical improvisation and argues that both could be viewed from a purely musical lens or as a pure communicative relationship between players; it depends on the listener's point of view (pp. 70–74):

> Therapists making music with clients are never just concerned with the therapeutic relationship in sound because this relationship is mediated by musical factors. The therapist's choices of instrument, tonality, timbre, harmony, and tempo are all affected by the musicality of the client's expression as well as the clinical needs, the dynamics, and the communicative patterns of the relationship. The same is true of the players in a jazz group. What they play is a combination of what they hear from each other, what they know about each other's predilections, and the relationship dynamics among them, including who is a better listener, who functions more as a leader or a follower, and who is a more dynamic personality. In fact, jazz can be as much as music therapy an example of interpersonal communication in music. (p. 71)

If jazz can be viewed from this standpoint, then it is in a position to inform the practice of clinical improvisation. Although the nature of the relationship between client and therapist, as well as their surrounding context, is different from that of jazz, the use of jazz aesthetics not only in terms of sounds but also including its interactional conventions can be of great benefit for clients.

The strength of good clinical improvisation comes from the ability to balance predictability and unpredictability. Monson (1996) contends that in a jazz performance, the "unpredictable may be euphoric or anxiety-producing (such as fear of getting lost), but the mixture of expectation and wilful departure traded around the bandstand is something the music absolutely thrives upon (p. 27). The same would apply in the therapeutic setting, for therapeutic change cannot take place if clients have no opportunity to step out of their "comfort zones." Even though stepping into the unpredictable can evoke fear and pain, these are necessary in the journey of personal growth. Jazz improvisations are often set on short cyclical forms (usually a standard song or blues that repeats indefinitely) and follow clear rules as to how variations will be

---

[2]For a more detailed discussion on the blue notes and short cyclical forms, see Chapter 7.

improvised among group members. By studying such principles (e.g., theme and variation, accompanying techniques, turn-taking, etc.), therapists can better understand how to bring clarity and shape in clinical improvisation and thus create an appropriate container for freer expression.

Jazz is also associated with African musical traditions, which are often based on rhythmic entrainment. When the musician or listener becomes entrained by the music, he or she can (in theory) achieve higher states of being or trance (Mereni, 1996). Although this may have significant implications for therapy, you cannot ignore its potential effect in sessions. Ruud (1995) explores Victor Turner's concepts of liminality and communitas as they appear in jazz music and discusses implications for clinical improvisation. Similarly to the blues or rock, jazz brings an opportunity to get into a groove or musical "flow," which can lead to an enhanced level of focus and musical engagement. This, in turn, sets the stage for therapeutic and often transformational outcomes.

The idea of groove and musical flow are also directly linked to Ansdell's (1995) concept of "quickening," which means "to give life to" or "to impart energy" (p. 81). He suggests that "music works therapeutically not by giving a mechanical stimulus but by lending somehow some of its qualities of liveliness and motivation to both body and spirit" (p. 81). A repetitive groove serves this.

Swing offers a sense of freedom and excitement and can sometimes lead into the realm of entertainment. Since jazz has strong ties to entertainment music, we may ask, What is the role of entertainment in a therapeutic process? Or, What is its relationship with music therapy? Although jazz can fulfill a need to escape and provide temporary relief from difficult feelings, it is important for therapists to remain aware of their clients' overall process and to be careful not to overuse the jazz idiom for such purposes. However, in some cases, temporary relief and distraction from pain may be the only thing a therapist can offer. Whatever the context, this issue should be considered when using jazz as an intervention.

Finally, the study of this chapter gives a more complete understanding of functional harmony, texture, and colour. With such an understanding, therapists will be able to be more flexible musically and increase their capability of adapting their music to meet the needs of their clients. By studying the full spectrum of harmonies and the laws of harmonics, you can learn to gain control of the build-up of tension and its release, which is a fundamental skill of a good improviser (Lee, 2003).

EXERCISES

In this chapter, only the fundamentals of jazz are explored. In order to assimilate the jazz style in more depth, the reader is urged to work with specialized jazz method books (such as Levine, 1989; 1995). Although jazz can be a wonderful idiom for clients to experience, it is one that takes a long time to master, for it involves much complexity, especially concerning harmony and voice-leading. Although this chapter was not designed for the beginning improviser, even beginning clinical improvisers can benefit from committing to a few months of jazz study, for even a simple walking bass line or swing feel on a cymbal can be a highly engaging element in the context of a music therapy improvisation. Thus, beginning keyboardists can study this chapter starting with the rhythmic aspects of the style and later explore harmonic progressions and sequences as they gradually master the use of simple (triadic) harmonies. For more advanced pianists, this chapter can be studied in tandem with Chapter 7, as both styles share much common ground.

SWING USING A CYMBAL AND SNARE DRUM

The jazz "feel" is inseparable from its rhythmic constituent, namely swing groove and syncopation. Compared to the blues' shuffle, swing has a looser feel, less heavy on the downbeats while emphasizing upbeats 2 and 4, and is generally facilitated by the drummer using a ride cymbal (Monson, 1996, p. 55). Integral to it is the walking bass line and the addition of a harmonic instrument, such as the piano or guitar. Together, they create the rhythm section for a number of jazz combos or orchestral ensembles. Trumpeter Wynton Marsalis compares rhythm section members to the parents of a family, as they are in charge of maintaining stability and responding to the immediate needs of the soloist (the child) (Marsalis, 2008, p. 31). This comparison also applies in the clinical setting, as therapists also have the responsibility of containing and responding empathically to their clients' expression.

The use of a swinging groove can add much excitement in musical improvisation, as it gives a constant drive. It produces a will to move. According to Monson (1996), the emphasis on swing's offbeats "has a noted ability to inspire people to rhythmic participation" (p. 28). Swing can also act as a rhythmic grounding mechanism, similar to that of an ostinato, as it fills the musical space with something constant and predictable without becoming overwhelming or complete on its own. The swinging groove may help to create momentum for clients who have difficulty sustaining musical interaction. In this section, we will explore the percussive elements of swing, while in the following section we will explore the role of the bass. These exercises are based on Strong (2006, pp. 127–154) and Monson (1996, pp. 51–66).

Solo

Swing Using a Cymbal

Using regular drum sticks, begin a steady pulse of quarter notes at a comfortable medium pace (between 100–130 on a metronome) on a ride cymbal.

Example 8.1

Once comfortable with your steady pulse, slightly accent beats 2 and 4 (the weak beats).

Example 8.2

Part of the swing feel is to accent weak beats rather than strong beats.

Finally, add a swing 8th note between beats 2–3 and 4–1.

Example 8.3

The swing 8th note is slightly accented also. Note that the triplets are only an approximation for slower and medium tempi. In reality, it sounds more like a late 8th note. The proper accents are key in conveying the swing feel; however, it is simpler to listen to authentic audio examples and imitate them in order to master it.

For faster swing tempi, the 8th note becomes closer to a straight 8th, as shown below:

Example 8.4

Practise playing in and out of swing time by alternating with passages of straight 8ths. In order to develop the jazz feeling and rhythmic precision, practise beating on alternating between straight 16th notes and triplets, with the help of a metronome set to a quarter note pulse.

While doing these exercises, take the time to fully explore the possible sounds you can make on the cymbal. Try striking the cymbal and immediately grabbing it with the other hand to dampen the sound. This can create short punctuations. Or, use the brushes or other types of mallets to alter the timbre. Play the cymbal in an unconventional way, experimenting with the sound of the metal frame. All of these techniques can be used to create variation and to respond creatively to a client's music.

Creating Syncopation Using a Snare Drum

Syncopation in a swing groove is created by interjecting between the beats with accents. Pianists use syncopation to create rhythmic interest and more movement when part of a rhythm section. The drummer also uses this technique, especially on the snare drum or toms. In a clinical improvisation, the snare drum can be used as the main interactive instrument that responds to the client's expression while the cymbal simply keeps a steady, grounding pulse.

Play the following example with a swing feel (triplet pulse). Play the cymbal with your dominant hand and the snare with the other:

Example 8.5

In order to focus on the snare drum, the swing pattern on the cymbal has been simplified to a quarter note pulse. More advanced percussionists can play a more complex cymbal groove.

At the end, a cymbal crash is demonstrated on the upbeat of beat 4. This is a stronger punctuation often used at the end of a section before repeating the form or beginning a new section of music.

Duet (B–I)

> *S,* improvise freely on any percussion instrument. *A,* support by playing steady quarter notes on a cymbal (without swing) and find a suitable pulse that sufficiently matches the mood and character of *S*'s music. Remember to give *S* time to explore within the musical space. After 30 to 40 seconds, transform the pulse into a swing groove and occasionally respond to *S* by crashing the cymbal at appropriate times while keeping the swing groove. *Note: It can be useful to grab the cymbal with one hand to dampen the sound in order to create short punctuation effects.*

It can be a rewarding experience to simply use percussion instruments in order to support clients. Therapists should be aware that in those instances, no harmonies are available to provide musical direction. Therefore, it is important to constantly look for communicative patterns that can emerge from clients' music, whether in the form of a rhythm or a melodic phrase. The key is not only to create a grooving atmosphere but also to interact and communicate musically with clients. Using only a cymbal (with the option of a snare) may be beneficial for clients who are averse to the sound of the piano or guitar. The following section is a continuation of the use of swing, this time using a walking bass line.

SWING USING A WALKING BASS LINE

Most jazz ensembles are supported by a bass player. The walking bass line is another essential feature of the jazz groove. It not only supports harmonically, but also provides a rhythmic drive. Like using the ride cymbal, this technique not only conveys the jazz "feel" but also creates a motivating musical atmosphere that can propel you to move. There are three types of motion used to achieve an authentic walking bass line: arpeggiated motion, step (or scale) motion, and chromatic motion.

Solo (I)

Arpeggiated Motion

> One of the most common bass line motions in jazz is to arpeggiate every chord beginning with the root note (Starr & Starr, 2008, p. 101). The following example demonstrates the movement from Cmaj7 to Fmaj7. Play it at a medium pace, emphasizing slightly the weak beats (2 and 4).

Example 8.6

Since the triad tones are the most important, it is possible to play a walking bass line composed entirely of arpeggios.

Not all notes of the chord need to be present, and the bass line's direction can move up and down according to the performer's choice.

Practise the arpeggiated motion on the following typical jazz progression in the next example:

Example 8.7

After mastering this version, make your own arpeggiated bass lines on the same progression.

Practise arpeggiated bass lines on other harmonic progressions. Going through the circle of 5ths (C, F, B♭, E♭, A♭, etc.) on dominant 7th chords can be a challenging but valuable exercise, as this chord sequence is used extensively in jazz.[3]

Scale Motion

Play the following walking bass lines demonstrating scale motion. Play them with a strict pulse, imitating a double bass:

Example 8.8

Scales are the most basic way to get from point A to point B. In these examples, the bass line clearly outlines the C major chord, with the triad notes placed on the strong beats.

The triad notes (root, 3rd, and 5th) are emphasized on strong beats. *Note: The general rule of always playing the root of each chord on beat 1 still applies.*

The scale type should conform to the chord you wish to play. In the second example, the chord is C minor; therefore, the appropriate modes and scales are Dorian or Aeolian (natural minor).

Practise the following bass pattern on this classic jazz progression:

---

[3]See "Circle of Fifths" below for a more detailed discussion on this sequence.

Example 8.9

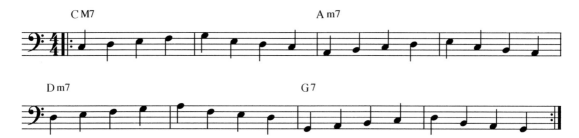

Although the above example is artificial (as an authentic bass line would contain more variation), this bass pattern is useful to outline a chord over two measures and links easily to other chords.

Chromatic Motion

Chromaticism is no doubt integral to the jazz idiom. It is used not only in melody and harmony, but in bass lines also. The following examples demonstrate the principle.

Play the following chromatic bass lines:

Example 8.10

Chromaticism is a great tool, especially when we run out of scale tones to arrive at the next root note.

Observe the use of the D♭ at the end of the first example in order to return to C. Playing the note a semitone above or below the intended resolution note (the root of the following chord) is typical of the jazz idiom. In this case, the pattern returns to C.

Generally, bass lines sound great in the lowest register of the piano.

Practise creating your own walking bass lines, moving between two chords on the piano at a medium or comfortable pace in 4/4 (four bass notes per measure). Cmaj7 to Fmaj7 or Dm7 to G7 are good starting points. At first, begin with simple arpeggios, then add scale motion and chromaticism. Play the full chords solidly in whole notes on each first beat of the bar in order to hear clearly what chord is being outlined by the bass (see examples below):

Example 8.11

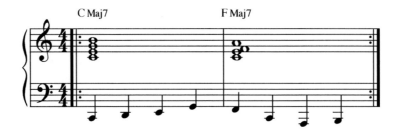

Example 8.12

Duet (I–A)

S, improvise freely on an nontuned percussion instrument. **A,** support **S** using a walking base line. Listen for a suggested pulse in **S**'s music, then play a prepared swing bass line in the lower register of the piano, outlining two chords (as in the solo exercises above). Repeat the pattern several times to get comfortable, then move away from it by walking the bass line into the midrange of the piano. Return to the original pattern and create an ending. *Note: It is important not to hesitate while improvising bass lines, as this technique requires an absolutely steady pulse. Remember that keeping the groove is more important than the actual notes.*

Repeat the previous duet exercise, but this time, **A,** add measures of complete rest in the middle of the improvisation to allow **S** to stand out briefly, then return to the original pattern and create an ending.

Again, based on the first duet exercise above, **A,** begin your bass line by outlining two chords, then as the improvisation unfolds, move away from tonality into a free jazz walking bass line that does not outline any recognizable harmonies. *Hint: Avoid outlining full triads, but instead include a lot of chromaticism.*

Once comfortable using walking bass lines, **A,** support **S** using both a walking bass line on the piano and a swing groove on a cymbal simultaneously. This combines all of the skills of the first two sections.

Creating a swing groove on the piano or cymbal is fundamental to the jazz idiom. It is sufficient on its own for clients to recognize the style. The above techniques are designed primarily for accompanying purposes, and therapists should remain clinically aware of their clients' possible need for variation of tempo, or even whether they can tolerate a constant rhythmic pace. For some clients the constant pulse of swing may hinder expression, while for others it may be a key motivating and stabilizing factor. Therapists should be ready to offer both constant grooves and improvisations without pulse even within the framework of jazz itself.

HARMONY

For any musician, including music therapists, it is very useful to study jazz harmony because of the large spectrum of colors and textures it offers. It is important to know our clients' preferences in terms of harmony in terms of not only major or minor modes but also density. We use the term "density" here in referring to both the frequency of chord changes and the level of harmonic complexity in each separate chord. The use of harmony is denser in jazz than in most popular styles. For example, a C major chord is seldom played as a simple triad. Instead, a denser sonority is preferable through the addition of the 6th or 7th, and sometimes more harmonic extensions are added, such as the 9th, 11th, and 13th, creating up to six or seven notes in a chord. The jazz idiom is especially suitable for clients who are highly responsive to dense and often dissonant sonorities. It can also be extremely engaging for others who are sensitive to color and timbre. Jazz harmony can unleash the imagination and bring a sense of freedom and novelty. The following exercises will explore three-note voicings, the addition of extended harmonies, and quartal harmony, informed by Levine (1989).

Three-Note Voicings (Root, 3rd, 7th)

In jazz, the most important defining tones of a chord are the root, 3rd, and 7th, regardless of whether the chord is major, minor, or dominant. The only exception is the permitted substitution of the 7th for a 6th in major and minor chords. In music therapy, such chords can be useful in maintaining a jazz framework while providing a less obtrusive accompaniment for clients playing on the piano or a xylophone. These basic structures provide a clear yet solid harmonic sense for a soloist.

Solo (I–A)

Play the following chord skeletons:

Example 8.13: On major chords

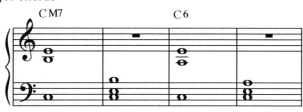

Example 8.14: On minor chords

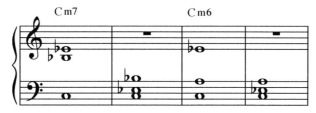

Unless specified, the 7th is always minor for minor chords and the 6th is always major. The major 7th chords are usually indicated by "M7", "maj7" or "ma7" in a fake book. Do not confuse C7 for a major 7th chord, for when no indications are present, we must assume that it is a dominant 7th chord.

Example 8.15: On dominant 7th chords

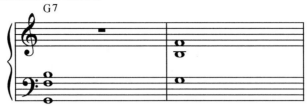

Note that the 7th on dominant 7th chords is always minor.

You may wonder why the perfect 5th is not included in the basic chord structure. It is simply left out in many cases, as it merely adds texture and thickness to the sound; it does not have any effect on the quality of the chord.

One of the quickest ways of becoming more familiar with the three-note voicings is to practise them in sequence in all 12 keys as II–V–I patterns, as in the following example:

Example 8.16

These voicings in this particular sequence (rising by semitone) are only one of several possible ways of practising. What is important is to include only the roots, 3rds, and 7ths of each chord and to keep the common tones between chords. In the II–V–I pattern, there are common tones alternating between the top and bottom notes in the right hand (the 3rd becomes the 7th of the following chord and vice versa).

Practise playing basic chord structures in a jazz fake book. "Autumn Leaves" or "All the Things You Are" are great starting tunes, as they are composed primarily with II–V or II–V–I patterns. Here is the harmonic skeleton of the beginning of "Autumn Leaves" in the key of A minor:

Example 8.17

Notice the beautiful sequence it creates (sequences will be discussed later in the chapter).

This sort of progression can easily serve as a basis for a melodic improvisation on the white keys of the piano or tuned percussion instrument.

Duet (I–A)

CD2 (12)   **A,** use a three-note voicing chord progression based on the first 8 bars of the author's jazz ballad (Example 8.18 below) to support a melodic improvisation by **S** (see also chord reduction Example 8.19 below). Play it slowly, imagining being accompanied by a bass player and drummer. **S,** improvise a melody on a tuned percussion instrument. **A,** listen carefully to **S**'s phrases and try to place the chords at appropriate times, coinciding with **S**'s phrases. As the improvisation unfolds, add melodic or harmonic embellishments in response to **S**. Create an ending with G7 resolving to Cma7.

Example 8.18

Example 8.19

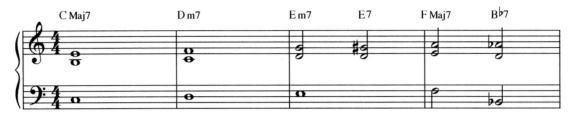

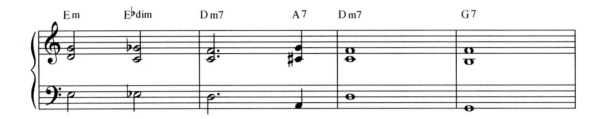

As a variation of the above exercise, **S,** improvise on a prepared tuned-percussion instrument using the following alternative scales:

Example 8.20: Blues scale

Example 8.21: Pentatonic scale

Example 8.22: Combination

Again, based on the examples from above, **S,** improvise vocally on a syllable (or words). **A,** improvise an accompaniment using the chordal skeleton above.

CD2 (13)   **S,** improvise using the F and B♭ notes on tone chimes. **A,** support and direct **S** with a rhythmic accompaniment in the Latin jazz style (bossa nova or samba), using the following example based on the "One Note Samba" by Antonio Carlos Jobim (Example 8.23). Direct **S** to play the F note for the duration of section A, then indicate when to change to the B♭ bell at the beginning of section B. *Note: This structured improvisation exercise also works with two supported participants, each holding a separate tone chime.*

Example 8.23

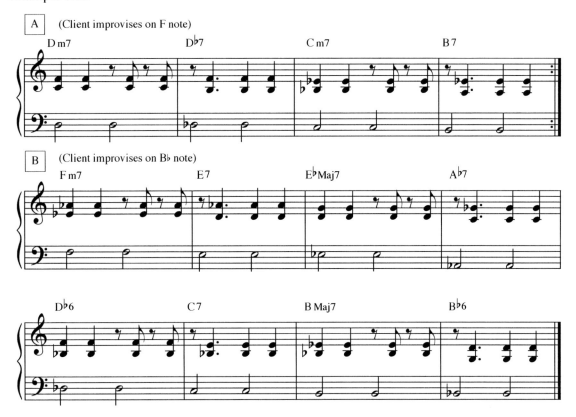

A, improvise a greeting song ("Hello" or "Good-bye") for **S** using one of the above progressions (Examples 8.19 and 8.23).

Extended Harmony and Triadic Upper Structures

The use of harmonic extensions (9th, 11th, and 13th) and/or triadic upper structures[4] can engage clients due to their almost unlimited array of feelings. They are especially useful to create rich soundscapes into which clients can bathe in the colours of jazz. Jazz chord voicings range from bright to dark, thin to thick, and consonant to dissonant. The use of triadic upper structures is a technique that facilitates the construction of complex chords. They make chords sound solid, distinct, and well-rounded. They consist of major or minor triads in the upper part of a chord and function to add color, texture, and density. Harmonic extensions usually are part of the upper structure of chords, while the fundamental tones (root, 3rd, 7th, or simple triads) are in the bottom structure. Since jazz chords can contain up to six or seven notes, in many cases the right hand plays the upper structure while the left plays the fundamental tones. These harmonic voicings are always based on a scale or mode.

Solo (A)

Play the following C major chords:

_____

[4]The term "upper structure" was coined by Levine (1989).

Example 8.24: On major chords

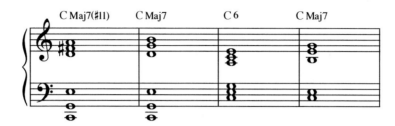

Several colours can be created simply by adding a major or minor triad (in any inversion) on top of the basic chord tones. In some examples, the 5th tone has been added in the bottom in order to create a warm and full sound. The D major triad in the first example outlines the Lydian mode with the F♯. The G major triad in the second example adds the major 7th tone as well as the 9th.

Note that only triads in which all tones are part of the Lydian mode will sound consonant[5] for major chords. The Lydian mode is preferred instead of the regular major scale (Ionian mode), as the 4th degree of the major scale clashes with the 3rd of the chord (F natural against E). Here are all the C Lydian mode triads; each is a possible upper structure for a C major chord:

Example 8.25

Any of the above triads can be put in any inversion above a C major triad. Try playing each one up and down the middle register of the piano while holding a C major triad in an open configuration (as in Example 8.25) or in root position. Notes of the upper structure triad may be doubled, especially when played in a higher register of the keyboard.

As a guideline, keep all upper structure chord notes near the middle register of the keyboard between middle C and G an octave and a 5th above, and do not play the left hand notes too far below the chord of the right hand.

To find other major chord possibilities, e.g., B♭, first play the B♭ Lydian scale (B♭ major with E♮ instead of E♭), then play the scale in triads as in the above example.

Think about the possible use of such chords in your work with clients. Where would it be clinically appropriate to bring denser sonorities or rich harmonies? Think of ways of incorporating the upper structure technique in your work within and outside the jazz framework. The following examples demonstrate this technique used on minor and dominant chords:

---

[5]The exception to this rule is the occasional borrowing from the Mixolydian mode for a "bluesier" piece.

Example 8.26: On minor chords

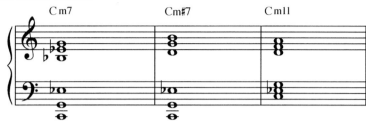

Generally, minor chords are based on the Dorian mode but can also take on a sharper sonority when based on the melodic minor scale.

Compare the sounds of these three minor chords. The E♭ triad on a C minor chord creates a regular minor 7th sonority. The G major triad in the second example outlines the melodic minor mode with the B♮. Finally, the third example consists of a minor chord a tone higher than the bottom triad (Dmin against Cmin). This creates a denser minor chord and is used often in modal jazz.

Here are all of the possible upper structure triads on a C minor chord based on the Dorian and melodic minor scales:

Example 8.27: C Dorian triads

Example 8.28: C melodic minor triads

Try a variety of inversions on any given upper structure triad. Some work better than others. Keep all upper structure chord notes near the middle register of the keyboard between middle C and G an octave and a 5th above, and do not play the left hand notes too far below the chord of the right hand.

On a dominant 7th chord, there are numerous possibilities for colors using triadic upper structures. The following examples are by no means exhaustive.

Example 8.29: On dominant 7th chords

In the case of dominant 7th chords, almost any major or minor triad will sound good as an upper structure, as long as none of the notes conflicts with the 7th or 3rd. Some of the most widely used upper structure chords come from the Mixolydian, Lydian-dominant, Half-step-Whole-step, or Altered scales (see Appendix C).

Note that in the second and last measures of Example 8.29, the 3rd of the chord has been taken out in the left hand, as it conflicts with the suspended 4th (C).

Here is a quick reference chart that shows how to proceed to create your own jazz chords using triadic upper structures (Appendix C provides all notated jazz modes):

Type of Chord	Left Hand	Right Hand
Major	Root, maj3rd, (5th), maj7th	Triad based on Lydian (or Mixolydian) scale
Minor	Root, min3rd, (5th), min7th	Triad based on Dorian or melodic minor scales
Dominant 7th	Root, maj3rd, (5th), min7th	Triad based on Mixolydian, Lydian-dominant, Half-step, Whole-step, or Altered scales

Prepare a chord progression using upper structures (between four and eight chords), keeping a common tone between all chords (see sample progression below). Follow the steps below:

1. Keep the fundamental tones (root, 3rd, 7th, occasionally including the 5th) in the bottom (left hand) structure. Open or closed voicings work equally well.
2. Each upper structure triad should contain the common tone (e.g., D major, F major, A major, and F♯ minor all contain A as a common tone — see example below).
3. Make sure the bottom and upper structure tones conform to an appropriate mode for each chord (refer to the diagram above or Appendix C for common modes for each chord type).

Example 8.30

Note that although each chord conforms to a particular mode, the relationship between each chord does not have to follow a logical harmonic progression, nor does each chord have to keep the mode of the previous chord.

Duet (A)

Similarly to Example 8.30 above, *A,* prepare a chord progression using upper structures (between four and eight chords), keeping a common tone between all chords. *S,* improvise on a hand bell (or a reed horn) tuned to the common tone.

A, support *S* by playing the chord progression following *S*'s tempo. Remember to stay on the chords long enough to allow *S* to experience their unique qualities. You do not have to change the chord every time *S* plays the bell.

A, follow the directions of the previous exercise, this time creating both an A and a B section, where B consists of a new series of chords with a different common tone. Direct *S* by pointing to the second bell or horn when the B section starts.

Quartal Harmony (Stacked 4ths)

Another way to create interesting sonorities is to construct harmonies using notes of modal scales by the technique of stacked 4ths. Although stacked 4ths are usually found in modal jazz from the 1960s, they can sound jazzy even without a tonal centre.

The use of this technique results in more ambiguous sonorities and an increase in harmonic density. It is a great way to avoid traditional triadic chords. It can be useful for clients who are easily engaged by unfamiliar sounds and more dissonant music.

Solo (A)

Play the following chords:

Example 8.31

Sometimes stacked fourths are in the upper structure of the chord, and sometimes they are at the bottom. For the first two major chord voicings, the notes are from the Ionian (major) mode, while for the final four minor chord voicings, the notes are from the Dorian mode.

Experiment playing chords using the white notes (D Dorian) and contrasting them with chords using the black notes (E♭ Dorian). Miles Davis's tune "So What" from his best selling album *Kind of Blue* is one of the first modal jazz pieces using this technique. With harmonies changing only once, improvisers have more melodic freedom. Play the following piano arrangement, examining the stacked 4ths in the solid chords.

Example 8.32

First practise playing stacked 4ths up and down the D Dorian mode. Do this with both hands. *All chords consist of white keys.*

Example 8.33

Then find all of the stacked 4ths from the E♭ Dorian scale:

Example 8.34

Create an improvisation that contrasts the D and E♭ Dorian modes.

Try playing a simple children's tune such as "Mary Had a Little Lamb" or "Twinkle, Twinkle, Little Star" using parallel stacked 4ths in the right hand.

Duet (A)

S, improvise on the drum and cymbal. At the piano, **A,** accompany in a modal jazz framework using stacked 4ths in the key of D Dorian (white notes only). Create a short rhythmic theme based on **S**'s rhythms. Add a walking bass line to the chords to create movement if it fits with **S**'s playing. *Hint: Remember to establish a clear key centre on D in the bass.*

S, improvise on the drum and cymbal. **A,** based on the form of Miles Davis's "So What," begin accompanying **S** in the key of D Dorian with stacked 4ths. Use a walking bass line to create movement if necessary. Then add a contrasting section using stacked 4ths in E♭ Dorian (a half-step above). After a short moment, return to D Dorian, thus completing an ABA form.

CD2 (14) **S,** improvise freely in the upper registers of the piano. **A,** use the technique of stacked 4ths in an atonal free jazz framework. Support **S** with a walking bass line. Add punctuations (through syncopated accents) with stacked 4ths in response to **S**'s playing. *Hint: Since harmony is of secondary importance, focus on texture and rhythm, using syncopation within a swinging groove to support* **S.**

COMPING ON CHORD PROGRESSIONS

As seen in other chapters of this book, creating predictable harmonic progressions is an important improvisation skill. It is essential in clinical improvisation, especially with clients who require a high level of musical structure. This section will explore the same concepts as seen in Chapters 2 and 3 (Baroque and Classical eras), but with examples from the jazz idiom, more specifically in the form of vamps, common chord progressions, and sequences. In addition, we will demonstrate how the progressions are realized by a pianist in a rhythm section. The technique is referred to as "comping" style. According to Monson (1996), "comping refers to the rhythmic presentation of harmonies in relationship to the soloist or the written theme of an arrangement" (pp. 43–44). Berliner (1994) points out that:

> Like the drums, the piano can punctuate the music rhythmically, yet it has the ability to mix short accentuating punches with long sustained sound. Introducing constantly changing shapes into the accompaniment, the pianist can repeat the same rhythmic pattern while altering chord voicings, or hold particular voicings constant while applying them to different rhythmic patterns. (pp. 332–333)

This section will integrate and build upon the skills explored in the previous sections of the chapter.

Vamps and the II–V Progression

A vamp is a chord pattern that repeats indefinitely while a soloist improvises on top. Some jazz compositions are entirely based on vamp patterns, while other compositions feature a vamp as an introduction or ending for the tune. These usually consist of one to four chords and are no longer than two bars. In the clinical setting, a vamp can provide the necessary harmonic grounding or holding mechanism[6] onto which a client can express freely. While evoking the jazz framework, it can also function similarly to an ostinato due to its predictability and constant movement.

Solo (I–A)

Play the following vamp:

Example 8.35

This pattern outlines the chords II–V in the key of C major (or I–IV in the key of D minor Dorian). Regardless of the key, this pattern is generally referred to as a II–V progression (Levine, 1995). Realized as D minor to G dominant 7th, the progression can be used to support an improvisation on the white keys of a piano or a tuned percussion instrument.

Learn the II–V pattern starting both on D (Dm7–G7) and E♭ (E♭m7 to A♭7), as the former can support an improvisation on the white keys of the piano while the latter can be used for black keys. Here are three possible versions in both keys:

---

[6]The terms "harmonic grounding" and "holding" are used as defined in Wigram (2004, pp. 95–97).

Example 8.37

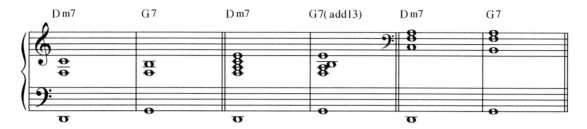

Example 8.38

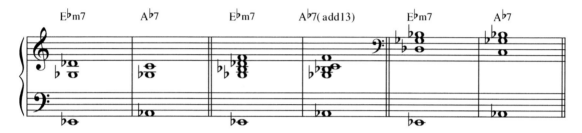

Practise them first as written, examining the voice-leading. Then add stylistic elements to put them more properly into the jazz framework. Add a simple walking bass line outlining notes from the basic triads of each chord, and play the right hand chords with short syncopated punctuations and occasional accents on offbeats as in the following example:

Example 8.39

Once comfortable with these transpositions, write new transpositions in different keys and try them at the piano.

Create your own vamp patterns by moving back and forth between two chords using a walking bass line, e.g., Cmaj7 to Fmaj7 or Dmin7 to A7. Play the chord in the right hand while experimenting with the left hand walking bass. Once comfortable, add syncopation with the right hand while keeping a steady walking bass.

Try a variety of less common two-chord vamps, such as Am7 to Gm7 or Cmaj7 to Amaj7. *Hint: Juxtaposed major or minor 7th chords are likely to sound jazzy in almost any combination.*

Duet (I–A)

> *A,* begin playing a vamp on the chords Dm7 and G7, using a walking bass line. Keep the swing groove steady, leaving space for *S* to improvise a melody. *S,* improvise a melody on the white keys of the piano.

> *A,* repeat the above exercise, this time on the chords E♭m7 to A♭7. *S,* improvise on the black keys only.

The I–VI–II–V Progression

The I–VI–II–V progression is one of the most common harmonic patterns found in jazz standards. Gershwin's "I Got Rhythm" is just one of hundreds of songs that use this progression extensively. It consists of a simple prolongation of the I chord, passing through the predominant (II) and dominant (V), which leads back to I in the following measure. This progression can serve as a great starting point when beginning an improvisation in the jazz framework, as it can form the basis of an entire section. There are numerous variations on this pattern. Only a few will be presented here.

Solo (I–A)

> This is the simplest version of the I–VI–II–V progression, using only basic triads:

Example 8.40

To play this progression in the jazz framework, it is necessary to make the harmonies thicker through the addition of the 7th. It is realized as follows:

Example 8.41

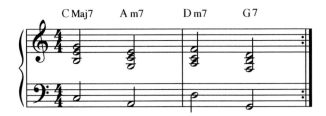

Most jazz pianists will include additional decorations through substitute voicings or the use of extended harmonies. The following version substitutes the minor VI chord with a dominant seventh chord, leading to II. *This type of substitution can also take place on the II chord, transforming the progression into a circle of 5ths (see "Circle of 5ths" below).*

Example 8.42

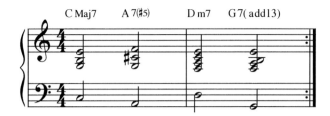

Finally, the progression can be played in a comping style, using syncopated and punctuated chords in the right hand and a walking bass line in the left. Play it in a medium swing tempo:

Example 8.43

More advanced pianists can explore a variety of I–VI–II–V voicings in the jazz framework. However, intermediate pianists can simply memorize the second version (triads with added 7ths) and practise it in a comping style similar to the above example (for swing, rhythm is more important than chord voicings when evoking the jazz idiom).

Descending 5ths Sequence

The descending 5th sequence is as old as the baroque era. It has permeated western music throughout its development and is still used in popular songs today. Although the jazz style began as a mixture of various cultural influences, its harmonic aspect comes in large part from European western music. It is possible to use such sequences in the clinical setting to create familiarity and predictability, as this sequence follows a logical chord progression that provides clear harmonic direction. In the jazz canon, there are hundreds of songs that use this progression. Two of the most famous standards are "Autumn Leaves" and "All the Things You Are."

Solo (A)

The following examples will demonstrate the descending 5th sequence in its simplest form and its gradual transformation into a jazz rendition. This first version contains only triads, with no added notes, following the sequence in the key of C major:

Example 8.44

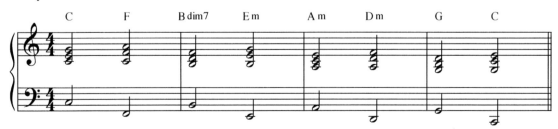

The second version substituted the doubled roots with an added 7th, as jazz chords usually consist of four-note 7th chords. All notes are taken from the scale of C major. This is the minimum amount of chord decoration needed to play this progression in the jazz framework.

Example 8.45

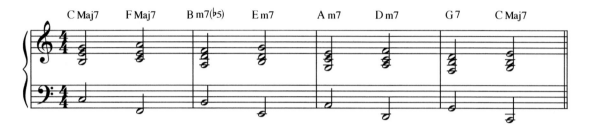

The progression can be further decorated (according to the performer's taste) with extended harmonies such as the 9th, 11th, or 13th, and altered (quartal) voicings:

Example 8.46

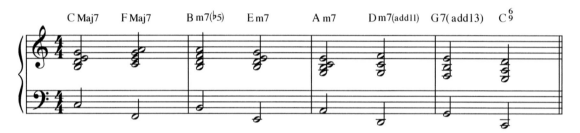

Finally, the progression is played following the jazz conventions in a comping style, using a walking bass line and syncopated chords in the right hand. Play it in a medium swing tempo:

Example 8.47

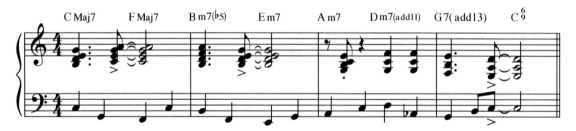

The descending 5th sequence can begin on any diatonic chord, not just the tonic. The IV or II chords (e.g., Fmaj or Dmin in the key of C) are popular ones.

This kind of sequence can also be played in a minor key, as in the beginning of "Fly Me to the Moon." Simply raise the 7th degree on the V chord (E7) to create the dominant of A minor. As in the major version above, the following examples will begin from 7th chord voicings of the progression and gradually move toward a jazz interpretation:

Example 8.48

Here is a more complex version of the same progression, using extended harmonies and altered (quartal) voicings:

Example 8.49

Several chords contain an added 9th or 13th. These extra tones dress up the progression and add a thicker texture to the sound.

Finally, here is an interpretation using a standard jazz comping (accompaniment) style. Play it in a medium tempo swing:

Example 8.50

Note the short 8th-note punctuations on the offbeats and the syncopated chords at the end of bars 1, 3 and 7, which anticipate the first beat of the following measure.

The first eight measures of the standard "Autumn Leaves" have a descending 5th sequence starting on the IV chord (D minor). Here it is presented in the key of A minor:

Example 8.51a

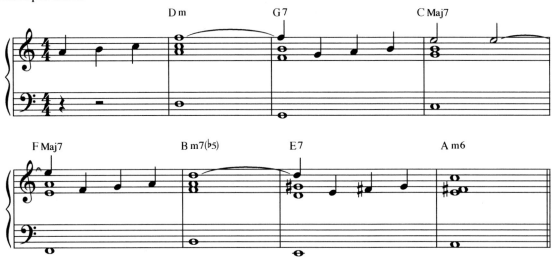

Here is a version based on the standard song "Autumn Leaves," using only three-note voicings (root, 3rd, 7th) starting on IV (Dm7) chord:

Example 8.51b

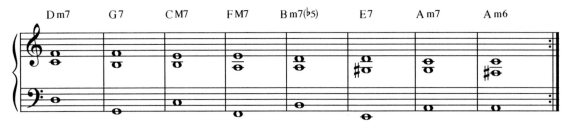

Transpose these sequences in three new keys of your choice. Try playing this sequence with a walking bass line by keeping the right hand voicings intact but walking to each root note on the first beat of every chord. Add syncopation in the right hand when comfortable.

The key to success for sequences is to remember the voicing used in the first bar or two and keep it consistent throughout. The voice-leading between the two chords is what defines what the hand will play for the following bars. Note that the pattern of common tones between the first and second chords in the right hand remains constant throughout the progression in Example 8.51b.

Duet (A)

S, start a swing groove using the cymbal. *A,* complement the pulse using the descending 5th sequence and add syncopation and a walking bass line once comfortable with the progression. If appropriate, add voice to complete the ensemble.

A, compose a piece for piano (or guitar) and percussion instruments that contains a descending 5th sequence in the B section. Each time the sequence chord pattern is played, leave a space for *S* to fill in (see Example 8.52).

Example 8.52

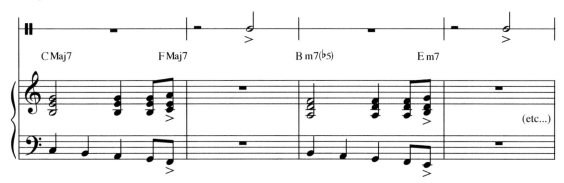

Circle of 5ths

The circle of 5ths is another useful progression, not only for jazz but for all tonal music, as it provides clear harmonic direction. Each chord can function as a V of the following chord in a dominant-tonic relationship. This makes it an ideal sequence for modulations. In jazz standards, this type of progression is often found in the B section or bridge of the piece.

Solo (A)

Play the following bass line:

Example 8.53

This type of sequence progresses through the circle of 5ths, allowing quick modulations or tonicizations.[7] The bass alternates by moving up a perfect 4th and down a perfect 5th, passing by all 12 keys.

Examine now a circle of 5ths sequence using dominant 7th chords in three-note (tritone) form.

Example 8.54

---

[7]These terms are taken from Sarnecki (2002), p. 171.

The circle of 5ths sequence is one of the most common in jazz. Note the tritone intervals in the right hand moving down chromatically as the 7th and 3rd of the first chord leads to the 3rd and 7th of the following one, and so forth.

The series of "V7 of V7" chords provides strong harmonic direction. It is used extensively in jazz standards based on *rhythm changes*[8], especially in the bridge (or B section). Examine the following sequence (Example 8.55) Note how the final chord of the sequence (G7) is the dominant which leads back to the home key (C) in the A section.

Example 8.55

When moving through the circle of 5ths on dominant 7ths, the same chromatic motion in the right hand can be used with any type of dominant voicing.

Example 8.56

The next example demonstrates the same principle, using a more triadic voicing of the dominant 7th chord:

---

[8] See following section (Form) for further discussion on *rhythm changes*.

Example 8.57: Circle of 5ths (Parallel Dominant 7th Chords)

This sort of chromatic chordal movement is one of the unique features of jazz. Using this type of sequence is one of the quickest ways to convey the idiom to clients.

Practise a variety of right hand dominant voicings that descend chromatically in parallel motion.

Duet (A)

> *A,* create an A section, supporting *S* by using a walking bass line pattern. *S,* improvise on a prepared tuned-percussion instrument or on the drum and cymbal. Once a clear theme has developed, *A,* create a contrasting B section consisting of a circle of 5ths sequence using a voicing of your choice.

The language of jazz makes possible an almost unlimited number of variations on simple sequences using chromaticism in the right hand and predictable bass lines jumping by 4ths and 5ths in the left hand. Such sequences are either descending 5th sequences or direct circle of 5ths sequences. Both are used extensively to provide harmonic direction and predictability in standard American songs. These voicings are at the core of the sound and are ideal for creating quicker-paced and more varied harmonic improvisations, which stand in contrast to a stable harmonic scheme of one or two chords used as a holding container,[9] such as a vamp. In choosing to use jazz sequences, therapists should consider whether their clients would benefit from a steady holding container or if they would benefit more from a constant change of harmonic colour.

FORM

Similar to the blues, most jazz forms are cyclical and repeat endlessly in a series of variations on a main theme or melody. They are usually short and simple, making them ideal vehicles for improvisation (Dean, 1989; Piazza, 2005). A jazz combo usually begins by stating the chorus or "head," which is generally a standard 32-bar song or a 12-bar jazz-blues. Each member of the ensemble then takes a turn to improvise variations on a chorus or series of choruses (which follow the same harmonic scheme as the head). At the end of the piece, the head is restated in its original form in order to recapitulate (Piazza, 2005, pp. 76–77). Consequently, the overall structure of most jazz performances is an ABA type, A being the statement of the head, with B being the improvised solos. This approach to form can easily be transferred to a music therapy setting by starting from a familiar song and taking it into an improvisation, then returning to the original song.

---

[9]See "Voice and Lyrics" in Chapter 6 for a more detailed discussion on two-chord holding progressions.

It is important to look not only at the larger form of an entire performance of music (e.g., head-solos-head), but also at the smaller components of form, such as a single chorus. The study of this compact form is a valuable tool for any improvising music therapist who wishes to gain an understanding of harmonic tension and release.

The 32-Bar Song Form (Rhythm Changes)

George Gershwin's "I Got Rhythm" has a prototypical AABA song form, with a chord progression that has been used for countless other jazz standards, such as Sonny Rollins's "Oleo" and Charlie Parker's "Anthropology" (Berliner, 1994, p. 78). This progression is referred to as "rhythm changes". Although there are many variations on rhythm changes, this section will concentrate on this version.

Solo (I–A)

Play the following example of a piece set in rhythm changes in the key of C:

Example 8.58

Observe the contrast between the A and B sections. This is achieved in several ways: (1) by using harmonies further away from the tonal centre C; (2) by diminishing the harmonic movement (one chord over two bars); and (3) by creating a harmonic sequence (circle of 5ths). Note that the last chord of the B section is the dominant. This prepares the return of the tonic chord. Tension increases as the progression moves away from the tonal centre. It then releases at the end of the B section, resolving back to the tonic.

In clinical improvisation, it is important to control the balance between tension and release (Lee, 2003). In order to achieve this harmonically, familiarity is first created by constructing an A section that establishes a home key. In the above example, the A section is made up of the typical progression, I–VI–II–V (see "Comping on Chord Progressions").

Once the safety and predictability of the A section is set, a B section is introduced. Then the A section is brought back. It is important to note that the AABA form does not necessarily have to be so neatly packaged in four phrases of eight bars. In fact, rarely would it happen in such a clean fashion in clinical improvisation. However, it is important to extract the above principles from it.

Using a jazz fake book, practise identifying the forms of songs and examine how contrast is achieved between the A and B sections.

Duet (I–A)

A, sing a familiar song of the 1930s or '40s (jazz standard), keeping it in its original form, At the end of the chorus, improvise an instrumental dialogue with *S,* following the harmonic progression of the song. *S,* improvise freely on any percussion instrument. *A,* leave space through the use of silence or a minimum of right hand movement (e.g., keeping the root of each chord in the bass and letting *S* play his or her own melody on top) in order for *S* to have a voice within the music. Recapitulate by singing the song one last time. *Hint: It is extremely important to memorize the chord progression in order to be able to focus on S's music during the improvisation rather than on the song form. This duet exercise can be applied to a group of participants (each participant improvising on a chorus).*

CD2
(16) *S,* play with a steady pulse on a drum and cymbal. *A,* listen to *S*'s rhythmic cells and if possible find a short melodic idea based on the rhythms. Use the I–VI–II–V chord progression of "rhythm changes" from above (Example 8.58) to establish tonality and stability in forming the A section. If necessary, repeat the chord progression indefinitely. As a B section, support *S* by using a chord sequence of your choice or remain with the original one from above. In the key of C, the chords of the B section are E7, A7, D7, G7. Return to the A section to complete the form.

Example 8.59

The Jazz-Blues Form

The blues form is so useful that it was borrowed and adapted in other genres such as jazz, rock, and country and continues to pervade in all kinds of music today. The blues has been integrated into the "genetic makeup" of jazz since the beginning, as the styles evolved simultaneously in New Orleans. The main difference between the two styles is that jazz-blues includes chord substitutions or added chords and is played in swing time. Improvised solos in the jazz-blues style tend to be more melodically adventurous (using modal scales), reflecting the increased complexity of the harmonic progression. In clinical improvisation, playing a song in a jazzier rendition can bring energy and excitement in a session. This, combined with swing rhythm, invites rhythmic participation and body movement.

Solo (A)

The following is a common harmonic variation of the jazz-blues form. First, play only the root note of each chord following a clear tempo; then add the chords in the right hand:

Example 8.60

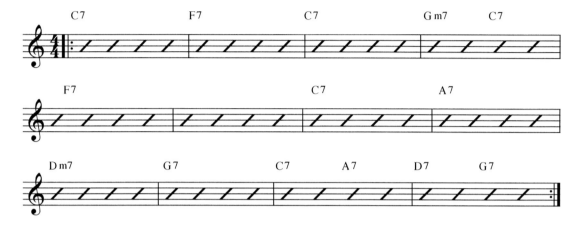

By learning how to "jazz up" the blues form, it is possible to extract principles and apply them to almost any other song — even classical music! However, some songs sound better than others when transferred to the jazz idiom. Here are a few techniques you can apply to "jazz up" a familiar song:

(1) Substitute regular major chords for dominant 7th chords.

(2) Vary the original melody by substituting some regular 3rds, 5ths, or 7ths with blue notes.

(3) Add additional chords such as a II–V progression leading to the next chord (a common tonicization) as in mm 4 of the jazz-blues form from above (Gm7–C7 … leading to F).

(4) Play the melody and harmonies in a syncopated way. Let some phrases finish just before the beat (on the final 8th note of the measure).

(5) Add a turnaround chord sequence at the end of a section: A turnaround is a short sequence of chords that adds movement and propels the form forward to the next section or repetition of the chorus.[10] They are typically based on the I–VI–II–V progression, often appearing as a series of V7 chords. The example above shows the use of the circle of 5ths (A7, D7, G7 … which lead back to C7). But upon closer examination, the bass notes are found to be the same as in the I–VI–II–V progression.

Practise playing the blues form using a walking bass line along with the basic chord tones in the right hand (3rd and 7th only). When comfortable with the progression, improvise melodically on the blues scale, supported by solid chords or root notes in the left hand.

---

[10] See "Turnarounds and Endings" in Chapter 7 for a more detailed discussion on turnarounds.

Using the above techniques, practise "jazzing up" another song that uses a simple harmonic scheme (I–IV–V), e.g., "Swing Low, Sweet Chariot" or "You Are My Sunshine."

Duet (A)

A, choose a popular song that contains only three or four chords (preferably a song that can be reduced to I, IV, and V harmonies), such as "Swing Low, Sweet Chariot" or "You Are My Sunshine," and prepare to play both the original and jazzy versions using three of the techniques mentioned in this section. First play the original version, then play the new jazzy version to *S* immediately, without pausing in between styles. Note that *S,* in this case, takes a more passive role by listening rather than participating actively in the music.

A, repeat the beginning steps of previous duet exercise: Play the original song, then the jazzy version, this time adding a third repetition as an instrumental or vocal improvisation with *S* in the jazz framework based on the harmonic progression of the verse or chorus. If the song does not lend itself well to improvising, substitute the song form with the jazz blues. Invite *S* to play on a small percussion instrument (following the beat or improvising freely), then return to the original version of the song to end. *These duets are meant to develop flexibility with the jazz framework (e.g., moving in and out of the stylistic framework).*

CONCLUSION

Jazz is not only compatible with music therapy in terms of ideology, but also contains highly practical tools to offer for clinical improvisation whether in terms of large-scale form — including its social processes and conventions — or the use of individual musical elements (harmonic textures, use of syncopation, etc.). Like the blues, jazz tends towards a groove-based way of improvising. This means that the therapist's role is often one of the accompanist who facilitates and keeps rhythm while the client takes the role of a soloist. However, in some cases, it may be beneficial to allow clients to be part of a rhythm section by allowing them to play the drums in a more equal musical relationship with the therapist, as it can be therapeutic and enjoyable to simply be part of a musical groove. Swing is an ideal intervention for the purpose of inviting dancing or rhythmic playing on instruments. Even beginning improvisers can develop the skills needed to facilitate it. The harmonic aspects of jazz can complete the whole but are not always necessary in the clinical setting. Finally, jazz is highly associated with entertainment and escape, which can serve a purpose in a therapeutic relationship. However, it should be used with care and consideration of the client's needs and preferences. Let yourself become inspired by the countless jazz recordings of the 1930s, '40s, and '50s, and consider practising some standard songs in a fake book, as these can enrich possibilities of repertoire to be adapted for clinical improvisation.

PART FOUR

WORLD

CHAPTER 9

India: Ragas

India is one of the most fascinating and intriguing countries in the world. With its dense population, intense climate, spicy cuisine, vibrant fashion, captivating rituals, bustling city streets, and lush countryside, it leaves most of its visitors feeling amazed and overwhelmed. Further woven into this country's colourful tapestry is the element of music. Dating back more than 4,000 years, the sounds of India tell a rich and captivating story. History describes how music was first mentioned in the *Vedas* (ancient Indian scriptures). Preserved through oral tradition and passed on from guru (teacher) to shishya (student), many of the hymns found in these ancient texts remain alive to this day. An important element bound closely to the development of music in India is that of spirituality, as throughout history, music was viewed as primarily a spiritual discipline raising one's inner self to divine peacefulness and joy. The art of music continues to thrive and develop in today's modern India, and although spirituality may not be at the forefront of every performance, it still holds an important place in many of the musical genres.

Among the many styles of music found in India today, ranging from folk to popular film music, the most common known to the western world is the raga. Interestingly, most westerners find themselves puzzled when trying to describe what a raga actually is. Perhaps this is due to the fact that the term "raga" has more than one meaning. Broadly speaking, the word "raga" refers to a style of music belonging to the Indian classical music system. From a literal perspective, the term "raga" translates to the word "colour" or "mood." It also refers to the ascending/descending scale and melodic framework used for improvisation in Indian classical music. There are several major differences between music from the eastern and western worlds. Keeping an open mind throughout this chapter is therefore highly recommended for anyone who is unfamiliar with Indian ragas, as letting go of any preconceived thoughts of what music should be will allow for a better understanding and appreciation of this mysteriously beautiful genre.

A good way of introducing ragas to yourself is to take a look at the nature of a raga performance. It is important to understand that ragas are a form of classical music in India and that traditionally performances are to be rendered in a peaceful and meditative environment. Musicians usually sit on the floor with their instruments, which typically consist of a drone, percussion, and melodic instrument. The drone player usually sits in the background, while the percussionist and soloist engage with one another at the forefront of the stage.

The structure of a raga in its most concise form is an ascending/descending scale with a simple melodic contour:

Example 9.1

Ascending/descending scale of raga Bhairav:

Example 9.2

Melodic outline (or composition) of raga Bhairav (Danielou, 1987):

At the beginning of the performance, the soloist slowly and methodically reveals the scale of the chosen raga. Once this is accomplished, the soloist and percussionist then move to the melodic composition of the raga that is essentially used as a foundation for extensive improvisation. Raga performances can last for periods of an hour or even longer, depending on the preference of the soloist.

A unique dimension belonging to Indian classical music is that each raga is meant to evoke a specific mood/atmosphere (such as joy, sorrow, love, etc.) for both the performers and listeners. This is achieved through meticulous execution of numerous characteristics embedded in each and every raga. The responsibility of bringing out these features essentially lies in the hands of the soloist, who creates the desired atmosphere. Another unique facet belonging to this musical style is that every raga is performed at specific times of the day or year. Performance times fall into one of the four quarters of the day: morning, afternoon, evening, and night.

Theoretically, Indian classical music possesses thousands of ragas; however, only a few hundred are commonly known today. Traditionally, ragas are taught orally from teacher to student; one phrase at a time, until the student has mastered every note. This process can often take a long time. A student may study one raga for years before moving on to another raga, which is the main reason why most Indian musicians perform only a limited number of ragas throughout their lives (Kaufmann, 1968). It is important to understand that this chapter offers only a basic introduction to ragas. Years of serious practice with a good teacher are necessary to achieve a high level of musicianship. The information provided in this chapter is intended as a starting point for anyone who wishes to gain basic knowledge on ragas and for music therapists who want to incorporate elements of Indian classical music into their clinical work.

There are two main raga families found in India. Ragas from northern India are known as Hindustani ragas, and ragas from the south, as Carnatic ragas. The information found in this chapter focuses only on Hindustani ragas.

RAGAS AND MUSIC THERAPY

Although music therapy from the western world is a relatively new concept in India, music in its purest form has played an important role in healing traditions of the eastern world for thousands of years. In India, raga therapy (also known as raga chikitsa) works on the premise that certain ragas have the ability to control specific nerves in the body. Some ragas have been known to help alleviate ailments such as fevers, stomach problems, and headaches (Sairam, 2005). An important difference to be aware of between the use of music in raga therapy and the information provided in this book is that the client in the former setting typically does not participate in the music-making process. In other words, the client is engaged in a form of receptive music therapy where he or she absorbs the music by listening. The information provided in this chapter is intended for clients who are engaged in active music-making.

One of the main reasons for incorporating Indian ragas into a music therapy session is to evoke specific moods and atmospheres. Although it would be impossible to re-create an actual raga performance in a clinical setting, it is possible for music therapists to incorporate elements of the raga (scale, ornaments, etc.) and to use these elements as a foundation for clinical improvisations in the style of ragas. By making decisions based on a client's apparent mood and with a sensitive approach, ragas can resonate strongly with many clients. Music therapists should also be aware that ragas were originally performed for spiritual purposes, and that not every client will respond to this style of music. Clinical improvisations in the style of ragas are likely to benefit clients who are searching for a connection with their inner self or who are in need of a peaceful and meditative experience.

Most traditional musical instruments found in Indian music are crafted in such a way that they produce a high amount of resonance when played. The sitar, for example, one of the most commonly found instruments in raga performances, holds several strings that should not be plucked. Known as sympathetic strings, their sole purpose is to vibrate when the main strings are played, thus creating a high amount of resonance. Although it would be wonderful to incorporate the sitar into a music therapy session, it is rather fragile and not easy to play. Fortunately, there are some Indian instruments that are readily accessible to trained western musicians. The harmonium, for example, is a small reed organ that uses air bellows to create sounds. It is portable and works well as a bedside instrument. The bansuri is a flute made of bamboo, very similar to the flute found in western classical music. Furthermore, a western instrument that has become quite popular in Indian classical music is the violin.

There are several options available when choosing musical instruments. A key element to look for when playing in the style of ragas is resonance. The exercises in this chapter are written for piano and tuned percussion. Lightly pressing the pedal and playing the notes gently can create a high amount of resonance on the piano. With a sensitive touch and an open ear, it is even possible to hear the rest of the strings inside the piano vibrating, thus creating a similar effect to that of the sympathetic strings on a sitar.

EXERCISES

DRONES

Indian classical music contains no functional harmony. Ragas are therefore based purely on melody and rhythm. Every note and melodic line created during a raga performance is thoughtfully chosen and played with dedication. In order to recognize and fully appreciate the relationship between each note in a performance, the soloist (and listener) must continuously be aware of the tonic of the given raga. A resonating drone therefore accompanies every raga performance.

Drones are typically played on a tanpura. This traditional musical instrument resembles an unfretted lute holding three strings tuned to the tonic and one string tuned to either the fourth, fifth, or seventh degree of the given scale (scale degrees will be discussed later in this chapter). To create a drone, the tanpura player gently strikes each string one after the other, repeating the four-note motif through out the entire performance. There are three different drones in C:

Example 9.3

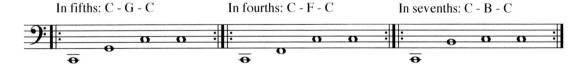

In fifths: C - G - C   In fourths: C - F - C   In sevenths: C - B - C

Delicately sustained in the background and without a set tempo, drones are rendered independently from the performance. The sole purpose of the drone is to continuously provide the tonic and second most important note without interfering with the delivery of the raga.

CD2
(17)   Solo – Tanpura (Drone)

In a clinical space where there is no **tanpura** available, it is still possible to create an effective drone on a piano or guitar. Playing slowly with a gentle touch and allowing the strings to resonate fully is essential in order to re-create that resonating quality so unique to drones found in raga performances. Drones can be incorporated in music therapy sessions to create a gentle and inviting musical space for clients; to provide a tonic (key centre) for a duet or group improvisation; or to serve as a soft container for a client's improvisation. This stylistic device can also be useful for clients who are not yet ready to engage in an improvised musical dialogue — the therapist can support gently without interference, thus allowing the client to express freely.

Solo (B)

> Sit at the piano and take a moment to absorb the silence preceding the music. Using the sustain pedal (pressed only one quarter of the way down), begin playing the following notes slowly and gently, repeating the pattern to create a constant sound.

Example 9.4

CD2
(18)   Solo – Piano (Drone)

> Try playing without a tempo. This may feel strange and perhaps even challenging at first. Concentrate on the sounds that you are creating, focusing on the resonating quality (vibration) of each note as opposed to its place in time. It may be helpful to close your eyes during this exercise.

> Once you feel as though you have established a successful drone, continue playing and take a moment to notice the atmosphere that you have created. Explore drones in a variety of keys.

Duet (B)

> *S*, play a melodic instrument on the white notes. *A*, play a drone on the lower register of the piano, creating a warm and inviting space. *S*, slowly begin exploring the tone material available. *A*, continue to support with the drone only, allowing time for *S* to explore within the musical space. Continue to support until *S* has finished exploring the tone material available.

CD2
(19) *S,* play the white keys on piano. *A,* play a drone in the lower register, using C as tonic with 5ths (C–G–C).[1]

Example 9.5

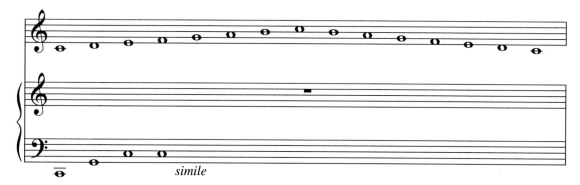

S, play the black keys on piano. *A,* play a drone on the lower register of the piano in 5ths, using F♯ as the tonic (F♯–C♯–F♯).[2]

Example 9.6

THAATS

Every raga belongs to a parent scale (or mode). In northern Hindustani ragas, there are ten parent scales found; these scales are known as thaats. Each thaat contains seven basic notes, called swaras. The names of these swaras are: Shadja, Rishabha, Gāndhāra, Madhyama, Panchama, Dhaivata, and Nishāda, better known as Sa, Re, Gha, Ma, Pa, Dha, and Ni. Indian swaras can be compared to the seven notes found in the western musical system (Do, Re, Mi, Fa, Sol, La, and Ti). Similarly to western notation, swaras can be altered from their natural position by a semitone. Lowered swaras are called komal, and raised swaras are called tivra.

---

[1] Playing a drone with C as the tonic will place the improvisation in the Ionian mode. A drone with D as the tonic will mean the Dorian mode; an E drone, the Phrygian improvisation; etc.

[2] Playing a drone with F♯ as the tonic will place the improvisation in F♯ major pentatonic and a drone with D♯ as the tonic, in D♯ minor pentatonic.

Swaras

Example 9.7

Although similar in appearance, Indian swaras and western notes are very different in intonation, the reason being that Indian classical music has no affiliation with the western equal temperament system. The Sa (or tonic) of a raga is determined by the vocal range of the singer or preference of the instrumentalist. Another important difference between swaras and western notes is that of microtones. Unlike most western musical instruments, Indian instruments are built in such a way that musicians can bend each note to obtain "very flat" or "very sharp" notes, thus creating 22 different tones within the octave, known as shrutis (Danielou, 1987).

The melodic composition (or framework) of a raga is created using the swaras of one particular thaat. Not every swara needs to be used in a composition — ragas hold a minimum of five or a maximum of eight swaras. Melodies in a raga (melodic outline/composition and improvised lines) are contained within the range of three octaves, with the lowest note resting in the area below "middle C" (usually G below middle C).

As previously mentioned, every raga is meant to be performed at a certain time of day and create a specific atmosphere. It has been found that ragas belonging to the same thaat often share similar characteristics. The following illustrates all ten Hindustani thaats, with a general description given for each. Each thaat is depicted with C as the starting note.

Solo (B–I)

Play each scale slowly and without pedal. Live in every tone as you play.

Example 9.8

Kalyan Thaat

Kalyan contains one altered note: the Ma tivra. It can be compared to the western Lydian mode. Ragas belonging to the Kalyan thaat are often performed in the early morning or early evening; the moods commonly evoked are light and soothing.

Example 9.9

Bilaval Thaat

Bilaval contains no altered notes. It can be compared to the western Ionian mode. Ragas belonging to the Bilaval thaat are often performed in the early morning or early evening; the moods commonly evoked are light and joyful.

Example 9.10

Khamaj Thaat

Khamaj contains one altered note: the Ni komal. It can be compared to the western Mixolydian mode. Ragas belonging to the Khamaj thaat are often performed in the early morning or early evening; the moods commonly evoked are light and grounded.

Example 9.11

Kafi Thaat

Kafi contains two altered notes: the Gha komal and Ni komal. It can be compared to the western Dorian mode. Ragas belonging to the Kafi thaat are often performed in the late morning or late night; the moods commonly evoked are light and calm.

Example 9.12

Asavari Thaat

Asavari contains three altered notes: the Gha komal, Dha komal, and Ni komal. It can be compared to the western Aeolian mode. Ragas belonging to the Asavari thaat are often performed in the late morning or late night; the moods commonly evoked are gentle and serious.

Example 9.13

Bhairavi Thaat

Bhairavi contains four altered notes: Re komal, Gha komal, Dha komal, and Ni komal. It can be compared to the western Phrygian mode. Ragas belonging to the Bhairavi thaat are often performed at sunrise or sunset; the moods commonly evoked are peaceful and serious.

Example 9.14

Bhairav Thaat

Bhairav contains two altered notes: Re komal and Dha komal. Ragas belonging to the Bhairav thaat are often performed in the morning; the moods commonly evoked are tender and contemplative.

Example 9.15

Purvi Thaat

Purvi contains three altered notes: Re komal, Ma tivra, and Dha komal. Ragas belonging to the Purvi thaat are often performed at sunrise or sunset and at night; the moods commonly evoked are serious and mysterious.

Example 9.16

Marva Thaat

Marva contains two altered notes: Re komal and Ma tivra. Ragas belonging to the Marva thaat are often performed at sunset and in the evening; the moods commonly evoked are uneasy and mysterious.

Example 9.17

Todi Thaat

Todi contains four altered notes: Re komal, Gha komal, Ma tivra, and Dha komal. Ragas belonging to the Todi thaat are often performed at noon and in the afternoon; the moods commonly evoked are dark and serious.

Thaats in music therapy can be used to determine what tone material would best suit a client's improvisation. Choosing a thaat that is congruent with a client's mood is likely to create sounds that feel comfortable, which in turn can encourage creative self-expression. To create an improvisation that is closest to the style of a raga, the music therapist should ensure that the tone material being used in the improvisation stays within the range of three octaves and that the time of day most common to the chosen thaat reflects the time of the session. However, it is nowadays common practice for a performer to play a morning raga in the evening and vice versa — therefore, the client's mood should take precedence over the time of day when choosing a thaat for clinical improvisation.

Choose a thaat along with an appropriate drone. For example, if choosing a Kafi thaat starting on F, the drone should be in the same tonality, therefore also starting on F.

Begin playing the drone slowly and gently. In this example, we are using a Kalyan thaat starting on C, with a C drone in 5ths.

Example 9.18

Once the drone is established, slowly play the chosen thaat ascending and descending, while maintaining the drone. If this is difficult, try it once more at a slower pace. Allow each tone to ring for a few seconds before moving to the next. Remember that the goal is to hear the quality of each note and to become familiar with the relationship between each swara and the Sa (tonic).

Example 9.19

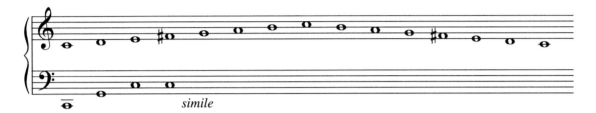

simile

CD2
(20) As you play, notice the atmosphere that you are creating. Repeat this exercise with every thaat. Experiment with various keys and drones. Also begin to include your voice.

Duet (B-I)

S and *A*, together choose a thaat with a drone. *S*, play a melodic instrument arranged with notes of the chosen thaat, and *A*, play the drone in the lower register of piano. *A*, play the drone quietly, creating a warm and inviting space. Once ready to engage *S*, begin by playing the scale, first ascending and then descending. *S* and *A*, focus on the sound of each note in relation to the tonic being provided by the drone. Notice the atmosphere that is being created with the chosen thaat. Repeat this exercise with every thaat. Experiment with various keys and drones.

S, play a thaat arranged in Bhairavi (C–D♭–E♭–F–G–A♭–B♭), and *A*, play a drone in 5ths C–G–C.

Example 9.20

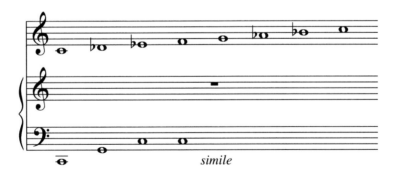

simile

S, play a thaat on the white keys of the piano, and *A*, play a drone in 4ths on the lower register with D as the tonic. This tone material creates an improvisation in the Kafi thaat.

Example 9.21

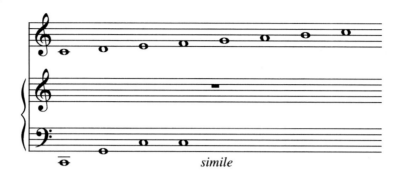

simile

ORNAMENTATION

Ornaments and grace notes play an important role in Indian classical music — some ragas even require specific types of ornaments in order to be rendered correctly. In theory, there are numerous ornaments and grace notes found in Indian classical music, some more common than others. The following describes some of the most common ones found in Hindustani ragas that can be integrated into clinical improvisations. It is important to understand that these embellishments should be sung or played on traditional Indian instruments. Reproducing these sounds accurately on a western instrument like the piano may therefore be challenging. It may be helpful to spend time listening to recordings of raga performances in order to gain a good understanding and appreciation of this stylistic device.

Mind

Similar to a western glissando, the mind is a glide from one note to another. It may be executed either fast or slow.

Example 9.22

Andolan

Similar to a slow vibrato, this is a slow oscillation of a single note moving from the actual note to a pitch slightly higher.

Example 9.23

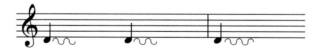

Kan

Similar to the western musical term "appoggiatura," this is a quick and delicate inflection before a tone.

Example 9.24

Murki

Similar to the western mordent, this involves two or more tones delicately played before the true pitch (Danielou, 1987).

Example 9.25

Ornaments and grace notes can be used as a technique to enhance the authenticity of the music in a clinical improvisation. The therapist can achieve this by meeting and matching what the client is playing and then adding embellishments where appropriate. Such attention to detail will intensify the character of the improvisation, which in turn may heighten the musical/therapeutic experience.

Solo (B–I)

> Chose a thaat and create a simple melody. (You may need to write down your melody for the purpose of this exercise.) Play the melody slowly a few times as written, while focusing on the sound of each note. In this example, we are using the Kalyan thaat, starting on C:

Example 9.26

Kalyan Thaat

Example 9.27

Melody created with Kalyan Thaat

> Once you feel comfortable with your melody, gently begin playing the drone with your left hand on the lower register of the piano. In this example, we are using a C drone in 5ths. When the drone is established, slowly play the melody with your right hand while continuing to maintain the drone. Repeat the melody several times. Remember to play slowly and gently.

Example 9.28

Begin adding a few ornaments to the melody. This may be challenging at first —
remember to keep it very simple. If this becomes too difficult, stop playing your left hand
and try ornamenting the melody without the drone. Once you have achieved this, resume
the drone. Remember that the drone should not be played "in time" — its purpose is to
provide the tonic of the musical exploration.

Example 9.29

CD2
(21)
Continue playing melody with ornaments until your playing is totally natural. Notice how
the quality of the melody and atmosphere changes when you approach each note with
care. Once you have exhausted the musical potential, cease the melody, sustain the drone
for a few seconds, and then gently end the improvisation.

Duet (B-I)

S and *A,* choose a thaat with a drone. *S,* play a melodic instrument arranged with the
chosen tone material. *A,* play a drone with the left hand on the lower register of the piano
and melodic lines with the right hand in the middle/high register of piano. In this
example, we will continue with the same tone material as in the solo exercise.

Example 9.30

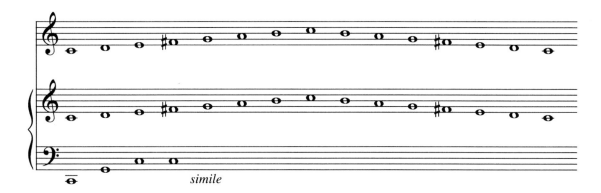

simile

A, play the drone quietly, creating a warm and inviting space. Once you feel ready to play, *S,* slowly begin exploring tone material available.

Once conversant, *S,* improvise different lines on xylophone. *A,* match *S*'s playing while continuing to add ornaments. *S* and *A,* continue until *S* has exhausted the musical potential. *A,* sustain the drone for a few seconds before ending the improvisation.

Example 9.31

simile

As most clients will continue to improvise new melodies throughout an improvisation, the therapist can support the client by meeting/matching what the client is playing and adding embellishments where appropriate.

Example 9.32

simile

FORM

Whether you are hearing Indian classical music for the first time or are a veteran of the genre, listening to an entire raga performance requires a relatively high level of commitment. In addition to being long, the rendition of a raga involves many details for the listener to absorb. Understanding the form of a raga and its many components is therefore likely to have an impact on the listener's level of enjoyment. In essence, the structure of a raga consists of many small parts, all of which can be categorized into a few larger movements. For the purpose of this chapter, we will focus on the larger movements that are most pertinent to clinical improvisation, namely the alap and the gat.

Alap

Every raga begins with an alap, which is an extended movement performed without rhythmic accompaniment. In the alap, the singer or solo instrumentalist is free to improvise (within the boundaries of the raga) with only the resonating drone as an accompaniment. This metrically free space allows the performer to slowly and methodically reveal the raga and its unique characteristics (scale, tones, melodic composition, ornaments, and mood). The duration of the alap is left to the discretion of the soloist and may last up to an hour or longer.

Each note in a raga is delineated as being either important and strong or unimportant and weak. Usually revealed in the alap, strong notes are played more frequently and dwelled on for longer durations, while weak notes are treated lightly and appear less frequently.

The strongest note is known as the vadi, the second strongest is known as the samvadi, and the other less important notes are known as anuvadi. The two strongest notes, the vadi and samvadi, are usually found a 5th or 4th apart. They stand out not only in the melodic framework of the raga but also in the improvised melodic phrases created throughout the performance (Kaufmann, 1968).

Creating an improvisation in the style of an alap provides a musical space in which the client can familiarize him/herself with the given musical instrument and tone material, allowing him/her to naturally choose a vadi and samvadi.

This open musical space can also provide an opportunity for the music therapist to observe to which notes the client is most drawn. The music therapist can then use this information to further engage the client in an improvised musical dialogue, leading the clinical improvisation into the gat.

Gat

Often following the alap, the gat is a movement where the melodic composition of the raga is used as a theme for melodic and rhythmic improvisation. At this point in the performance, the soloist is accompanied by a percussion player, usually a tabla player, who reveals and maintains the rhythmic cycle of the given raga.

During this part of the performance, the soloist and accompanying tabla player often engage in exciting musical dialogues, both demonstrating highly skilled playing on their respected instruments (Kaufmann, 1968).

The gat may be performed in a variety of tempi, depending on the nature or the raga and preference of the soloist. The vilambit gat is played at a slow tempo, the madhya gat is at a medium tempo, and the drut gat sits at a fast tempo. A raga performance may end with the gat or move on to other movements.

Creating an improvisation in the style of a gat provides a space for the client and music therapist to engage in an improvised melodic dialogue, using melodies/themes created by the client during the alap.

It is important for the music therapist to closely observe the client's playing and to also use the tones that he/she is most drawn to in this part of the clinical improvisation.

Solo (I–A)

Choose a thaat and drone for your exploration. In this example, we are using kalyan with C drone in 5ths.

Gently play the drone with your left hand. Once the drone has been established, slowly play your chosen tone material with your right hand, ascending and descending.

Example 9.33

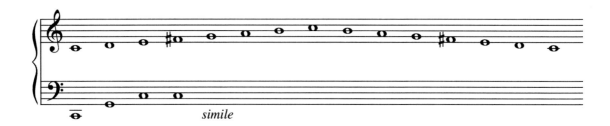

Continue exploring this tone material thoroughly by playing narrow and wide intervals and ascending/descending patterns, noticing to which notes you are most drawn. Gradually build a melody based on these notes.

Repeat this melody several times while always maintaining the drone. In this example, we will continue with the melody stated in Example 9.31:

Example 9.34

Once conversant with your melody, cease playing and take a moment to concentrate on the alap you are about to create. Notice which two notes you are drawn to: your vadi and samvadi.

Once this is established, quietly begin playing the drone. Using the ornaments and grace notes you have learned, slowly begin playing your melody, embellishing each note, with special attention to the vadi and samvadi.

Remember to take your time, only playing through your melody slowly and methodically. In the following example, B is the vadi and Fs, the samvadi.

Example 9.35

When you have played through your melody once, sustain just the drone for a few seconds before ending the music.

Duet: Alap (I)

Together, choose a thaat and a drone for this musical exploration. *S,* play a tuned percussion instrument prepared with the chosen tone material. *A,* play a drone and melodic lines on the piano. In Example 9.37, we are using the Kafi thaat in C.

Example 9.36

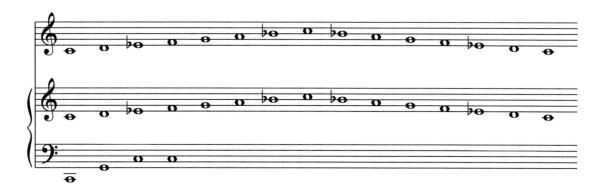

Duet (A)

A, gently play a drone, creating a space in which *S* can improvise. *S,* begin exploring tone material, using wide and narrow intervals and ascending/descending patterns. After a minute, begin to focus on a preferred tone or combination of tones. *A,* pay attention to the note *S* is most drawn to. *S,* improvise melodies based on these notes. Play slowly in order to give *A* the chance to match each pitch. *A,* support with the right hand by mirroring and matching the melodies while always maintaining the drone.

Example 9.37

Using ornaments and grace notes, *A,* slowly and methodically embellish each note of the melody created by *S*. *S* and *A,* play the melody only once, taking as much time as needed to emphasize the vadi and samvadi and to create the desired atmosphere for the improvisation. In example 9.39, the vadi is D and the samvadi is A.

Example 9.38

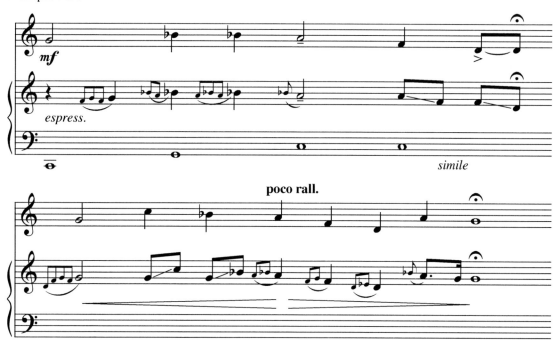

S, cease playing once the melody has been played once through. **A,** sustain the drone for a few more seconds before ending the music. Now move on to an improvisation in the style of a gat.

Duet: Gat (I–A)

CD2
(22)
A, sustain the drone until **S** is ready to further engage in an improvised musical dialogue, in the style of a gat. **S,** begin improvising melodic lines based on the melody from the alap. **A,** Listen to the pulse of **S**'s playing and gradually play the left hand drone note in that pulse.[3] In this example, we are dividing the melodic lines into four beat sections, similar to a 4/4 time signature.

Example 9.39

---

[3]It is important to note that drones are not normally played to a rhythmic pulse. For this type of improvisation, however, it is necessary for **A** to play the drone with rhythmic character.

A, once a rhythmic pulse has been established, meet and match *S*'s playing, adding ornaments and grace notes where suitable. In order to maintain a sense of consistency, *A,* you may also incorporate the original melody into the improvised dialogue. *S* and *A,* engage in a call and response dialogue, gradually increasing the speed if appropriate. The following is a short example of an improvisation in the style of a gat:

Example 9.40

When *S* comes to the end, *A,* continue for a few more seconds before ending the improvisation.

TALA

The rendition of a raga requires two fundamental and equally important musical elements, melody and rhythm. In raga performances, the percussionist sits alongside the solo instrumentalist. Together, they reveal the intricacies of a given raga, often challenging one another to perform at the peek of their abilities. It is a beautiful and complex marriage. The following describes the basics of rhythm in raga performances.

Once the soloist is done exploring the alap, they move on to the next part of the performance, where the accompanying percussionist (usually a tabla player) begins playing a precisely structured rhythmic pattern, known as the tala. There are many different talas found in Indian classical music, each containing a fixed number of beats divided in two or more phrases. Every raga performance is set to only one tala — the tabla player will continue to repeat the chosen cycle of beats until the soloist has reached the end of the performance. Here are common talas found in Hindustani ragas:

Name of Talas	Number of Beats	Division of Phrases
Dhadra	6	3+3
Rupak	7	3+2+2
Kaharva	8	4+4
Jhaptal	10	2+3+2+3
Ektal and Chautal	12	2+2+2+2+2+2
Dhamar	14	5+2+3+4
Tintal	16	4+4+4+4

The phrases in each cycle are clearly defined by the different types of strokes played on the tabla, know as bols. The names of the bols found in a tala are essentially syllables that, when spoken, resemble the sounds that they make on the tabla. The bols, for example, of a 16-beat tintal played on tablas are as follows:

Count: 1   2   3   4 – 5   6   7   8 – 9   10   11   12 – 13   14   15   16

Bol: Dha dhin dhin dha Dha dhin dhin dha Dha tin   tin   ta   Ta   dhin dhin dha

The beginning and middle of each cycle in a tala is defined by the sam and the khali. The sam is the first beat of the cycle — it is known as a strong beat and is usually played with a strong stroke on the tabla. The khali is typically found in the middle of the cycle. It is a subtle beat, usually played as a silent or weak stroke on the tabla. In the tintal cycle, for instance, the first beat is accentuated and the 9th beat is silent. The number of beats in the tala as well as the tempo are always congruent with the length and nature of the raga being performed. The tala may accelerate as the raga develops, depending on the situation and preference of the soloist.

Improvisations in the style of talas are possible when a client is able to improvise strong melodies on his own, allowing the music therapist to heighten the element of rhythm. This can be achieved on melodic instruments, such as the piano and vibraphone, or with a combination of percussion and melodic instruments, such as bongos and vibraphone. Another option is to have a co-therapist also taking part in the improvisation, playing precise rhythmic patterns on a percussion instrument while the therapist and client play on melodic instruments. To create an improvisation that resembles that of a tala, the music therapist needs to structure the music so that it sits in one consistent meter such as 7/4, dividing each "measure" into shorter phrases like 3+2+2 — this would resemble Rupak tala in 7.

Solo (B–I)

Sit on the floor with a pair of percussion instruments; if there are no tablas available, bongos are a good substitute. With your hands, play the bongos slowly, one strike at a time. Try to find different sounds such as low-/high-pitched, short and dry/long and hollow, etc. Practise these sounds until you are familiar with their different strokes.

Choose a tala from the list above — in this example, 10-beat Jhaptal. At a slow tempo (approx. 80 bpm), try playing the short phrases (2+3+2+3), defining each phrase with the different sounds that you have discovered. In order to keep track of where you are in the cycle, count out loud as you are playing. It may be helpful to do this with a metronome.

Example 9.41

Practise this exercise with the other talas.

Solo (I–A)

At the piano, choose one of the talas above with two different sounding chords. Playing chords over a fixed drone will create the effect of modal music, which is akin to Indian classical music in that neither style contains functional harmony. In this example, we are using a 7-beat Rupak tala (3+2+2).

With your right hand, play the chosen chords slowly, one after the other.

Example 9.42

Once comfortable playing these chords, divide each measure into a 3+2+2. Count out loud and use a metronome to help you stay on track.

Example 9.43

Now add the resonating drone with your left hand. This may be challenging at first because your right hand is playing in time while your left hand is playing freely. To make things easier in the beginning, play the same rhythm in both hands. Here we are using a D drone in 5ths, creating an accompaniment in Kafi thaat. Remember to play the drone quietly.

Example 9.44

To take the exercise further, let go of the chordal accompaniment, continue playing the drone with your left hand, and try improvising melodic lines with your right hand.

Example 9.45

Explore the other talas, using different types of chords and drones.

Duet (I–A)

S and *A,* choose a tala and a thaat with a drone. In this example, we will use a 7-beat *Rupak* (3+2+2) with a Bhairavi thaat. *S,* play a melodic instrument arranged in Bhairavi; on piano, *A,* play a C drone in 5ths with the left hand and chords with the right hand, using same tone material as *S*.

Example 9.46

7-beat Rupak: 1–2–3 1–2–1–2   1–2–3   1–2 1–2

Rupak is unique among the talas in that, rather than having a subtle middle beat, it has a subtle first beat. For this exercise, *A,* alternate between playing and omitting the first beat (or chord) on the piano.

CD2
(23) **A,** (piano – bass) gently begin playing the drone, creating a warm and welcoming environment. **S,** (piano – treble) explore the tone material while **A** maintains the drone. When you can feel a pulse coming from **S**'s improvisation, **A,** play the drone notes with a pulse, using a rhythmic pattern that complements **S**'s music. **A,** you may also gradually add a chordal accompaniment with right hand.

Example 9.47

S and **A,** continue to improvise together until **S** is finished. **A,** continue to play the drone freely for a few seconds before closing the improvisation.

CONCLUSION

Incorporating world music into music therapy can be an exciting experience for client and therapist. Opening your ears to new sounds and experimenting with different instruments can create opportunities for the unexpected, which is often when growth can take place. It is important for music therapists to have a good understanding of a musical style before incorporating it into a session. Being aware of the context in which a musical genre was created — its emotional content — is essential in order to make informed decisions in a clinical setting, as connecting a client's mood with the archetypal emotional content of a musical style is likely to have a positive impact on the client's experience. Music therapists should always make serious efforts to provide music that is most authentic when bringing world musical genres into a session. Using traditional instruments when possible, approaching western instruments in a "nonwestern" way, and trusting the musical genre itself are important facets to remember during the process.

Music therapists should always be sensitive towards a client's cultural background when incorporating music from a different culture. It should not be assumed that a client would relate to music from the culture in which they originated. It is also not guaranteed that clinical improvisations in the style of ragas will please every client who is Indian. Some individuals who are familiar with ragas may find it difficult to express themselves if the music being offered is not rendered as a raga performance should be, or they may simply not like that style of music and would rather hear something different. Taking an opposite stance, clients who are completely unfamiliar with a musical genre may find it easier to express with such music, as novel sounds may relieve them of expectations or inhibitions. It is the music therapist's responsibility to know and assess each client before deciding what kind of music is best is suited for each clinical scenario.

Indian ragas hold great potential for music therapy. Over the course of many generations, this style has been perfected to the highest standards of performance and creativity. Those who keep ragas alive today continue to believe that this music holds the ability to connect human beings with their inner selves and the greater universe. We are fortunate to have access to this rich history, inspiring beliefs, and beautiful music in the western world. Having the opportunity to share this music with clients is something not to take lightly. Indian classical music is challenging — it forces western musicians to hear sounds in different ways. Even though it may take time to reach a level of performance where you are ready to use this musical style in a session, it is worth the effort of time, focus, and practice. Having the ability to capture the beauty of this music and offer it to clients is what makes the profession of a music therapist unique. The experiences we create can last a lifetime, both for the client and therapist. Close your eyes, breathe, and listen — let the sound vibrations guide you and allow the music to find its natural path.

CHAPTER 10

Korea: Folk Music

The music of Asia is rich and diverse, which reflects its unique history and traditions. Korean music is perhaps the least well known, yet it has a rich cultural heritage accumulated through its 5,000-year history. Korea's civilization is a manifestation of a value system that is unique in the world. The diverse emotions of joy, anger, sorrow, and pleasure are all genuinely expressed and sublimated through its musical style. The aesthetics of traditional Korean music show significant differences from those of other Asian countries. Jun (2006) classifies musical artistry into the following elements, which we believe create the distinct qualities of traditional Korean music:

Magnificence
Grandeur
Nobility
Simplicity
Extension
Natural
Deep sorrow
Excitement
Pleasure
Humor

There are two separate components of Korean music. The first is traditional music originating from cultural history. It is classified by two subcategories: Jung-ak (court music) and Min-yo (folk music). In this chapter, Min-yo, including its musical elements and instrumental realizations, mainly will be examined. The second area is traditional music that has been influenced by the West. These two aspects have been used singly and in combination in the development of contemporary music in Korea.

Korean traditional music was originally communicated orally, though there are some forms of complex transcription found in Jung-ak court music. The uniqueness of the traditional music is that there are no significant differences between composer and performer. As in many other cultures, music was born through the experiences and representations of its evolving culture and embedded in everyday life. Through this evolution, improvisation became integral to how music was considered and used. Jun (2002) describes how composers of Korean traditional music were not explicit in the way we understand them today. They were part of a group of musicians who created collectives that would describe and represent the needs of the community in which they lived. The composer was therefore a part of the fabric of life and not in any way elitist. During the 1940s, Korea began to use formalized western notation. With that, traditional music began to be transcribed, thus ensuring its survival. It allowed the music to be preserved, analyzed, and arranged in new and different forms.

Music influenced by the West is the most popular in daily Korean life today, although there are still many musicians pursuing traditional music. The impact of western culture on Korean life is in part due to the effects of globalization. This does not mean, however, that Korean music has lost its traditional musical identity; rather, it highlights the current trends of combining traditional Korean and western-influenced music. Such innovative movements have added to Korea's already rich musical landscape.

KOREAN FOLK MUSIC AND MUSIC THERAPY

Korean traditional music is a unique style that can be a valuable resource for music therapy. One of the immediate problems when trying to capture the essence of Korean music is the use of traditional instruments. Most contemporary music therapy practice in Korea is based on the use of western percussion instruments. This will of course produce different timbres that in turn will affect the therapeutic outcome. There are, however, a number of traditional percussion instruments used by music therapists.

Today, traditional instruments are mainly used for performances of folk music. One specific style is called Poong-mool, which depicts nature and landscape. Another, Nori, depicts light and amusing activities of life. Out of these developments came the Sa-mool Nori style, the musical components of which represent elements of nature such as thunder, lightning, rain, and wind. These are the instruments most commonly used in music therapy sessions because of their textures and representative sounds. The following instruments are used for Sa-mool Nori:

Jing	Small portable gong
Ggang-ga-ri	High-pitched cymbal
Jang-goo	Portable drum in the horizontal position that can be played on two surfaces with either one or two sticks
Book	Drum in the western style played in the vertical position

These instruments were used originally for amusement, dancing, and audience engagement. They are easy and accessible to play and as such could have an impact in broadening the musical palette for clinical practice. This chapter will assume that western instruments are to be used, although we suggest that if possible you acquire traditional instruments also.

Traditional Korean music is frequently used for work with the elderly, although it can be equally well executed for other populations. We urge you to try the following exercises for all client groups. Many traditional music pieces have been transcribed to fit western notation. Hence, these pieces can be played using western instruments (e.g., piano and guitar). Such transcribed pieces can be used for all client populations and are an excellent resource for improvising in the Korean traditional style. There are certain pieces, as in all cultures, that are known by all. These would be the equivalent of western songs such as "Amazing Grace." Some of these well-known songs will be explored in this chapter within a western musical notation.

EXERCISES

To begin, we will explore the musical elements that constitute Korean music. Koreans often express and communicate their feelings in an indirect manner, and their words often contain multiple meanings. This is why the Korean language and alphabet, known as Hangul, contains many adjectives and metaphoric words. Similarly, in music, a tone does not have an absolute value but can be stretched in subtle ways that cannot always be captured through western notation. Thus note values, rhythms, and overall textures can be changed, adapted, and realized in many different ways. Variation form and ornamentation are both important aspects that define Korean traditional music. Along with these is the unpredictability of improvisation that is central to the musical beauty of its style. These characteristics hold clinical value due to their distinct aesthetics and unique flavor.

MELODY

Korean melodies are multilayered and complex. They are usually interpreted according to the performer's whim and can best be compared to the beauty of a curved line. The emotional content is that of being composed and reserved. Melodies are simple and have a relaxed flow that is often not dependent on strict meter. They can be compared to the splashes of colours and lines in an oriental painting.

Solo (B)

> Play and experience the melodic contours of this traditional melody on an instrument of your choice.

Nil-li-ri-ya

Example 10.1

> Using the pentatonic scale in E♭ (E♭, F, G, B♭, C), continue and expand the melody into a new section that is similar in style but that creates contrast. Keep your melody simple and focused.

> Now use a simple harmonization on the piano or guitar. Explore the melody and indulge in its lyricism. Always play with a sense of rubato.

Duet (B)

> *S,* play a small cymbal, creating quiet washes of sound. *A,* use the melody as in the ABA form described above to create an experience for *S*. If using voice or an orchestral instrument, sing/play with a clarity and simplicity that will enhance *S*'s playing.

> Now repeat the experience using the piano or guitar, adding a simple harmonization as realized in the above example.

RHYTHM

Jangdan

One of the special characteristics of Korean music is that of the diverse performance techniques of combining beat and melody into rhythmic cycles known as Jangdan. Lee (2004) describes it as a repeated rhythmic phrase played at regular intervals. Its rhythm is embedded in the timing of the beat and tempo and is played with a regular fixed pulse. Whereas western rhythms have a relatively simple meter, Jangdan contains more complex combinations, based on the tempo, form, and character of a piece. It also contains repeated rhythmic patterns that cycle within a specific unit length. This length can be prolonged or shortened according to the characteristics of the music. For example, a melody composed of the same scale can take on a completely different feeling depending on which type of Jangdan is used. In addition to the established forms of Jangdan, the performer's interpretation can produce creative and unique structures. Jangdan are sometimes associated with specific areas of Korea known for their local attributes. There are approximately nine folk song forms of Jangdan:

(1) Jin-yang jo
(2) Joong mori
(3) Joong-joong mori
(4) Ja-jin mori
(5) Whi mori
(6) Ut mori
(7) Ut-joong mori
(8) Saemachi
(9) Goodkuri

Solo/Duet (B–I)

Saemachi and Goodkuri are the most frequently used when traditional folk songs are performed.

> Play each example either as a solo on bongos two hands or as a duet on two separate drums. Repeat until the pattern becomes familiar and then use as a basis for a rhythmic dialogue.

Example 10.2

Saemachi

Example 10.3

Goodkuri

Use the above examples for practising rhythmic patterns while either clapping or drumming.

SCALES

Korean traditional scales can be classified into three major categories: heptachord (seven-tone scales), pentatonic (five-tone scales), and the three-tone scale. Hong (1987) explores and describes the three-tone scale known as the Saeya scale. There are many pieces based on the pentatonic and three-tone scale in traditional Korean music. The pentatonic scale, considered one of the most representative of the style, consists of five scale degrees: 1, 2, 3, 5, 6 (C, D, E, G, A in the key of C). Moreover, each tone can function as a tonic to form independent pentatonic scales.

Solo (B–I)

Play a C major pentatonic scale (C, D, E, G, A, C) up and down the keyboard. Play it in the span of two octaves.

Transpose and play the pentatonic scale in all 12 keys, moving up the keyboard chromatically.

Practise the scale in octaves, first right hand only, then octaves with both hands.

Incorporate the Saemachi and Goodkuri rhythms in the scale exercise using the 9/8 and 12/8 rhythms (Examples 10.2 and 10.3). Improvise free melodic phrases in the pentatonic based on the Saemachi and Goodkuri rhythms.

FOLK SONGS

Arirang

Arirang is one of the most popular traditional folk songs and reflects Korea's culture and the collective emotions of life itself. The song is based on the pentatonic scale on C. The lyrics describe feelings of sadness and regret. Both music and lyrics are well known by Koreans. The lyrics contained in the opening verse portray the meaning of the song:

Arirang, arirang, arariyo,
The man whom I love leaves on Arirang road,
If you leave me and break my heart,
I wish that your leg, not your heart, were of stone.

Solo (B–I)

Play and/or sing the melody, becoming familiar with the structure and feel of the song.

Example 10.4

Play and/or sing and accompany yourself on either piano or guitar with the simple harmonic realization suggested.

Duet (B–I)

(Piano four hands: *S,* treble; *A,* bass) *S,* improvise a free-flowing melodic line with one hand only. *A,* reflect and accompany by introducing the Arirang melody with either the above harmonic realization or one of your own. Keep the direction of the music simple and allow the melody to move in and out of freer improvising.

Solo (I)

The next realization introduces chromatic harmonies, thus adding further richness to the melody. Create harmonic explorations with added chromatic chords, notating them in your practice resource binder.

Example 10.5

Duet (I)

CD2
(24) **S,** improvise on a tuned percussion instrument prepared on a C pentatonic scale.
A, use the above realization as a basis for an improvisation.

Solo (I–A)

The final version of the song (Example 10.6) is full and rich. The style of the accompaniment provides a rich density with a synthesis between pentatonic and chromatic harmonies. Create your own melodies and play in other time signatures. Use your voice to create submelodies to the song, either with words or vocalize.

Example 10.6

Duet (I–A)

CD2
(25)   **S,** play a large cymbal or gong with long, broad sweeps. **A,** use the above interpretation to meet **S**'s playing. If possible, play the melody in octaves in order to pierce through the sound of the gong if **S** plays with strength.

Saeya, Saeya, Pa-rang Saeya — Hey bird, hey bird, hey blue bird!

This song is traditionally passed down through generations. The lyrics contain sarcasm and show the resentment against the Japanese occupation of 1910–1945. The song is simply structured around three notes: D, E, and A.

Example 10.7

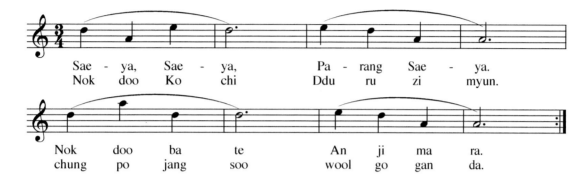

| Sae - ya, | Sae - ya, | Pa - rang | Sae - ya. |
| Nok doo | Ko chi | Ddu ru | zi myun. |

| Nok doo | ba te | An ji | ma ra. |
| chung po | jang soo | wool go | gan da. |

The translation of the lyrics is as follows:

> Hey bird, hey bird, hey blue bird,
> Don't stay on the mung bean field,
> If the flower of the mung bean is shed,
> A merchant [the Korean people] will cry and leave.

Solo (B–I)

Play the following melody and ostinato accompaniment.

Example 10.8

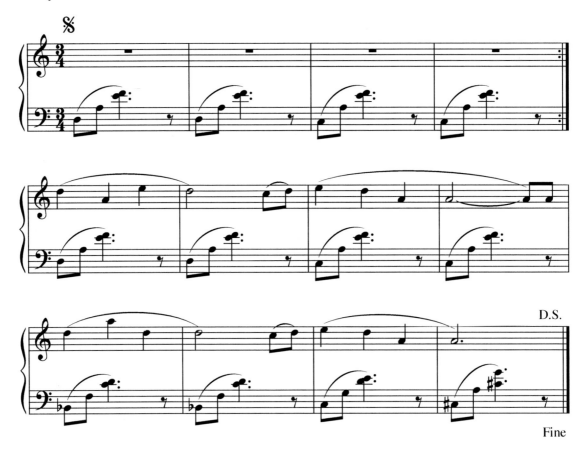

Chose other sets of three tones and create further simple melodies on the same ostinato. Create other ostinatos based on the same progression, creating phrases that are full of space and resonance. Keep the overall slow nature of the music constant

Duet (E)

CD2 (26)   **S**, use three chimes (D, E, and A) and create structured and improvised forms around this piece. **A**, create possible words that might be appropriate, moving between the structure of the song (A section) and freer, less-directed (B) sections.

Han Oback-Nyoun — Around 500 years

This folk song comes from the Kang-won province and expresses feelings of sorrow. The thoughts expressed through the lyrics are sublimated delightfully throughout the song:

> Of course, that is it! Of course, that is it!
> What are you concerned about, living around 500 years,
> The world filled with lots of regrets and unkind you, dear,
> Because I am leaving here with my heart left, I drop my tears.

As the melody is pitched low, it is easy to sing. The song is based on the G pentatonic scale: G, A, B, D, and E.

Solo (B–I)

> Play the melody only, slowly and repeatedly (Example 10.9). Note the ornamentation and flow of the melody, especially in bar four when the meter becomes two instead of three, thus adding a subtle syncopation. This kind of melody is very typical of Korean song. Play with a sense of rubato and melodic freedom, adding your own ornaments.

Example 10.9

> Now play the full version with the organum bass. Note how grounded and dignified the song now becomes. Explore this piece further with different melodies juxtaposed with the organum bass.

Duet (B–I)

CD2
(27)   **S,** improvise a regular and steady beat on a drum or bongo. **A,** play a strong pulse created by the organum, potentially creating a drum song. Try another arrangement with drum and cymbal.

Solo (I)

Play the same song, now with a more lyrical accompaniment. Improvise away from this piece into more open lyrical phrases.

Example 10.10

Duet (I)

CD2
(28) *S,* play a tuned percussion instrument prepared with a G pentatonic scale. Create simple lyrical phrases. *A,* use the above version to connect with *S*'s playing, encouraging and using your voice to create a dialogue.

Onghaeya

Farmers originally sang this labor folk song while threshing barley. The word "onghaeya" is used for the repeated refrain and became the title of the song. When farmers work using a flail (a tool for threshing rice or barley), they line up in pairs, threshing barley alternately while standing. *Onghaeya* is written in the form of call and response. The lyrics of the song translate how the farmer's hard craft can also be pleasurable. The song is based on the pentatonic: G, A, B, D, and E.

The translation of the lyrics is as follows:

Onghaeya, Onghaeya, you are doing good, onghaeya, only two of you,
Aehe, aehe, onghaeya, Ujulssigo, Onghaey, onghaeya, jujulssigo onghaeya,
A quail caused a problem at barley field, onghaeya, playing good, onghaeya.

Solo/Duet (B–I)

Play the call and response of the song on piano, two voices, or two tuned percussion instruments (one or two players).

Example 10.11

Call and response and question and answer are important techniques in establishing the therapeutic relationship and creating dialogue. Use this song and then explore further phrases in the same and different keys. Begin to build a catalogue of call and response phrases that could be used as a basis for further improvisations.

Duet (B–I)

S and *A,* play two similar tuned percussion instruments, both prepared with the G pentatonic scale (G, A, B, D, E). Use this example as a question and answer dialogue, further exploring this dynamic into further freer improvisations.

Solo

Play this arrangement emphasizing the strong nature of the call and response between hands.

Example 10.12

Duet (B–I)

> *S,* play bongos with the phrases of the piece between right and left hand the same as the piano. *A,* play the exact rhythm as *S* creates a piece that is in synchronicity with each part. After developing this, create a question and answer for each phrase between *S* and *A,* forming an A section. Develop into a more lively and developed improvisation (B section), returning to A to complete.

CONCLUSION

The foundations of Korean traditional music and western music are different. Western music is based on scales and harmony, whereas Korean music is based mainly on the Jangdan, although scales are considered also. Korean traditional music can be separated into two social categories: Jung-ak (court music) and Min-yo (folk music). This chapter solely explored folk music.

Jangdan enables players to create variations in a piece of music, whereas Jung-ak is presented with the same rhythmic pattern and little improvisation. The rhythms contained in Jung-ak are relatively more fixed; however, the rhythms of folk music are at times varied and can create different and diverse atmospheres in one piece. Min-yo is a delightful piece when Jangdan is applied appropriately. Hence, music becomes more appreciated if a variation of Jangdan is at the heart of it.

In this chapter, we have explored five folk songs. There are limitations in presenting this music in western notation as the songs were originally passed down aurally. Remember that to truly create the essence of Korean folk music, it is important to listen to as many recordings and live performances as possible. You should aim to understand the freedom of the music within the parameters of the pentatonic scales and rhythmic boundaries of the Jangdan. Playing this music on western piano, guitar, and percussion instruments will yield only a partial essence of the music and its potential for clinical/musical directness.

We hope that by bringing into clinical work Korean folk music, this style may add to the palette available to the music therapist. The folk music presented here is alive, fresh, accessible, and brimming with life. In exploring this music, always keep a sense of its simplicity and allow the music to speak with authenticity and clarity of direction.

CHAPTER 11

Argentina: Nuevo Tango

The tango is a style of music associated with sensuality and passion and was originally intended for dancing. The traditional tango is sometimes confused with the popular ballroom tango dance, a much more extravert and flamboyant version developed in later years. This chapter will focus on the nuevo tango, also a later development based on the traditional tango yet made for listening rather than dancing.

Although it is difficult to define the exact roots of the traditional tango, it appears that its identity materialized in the lower-class districts of Buenos Aires, Argentina. Nidel (2005) describes the country's trials in the 20th century during Astor Piazzolla's time:

> South America's most sophisticated country is an ongoing enigma. Argentina's political legacy in the 20th century was one of misguided ideals, lost opportunity, squandered wealth, and corrupt governments. The obsessive yearning for recognition in the first world and tying its currency to the dollar in the 1990s led to monetary crises that bankrupted Argentina, which has created a massive depression. (p. 316)

Buenos Aires was a city of immigrants from a variety of ethnic backgrounds. Many suffered from various socioeconomic difficulties, and some even "looked desperately for a distraction to ease their sense of rootlessness and disfranchisement as 'strangers in a strange land'" (Oclander, par. 1). Oclander gives an interpretation of the original meaning of the tango:

> Ironically, as these lonely immigrants and societal outcasts sought to escape from their feelings, they instead developed a music and dance that epitomized them. The wail of the tango, it is said, speaks of more than frustrated love. It speaks of fatality, of destinies engulfed in pain. It is the dance of sorrow. (par.1)

Although many historians argue about the origins of the music's aesthetic features, it is generally accepted that they derived from the music of the African slaves, "the popular music of the pampas (flatlands) known as the milonga, which combined Indian rhythms with the music of early Spanish colonists; and other influences, including Latin" (Oclander, par. 2). Regardless of its origins, Nidel (2005) contends that West African rhythms, dances, and songs were key elements that contributed to the genre's development (p. 317). Since Argentina was a major multicultural centre at the turn of the 20th century, the tango was infused with a multitude of world musics, including the sounds of European popular and classical music. Therefore, the tango resulted in a beautiful marriage of world rhythms and western harmony.

The nuevo tango represents the new form of tango attributed to Astor Piazzolla, who solely revolutionized the music of Argentina beginning in the 1940s by adding electronic instruments, such as the electric guitar, and incorporating contemporary classical and jazz compositional elements into the music. His influence upon the music of Argentina was so revolutionary that he is now regarded by many as a national icon.[1]

---

[1] However, some conservative Argentineans tend to cling to their traditional tango roots and refuse to acknowledge Piazzolla's work as an authentic form of tango. This was confirmed by a personal communication with a traditional tango dancer Mario Aranedas.

Since the development and evolution of the nuevo tango is inseparable from Piazzolla's personality and influences, it would be useful to examine some of the composer's relevant biographical details. Although he moved to Argentina at the age of 16, a significant part of his personality was shaped by growing up in the Lower East Side of New York City as an Italian-American during the 1920s. According to Azzi and Collier (2000), "He was expelled from one or two of his early schools for fighting and was free with his fists in the streets, where he spent much of his time" (pp. 7–8). Azzi and Collier (2000) also provide insight into the composer's personality through the testimonies of friends and relatives. Vera Brandes, a record producer, thought that:

> Astor was the same as his music. Totally passionate, vigorous, full of love, tenderness, humor, drama, suffering, joy, intensity, emotion, physical and spiritual at the same time, as unpredictable as life itself. [...] Pianist Monica Cosachov, by contrast, senses that he had "a terribly tortured world inside," and certainly he could be both exploitive and aggressive, sometimes indifferent to common conventions of behavior, occasionally cruel. His daughter considers him a man "like all geniuses, with some big weakness on the human level." (pp. 135–136)

Piazzolla himself provides us with some insight into the nature of his music by speaking about the tango's defining instrument, the bandoneon, and comparing it with an accordion. "The accordion has an acid sound, a sharp sound," he said in New York in 1988. "It's a very happy instrument. The bandoneon has a velvet sound, a religious sound. It was made to play sad music" (Azzi & Collier, 2000, p. 153).

His musical style is based on the traditional tango dance, famous for its expression of extreme passion, melancholy, and nostalgia. What makes his style unique is that it combines influences of not only the western classical tradition but also jazz. Composers Alberto Ginastera and Bartók, known for their use of bitonality and tone clusters, were also a significant influence. In fact, he studied for some time under Ginastera and Nadia Boulanger. It is no surprise, then, that the resulting aesthetic is a beautiful mixture of world music both contemporary and old.

One of the most noticeable features of his music is the presence of extended harmony, dissonance, and modal clusters, borrowed from composers who influenced him. His music also includes a large amount of improvisation through melodic embellishment and rhythmic variation, which gives the music a sense of freestyle expression as can be heard in jazz. The composer also makes use of a number of baroque elements. Immediately identifiable are the circulating bass lines and harmonic sequences, which correspond to the passacaglia technique of the baroque period (Azzi & Collier, 2000, p. 157). Piazzolla's influence from J.S. Bach inspired him to include much counterpoint in his voice-leading. This allowed musicians and listeners to focus their listening on any musical part and enjoy the individuality of each musician. In his works for quintet, for example, countermelodies are played by the guitar or violin underneath the principle melody. Some compositions even include fugal sections. Azzi and Collier (2000) describe his mature style:

> As his music making matured, Piazzolla deployed a full range of composing skills: canonic writing (or at least imitation), polyrhythms, polytonality, fugues, dissonances, occasional atonal effects, and impressionistic dreamscapes reminiscent of Ravel (p. 158).

Most of Piazzolla's shorter works follow a binary type of form consisting of two contrasting sections, rhythmic and lyrical:

> A common feature of many of his shorter pieces thereafter is a two-part division: one section, with a heavy rhythmic emphasis or thrust, and another, where a melodic line

predominates. While such a scheme had been common enough in tango music from at least the 1910s onward, Piazzolla gave it his own peculiar stamp. In his rhythm-led sections, the melody is often fragmentary, jagged, jerky; in the melody-led sections, it is frequently meditative, romantic, or passionate. (p. 160)

These sections usually alternate in the semirondo form ABABC (where C is a coda), but there are many exceptions, for some pieces do not contain lyrical parts while others have barely any rhythmic parts. However, most of Piazzolla's works have clear formal sections easily identifiable by a melodic motive, harmonic pattern, or character.

THE NUEVO TANGO AND MUSIC THERAPY

Piazzolla is a perfect example of a man whose imagination and struggles forced him to take a unique creative path. While struggling to find his own voice in composition, he was encouraged by Nadia Boulanger to accept his own musical roots: those of the tango. In Piazzolla's own words:

> She taught me to believe in Astor Piazzolla, to believe that my music wasn't as bad as I thought. I thought that I was something like a piece of shit because I played tangos in a cabaret, but I had something called style. I felt a sort of liberation of the ashamed tango player I was. I suddenly got free and I told myself: "Well, you'll have to keep dealing with this music, then." (Saavedra, 1995: A Tanguificated Fugue, par. 3)

Relating this to music therapy, do we not as therapists help our clients in their process of self-awareness and discovery? In therapy, clinicians have the opportunity to help clients find their own voice. Like the relationship between the composer and Nadia Boulanger, in the therapy setting we create a space for reflection and self-searching. As we discover more about our clients, we are able to gain insight through the music they resonate with and through this process our clients are able to discover or reconnect with their authentic selves. Not long after studying with Boulanger, Piazzolla found that his direction in life and his music became well known worldwide. Today, his music is performed regularly in many concert halls. Therefore, if Piazzolla knows the meaning of having been lost, fragmented to pieces, and found again by looking at himself in a new light, what could his music mean for clients who experience it in the clinical setting?

Piazzolla's personality (on both a musical and human level) contained within it many opposites: an inner loneliness despite having a huge social entourage, a loving and affectionate person who at times could become aggressive and cruel. He expressed sadness and melancholy yet possessed such a zest for life, full of passion and vitality. People in therapy are always at risk of being judged by their diagnoses. Although some clients are depressed or exhibit antisocial, defiant behaviors, there is always another side to them, perhaps a sensitive, loving, and caring one, that due to circumstances was not able to be expressed or was overshadowed by defense mechanisms. Piazzolla's nuevo tango appears to embody all of these extremes: the good, the bad, the restless, the calm, the extrovert, the introvert. By studying his music, you can gain a sense of how to synthesize a multiplicity of emotions into a coherent whole. And by viewing our clients in this way, we believe that some insight can be gained about them: mainly, that each client is multifaceted and that all of their personalities can be expressed in the form of music.

Piazzolla's tangos have a clear aesthetic quality, namely that they open the possibility of juxtaposing several contrasting moods. Could the bold contrasts of lyrical and harsh rhythmic sections allow you to experience the duality often found in your feelings — for example, anger vs. sadness, or anxiety vs. loneliness? The style's harsh sounds are often balanced with lyrical melodies, which allow the pouring of emotions. Since the tango originated in a country that at the time was in a state of social distress, it could be argued that it has the potential to be a catalyst for feelings of anxiety and depression. Indeed, the music's entrancing rhythms are almost irresistible.

Its rhythmic, dancelike character can inspire clients to participate by playing the drums and perhaps dancing, while the lyrical sections may inspire more introverted expression played on the cymbal, tone bells, or even piano.

Finally, Piazzolla's harmonic palette is predominantly minor and avoids the more brilliant sounds of major keys. When minor keys are prolonged for a long period of time, this may give more meaning to major sonorities when they arise. In the clinical setting, therapists have the opportunity to manipulate the mood of the session by balancing major and minor keys, choosing to delay major resolutions for as long as needed through the use of tango music. It can be a powerful tool for the relief of tension after a long period of intensity and melancholy.

EXERCISES

Although this style of music can be inspiring, it is not an easy one to master. It is made for the more advanced pianist, as it requires a high level of rhythmic and harmonic skills. However, we believe that even by taking the time to learn just the basics, you can derive much fulfillment and many positive results in clinical improvisation. As in the jazz chapter, it is highly recommended that you master the first exercises before continuing to other sections.

In the clinical setting, it is most useful to play the tango in the keys of A, D, and E minor, as they match the available pitches on tuned percussion instruments such as the xylophone and metallophone. When playing in the key of D minor, these instruments can be prepared by substituting the B♮ for a B♭ to create the D Aeolian scale. For E minor Aeolian (natural minor), the F♯ must be used:

Example 11.1

For the purpose of clarity and consistency, most exercises will be written in the key of A minor.

TANGO BASS PATTERNS

As in most styles of music, the bass line normally provides the basic pulse while supporting the harmonies. Although Piazzolla's tangos do include musical development, they can be seen as a series of contrasting sections, each with a characteristic rhythm and harmonic sequence. The tango contains two main types of bass figures: syncopated ostinatos and walking bass lines.

It is important to consider the effect that each creates. Syncopated ostinatos evoke the dancelike character of the music, while walking bass lines bring a sense of forward movement. The basic rhythmic pulse of the tango consists of a 3+3+2 (8th note) feel, as demonstrated here:

Example 11.2

Solo (B–I)

Tango Ostinatos Using the Aeolian 6th

Examine the piece "Ausencias." Play it slowly and lyrically.

Example 11.3

Play the left hand only and note the emphasis on the Aeolian 6th (Db) through the use of syncopation. Together, the hands create the typical 3+3+2 pulse.

The following two ostinatos are based on the above piece. Play them lyrically and transpose them in the keys of D and E:

Example 11.4

Example 11.5

These ostinatos can support a changing harmony in the right hand functioning similarly to a pedal point. The second version (Example 11.5) may be more suitable for an advanced pianist. Supported by one of these ostinatos, try playing melodies that outline the chords of A minor, D minor, and E7 (I, IV, V in the key of A minor).

The next ostinato is based on the piece "Sin Rumbo." It features a chromatic line that rises and falls, passing by both minor and major 6ths.

Example 11.6

Improvise a lyrical melody in A Aeolian (white notes only) using the above ostinato. Transpose this ostinato in the key of D and E. This time, improvise a melody in the respective Aeolian modes. Increase the tempo and improvise more percussively, adding syncopation in the right hand. What potential do you think this ostinato may have in the clinical setting?

Duet (B–I)

CD2 (29) *S,* play lyrically and slowly on a tuned percussion instrument prepared on the white notes. *A,* match *S*'s tempo and mood by adding an ostinato in the key of A natural minor (Aeolian) and respond to *S*'s phrases with short melodic phrases or solid chords on the white notes of the piano. If *S* plays constantly, leave more space. *Chords may complete the whole rather than interrupting **S**'s phrases with another melody.*

S, improvise on a drum and cymbal. *A,* match *S*'s tempo and mood with an appropriate ostinato from the exercises in the key of A minor. Remain relatively stable in tempo even if *S* plays more sporadically in and out of tempo. After having established a tonal centre, offer a contrasting B section using a different ostinato in a new key (e.g., from A minor to D minor). Return to the original ostinato in the key of A to close the improvisation.

Walking Bass Lines

Walking bass lines consist of steady quarter notes. Compared to the walking bass lines found in jazz, tango bass patterns are generally shorter and more predictable. They are used in tangos of all tempi.

Solo (I)

Play the following ostinatos (Examples 11.7 and 11.8). Practise them with a bouncy (detached) tone. Try them also in octaves:

Example 11.7

Example 11.8

Here they are demonstrated in Piazzolla's "La Muerte del Angel" (Example 11.9) and "Michelangelo 70" (Example 11.10):

Example 11.9

Observe the rhythmic displacement in the right hand in mm 1–2 and the accented notes. The walking bass line provides a steady beat onto which a syncopated melody can be played. The same idea applies to the next example; this time the ostinato is played in octaves.

Example 11.10

Again, the displaced rhythms and syncopations are reserved for the melody in the right hand. The bass moves from the tonic to the 3rd, rocking back and forth and creating movement while sustaining a clear sense of the tonic key. The octaves add strength and can serve to support percussive instruments.

Duet (I)

> **S,** play percussively on a xylophone or metalophone, keeping a strict tempo. **A,** support with a walking bass ostinato. After some time, transpose the ostinato up a perfect 4th (e.g., from A to D). Do not deviate from **S**'s tempo. To end, return to the original transposition and gradually slow down the tempo of the ostinato, guiding the improvisation to a stop.

> CD2 (30)   **S,** play percussively on a drum and cymbal. **A,** support in a similar way as in the above duet, establishing a clear A minor key. This time, add a short melodic theme similar to the ones in "Michelangelo 70" or "La Muerte del Angel." Eventually, transpose the ostinato into a new key (e.g., up a 4th or down a 5th). Finally, create a dominant preparation, keeping the bass note on the dominant (E) and bringing the improvisation to a climax; then return to the home key (A minor) with the original ostinato and end.

MOTIVIC CELLS

Many of Piazzolla's most famous pieces contain a short melodic or rhythmic fragment that is developed throughout. One of the most famous is found in "Michelangelo 70." These fragments are easily remembered and provide a strong sense of unity. It is usually best to work with short melodic fragments of only three to six notes. This way, both therapist and client can remember them easily. Simple motives allow for greater freedom and can be easily developed into more complex patterns as the improvisation unfolds.

Solo (I–A)

Play the following theme from "Michelangelo 70":

Example 11.11

There are only four notes in this motive, but the rhythmic displacement and accents are the key elements of interest. Play it with the added bass and harmonies from Example 11.10 from the previous section. Note how the theme keeps repeating without variation even though the harmonies change underneath.

Some motives require slight variation in order to match the chords. Here is another motive typical of Piazzolla's style:

Example 11.12

This motive outlines an A minor chord and ends on an ornamented Aeolian 6th (F).

Below are two versions of the motive, the first on the tonic chord and the second on the dominant. The motives are slightly altered in order to fit the chord changes, but the characteristic Aeolian 6th remains:

Example 11.13

Practise the above motives accompanied by a bass ostinato or walking bass line that outlines the tonic and dominant chords.

One of the best ways to develop a motive is to play it within a predictable chord sequence[2] by transposing it up or down by step. The following example transposes the original motive down by step.

Example 11.14

Create your own simple motives based on outlining a chord. If possible, include the Aeolian 6th as a featured note. Practise transposing them stepwise up and down the keyboard in the key of A minor (on the white keys of the piano).

Although motive transpositions are effective in creating coherence in music, it is sometimes more important to keep the rhythmic aspect of the motive intact rather than the original notes. Therefore, if playing the exact motive within a sequence is too difficult when improvising, simply imitate the same rhythm and play alternate melodies that fit with the harmonies.

Create an improvisation based either on a motive that remains the same (no transposition) while harmonies change or one that varies slightly in order to fit the chord changes.

---

[2]Sequences will be discussed in more detail later.

Duet (I–A)

CD2 (31)   **S,** play freely on the white notes of the piano (this duet also works on a tuned percussion instrument). **A,** listen for a significant melodic fragment or theme (a reoccurring rhythm or a tendency on **S**'s part to gravitate to a certain note or group of notes). Create a melodic motive based (if possible) on what **S** played and continue to present it repeatedly. Add an ostinato to establish an A minor key. Continue to develop the motive. Transpose the ostinato up a 4th to create harmonic variety, then return to the original version and prepare an ending.

S, play on a drum using one of the suggested rhythmic figures below (Example 11.15) as a basis for an improvisation and repeat it periodically throughout the improvisation. **A,** create a melody based on the chosen rhythm. Support your melody with an ostinato or walking bass. At first, play the motive alternating between its tonic and dominant version, (similar to Example 11.13 from the solo exercises). Then continue to develop the motive, playing it in various transpositions or in a sequence. Return to the tonic and dominant versions of the motive and prepare an ending.

Example 11.15

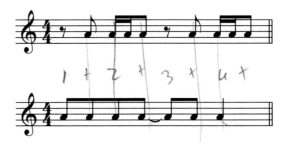

SYNCOPATED RHYTHM

Rhythm and syncopation are at the core of the tango. Without the tango's rhythmic feel, the music loses its vitality. Syncopated rhythm adds energy and life to music in almost all circumstances. This section explores this aspect of Piazzolla's music in more detail, focusing on syncopated rhythmic cycles, inverted rhythmic cells, and rhythmic displacement (polyrhythms) and considers potential therapeutic applications in clinical improvisation.

Syncopated Rhythmic Cycles

The rhythms of the tango, as in jazz and blues, are highly syncopated (but played straight rather than swung or shuffled). Since the nuevo tango has its origins in dance, its rhythms are often dancelike, repetitive, and entrancing. They may be an ideal tool to use with clients who alreadpossess a strong sense of rhythm and steady pulse.

Solo (A)

Play the following example at a moderate to lively tempo:

Example 11.16

As seen in the first exercises of this chapter (ostinatos and walking bass lines), the left hand keeps the basic pulse of the tango. The right hand plays accents at odds with those of the left hand, creating a dynamic syncopated feel. Continue to repeat the above pattern indefinitely, allowing yourself to experience the effects of the syncopated rhythms and the constant pulse.

Inverted Rhythmic Cells

Inverted rhythmic cells are rhythms that appear to go against the natural flow of the musical phrase. These rhythms usually start with quicker figures on strong beats, ending on longer tones (e.g., two 16ths followed by an 8th note, rather than an 8th note followed by two 16th notes). Here are some examples based on an analysis of several of Piazzolla's pieces.

Solo (A)

Play the following inverted rhythmic cell:

Example 11.17

Normally strong beats (1 and 3) are emphasized, but here the 16th notes lead to an accented weak beat (2). This gives the music a more forceful and percussive effect. Here are other examples:

Example 11.18

Practise improvising using one or two of the above rhythmic cells. Rather than focusing on which notes to play, simply focus on the rhythms. Play them with a walking bass line or ostinato.

Rhythmic Displacement (Polyrhythms)

Rhythmic cells can also be displaced over several measures, creating polyrhythms over a steady walking bass line. These are part of the syncopated nature of the tango.

Solo (A)

The following example from "La Muerte del Angel" demonstrates a typical rhythmic motif:

Example 11.19

Practise clapping this polyrhythm with both hands using the left hand to keep the beat while the right hand plays the rhythmic cell (accenting the long notes) as demonstrated below:

Example 11.20

Here is another typical rhythmic displacement:

Example 11.21

Once you are comfortable with Examples 11.20 and 11.21, practise them at the piano by playing a right hand pattern with a walking bass line. Chords or a melody in the right hand may suffice to convey the tango feel.

Think of possible clinical reasons for using the technique of rhythmic displacement in your work. In what situation would it be beneficial for a client? When could it be inhibiting or work to the therapist's disadvantage?

Duet (A)

S, play a steady quarter note pulse on a small percussion instrument such as a tambourine. *A,* support on another drum by first matching *S*'s tempo and dynamic level. After a few seconds, add rhythmic displacement, creating a pattern of 3 against 2 (see above Examples 11.20 and 11.21). How did *S* respond to the syncopation? What could be the purpose of breaking a client's steady pulse on an instrument? When could it be contraindicated?

CD2
(32)

Repeat the above exercise; this time, *A,* support on the piano rather than the drum.

S, play a steady 8th note pulse on a drum at a medium tempo and try to keep it stable no matter how *A* responds. *A,* match the 8th note pulse by creating a short melodic theme, using primarily 8th notes in the right hand. Add an ostinato to the melody. After a few repetitions of the theme, add syncopation by accenting melody notes that fall on the weak beats. Attempt to influence *S*'s response on the drum.

S, play a continuous rhythmic cell consisting of a long–short–long–short (quarter–8th–quarter–8th) pattern at a medium tempo (see Example 11.20). *A,* find a 4/4 pulse into which this pattern fits, transforming *S*'s rhythmic cell into a displaced rhythm. *Hint: You can first listen for the 8th note pulse in* **S***'s rhythm and then play quarter notes.* How did *A*'s steady pulse affect *S*'s playing? Are there any situations where it would be beneficial to change the musical context of a client's rhythm by introducing an unexpected pattern?

CHROMATICISM

It is impossible to think of the tango without its chromatic melodic embellishments. These often imitate the portamento that the voice or cello creates for an emotional effect. This technique can be used to add passion or more expression to a melody. Piazzolla's melodies incorporate chromaticism in their very essence, and he uses this technique not only in the top voice but in the inner voices as well, often implying harmonies.

Solo (I)

Melodic Embellishment

Play the following melodic phrases:

Example 11.22

The use of chromaticism in the melody may work best when clients play untuned percussion instruments. This way, unwanted dissonances can be avoided. However, if a client is playing a melodic instrument (e.g., xylophone or piano), chromaticism works well in the inner voices and can serve as harmonic colouring.

Practise adding chromatic passing notes in the melody of a familiar song, such as "Amazing Grace" (Example 11.23) or "Green Sleeves" (Example 11.24). The idea is to use chromaticism to fill melodic leaps of a 3rd or larger interval. Remember not to overuse chromaticism. It is best to reserve it for the beginning of phrases only.

Example 11.23

Example 11.24

Chromaticism used as an embellishment in the bass is less likely to interfere with the client's melody. It often consists of four 16th notes beginning on the last beat of the measure, filling in the interval of a major 3rd (e.g., F–A):

Example 11.25

Practise adding this typical bass figure at the beginning of phrases by starting a major 3rd lower than the note to which you wish to resolve. Create a lead in for the chords of A minor, D minor, and E minor, by adding this embellishment. If the client responds well to chromaticism, this figure could be used in order to prompt or respond to the client's phrases in the event of a musical dialogue.

Chromaticism in Inner Voices and Melodic Contour

The tango uses chromaticism not only to embellish melodic lines but also to imply harmonies or even to create an effect similar to that of a musical "sigh." When heard in descending motion, chromaticism can represent sadness or melancholy. They can also be used as fillers when there is a break in the melody. The following excerpts illustrate various uses of chromaticism in Piazzolla's music.

Solo (I–A)

Play the following example of a descending chromatic line in the inner voices from the song "Vuelvo al Sur":

Example 11.26

This type of descending chromaticism in the inner voice adds harmonic interest and adds a mournful sigh to the end of a phrase. Play just the left hand notes in order to fully experience the effect of the descending motion against the bass. Transpose these two measures in the keys of A, D, and E minor and use them as a basis for an improvisation.

The next example, from "Sin Rumbo," shows an ascending and descending chromatic filler in the inner voices:

Example 11.27

This example demonstrates the technique of filling space when the melody is at rest. Although it may be useful to fill in the space, in a clinical situation try to use this idea rather as a response to a client playing (e.g., after a crash on the cymbal). In situations when clients play only a single note or play and wait for further prompting from the therapist, this filling technique can be used to entice the client to continue playing while remaining in the tango framework. Again, transpose this measure into the keys of A, D, and E minor and create your own improvisation based on this inner voice movement.

The following exercises are designed to develop the use of chromaticism in the melodic contour of phrases. In order to keep the principle simple and clear, all of them are based on moving away and returning to the 5th degree of the Aeolian scale. First, become familiar with the most important neighbor tone, a semitone above the 5th.

Example 11.28

This is the Aeolian 6th. It finds its resting point when it resolves back to the 5th. The next example moves farther up chromatically to reach the major 6th (F♯).

Example 11.29

Listen to the difference between the minor 6th and major 6th against the root (A). Now add yet another chromatic step above to reach the point of highest tension, the minor 7th:

Example 11.30

Now try the same exercise on the dominant 7th chord (E7). Remember to keep the chromaticism based on the 5th degree of the key; not the 5th of the chord!

Example 11.31

Once you are familiar with this principle, practise improvising a chromatic tango melody harmonized with alternating I and V chords in the key of A minor, following the given scheme:

Example 11.32

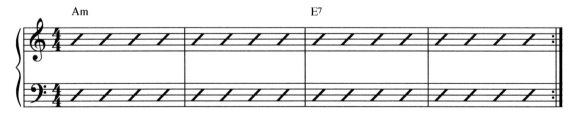

The above exercises can also be practised in the inner voices, as in the following examples (11.31–11.35):

Example 11.33

Example 11.34

Example 11.35

Again, note that each one is based on moving away and back to the 5th of the chord. Experiment by deviating chromatically away from the 5th in both directions, as in Example 11.35.

Duet (I–A)

S, play lyrical chromatic melodies in the upper register of the piano while **A** supports on the bottom register. **A,** respond to **S**'s phrases by either imitating or transforming them. *A chromatic line can be transformed by changing its direction from ascending to descending. It can also be imitated but at a faster or slower speed, or by changing the touch from loud to soft.* Add an ostinato in the bottom register to support the melodic dialogue.

S, play a melodic motive (3 to 5 notes in length, e.g., CBDC) on a tuned percussion and repeat it frequently. **A,** harmonize the motive using the inner voice technique in the above solo exercises.

S, play a lyrical melody in the upper register of the piano. **A,** support with a tango progression in the key of A minor at a slow or medium tempo, using chromaticism in the inner voices. Example 11.34 illustrates a possible A section using an ostinato with chromaticism followed with a contrasting B section consisting of a chord progression based on a sequence:

Example 11.34

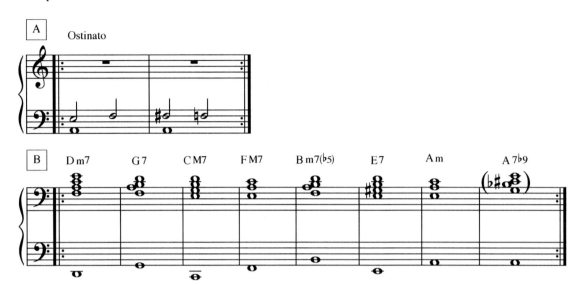

A, in the A section, play melodically with the right hand to respond to *S*'s phrases. In order to create contrast, in the B section play the chords with a 3+3+2 pulse. *The final chord is bracketed, as it is used only to repeat the progression smoothly.* Stay on A minor to return to the ostinato from the A section.

CD2 (33) *S,* play quietly and tentatively on a tone bar or a cymbal. *A,* add a filler of rising and falling chromatic lines in the inner voices after each of *S*'s notes. It is not necessary to establish a clear tempo or pulse. Give *S* a cue by nodding your head gently in order to invite him or her into the music without using words. *This is good practice for situations that require more guidance on the part of the therapist.* Establish a predictable pattern (*S* plays, *A* responds). Develop a short chromatic motive in order to unify the composition/improvisation.

S, play on a tuned percussion prepared with a short chromatic fragment on the notes E, F, F♯, G, A. *A,* support with a harmonic progression revolving around I and V (A minor–E7). Create a theme based on *S*'s chromatic fragment.

CHORD PROGRESSIONS AND SEQUENCES

As seen in previous chapters, chord sequences create a stable and predictable form for musical improvisation. They are found in almost all nuevo tango compositions. Typical chordal sequences are 1, 2, or 4 measures in length and consist of descending 5ths or descending chromatic lines in the bass. These are usually repeated before a new contrasting section is introduced. Most progressions are derived from baroque and jazz harmonic sequences and usually involve movement from IIm7(♭5) to V7(♭9) (a half-diminished 7th chord to a dominant chord with an added flat 9), as shown:

Example 11.35

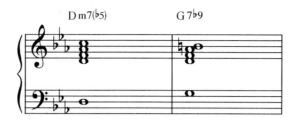

These flat notes are partly responsible for creating the darker sonorities of the tango. What prevents such sequences from becoming stagnant or redundant is that they are balanced by frequent key changes. Therapists who have mastered sequences in all keys may best benefit from using them in clinical improvisation, for they are likely to create interesting musical developments that will increase the energy of the music.

Descending 5th Sequence in a Minor Key

Solo (I–A)

    The following example from "Vuelvo al Sur" is based on a descending 5th sequence.

Example 11.36

    The progression can be repeated indefinitely without becoming stagnant. Originally, it was played with a strong 3+3+2 pulse in the piano, but it could also be used lyrically.

    Notice the tension and release inherent in the top voice in the form of musical "sighs." Play the progression several times and immerse yourself in its sounds.

    Here is a harmonic distillation of these eight measures:

Example 11.37

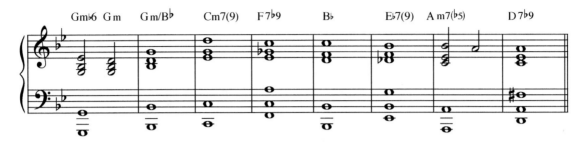

Starting in measure 3, the bass moves from C–F–B♭–E♭–A–D, which prepares the return to the tonic (Gmin). The equivalent scale degrees would be IV–♭VII–III–VI–II–V–(I).

Practise a simple form of the descending 5th sequence in the key of A minor. *Note that it begins on the IV chord (D minor).* The slurs indicate where the sequence repeats. It also shows the resolution of the sigh in the melody:

Example 11.38

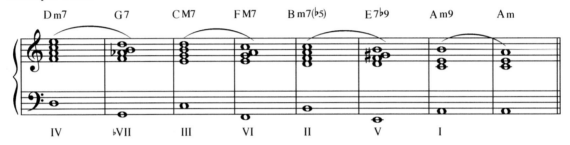

Transpose the sequence in the keys of D and E minor. Once you are comfortable in any of these keys, play the chords in a broken manner. Make your own version of the sequence beginning on other chord inversions. Here is a simple version of the same progression using only three notes per chord:[3]

Example 11.39

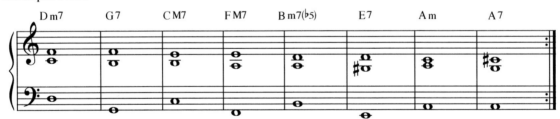

This consists of the skeleton of the descending 5th sequence. You may recognize it also in the music of J. S. Bach or many jazz standards, such as "Autumn Leaves." The final chord has been changed to A dominant 7th in order to create a smooth repetition of the sequence.

Practise the above sequence as written and then try adding your own melodic phrases in between the chords. Make each phrase lead into the top note of the next chord as in the following example:

---

[3]This progression is also featured in Chapter 8, in the context of a jazz improvisation.

Example 11.40

Chord Progressions Using a Descending Chromatic Bass Line

Solo (A)

Examine the following sequence:

Example 11.41

Here is a harmonic distillation of the sequence:

Example 11.42

The minor 9th is a prominent feature of most progressions. It creates a darker sound and helps to create mournful sighs when it resolves down a semitone. It also creates chromaticism in the voice leading.

This is a typical descending progression that could be related to the sadness that the music sometimes expresses.

Here is another progression based on a descending chromatic bass line. Although it is not a strict sequence, it is a typical tango progression that can be used as a basis for a section of a piece of music or improvisation:

Example 11.43

The half notes in the top voice have been added to show places where a musical "sigh" can be added. Sighs can be placed almost anywhere in a progression, provided that the first note holds more tension than the resolution note.

Miscellaneous Chromatic Sequences

Solo (A)

The following example (a reduction of the original rendition of "Vuelvo al Sur") shows a chromatic sequence based entirely on minor chords. This sequence was used to create a colourful introduction to the song:

Example 11.44

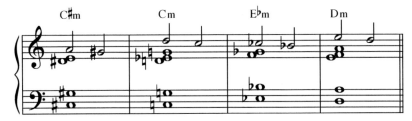

This is an example of the sudden colour changes that Piazzolla employs in order to create new harmonic interest or to give a sense of instability. By moving suddenly to an unrelated chord, it may be possible to get the attention of clients who may lack focus or begin to lose interest in the music.

Again, this progression features musical sighs in the top voice, either moving the Aeolian 6th to the 5th (first measure) or the 9th to the octave (second measure), creating tension and release. Practise transposing the first measure in three different keys. Try playing it as a sequence (by transposing it up or down a semitone).

Duet (A)

CD2
(34)
S, play percussively on a drum and cymbal in a tango (3+3+2) pulse. *A,* support *S* with an eight-measure chord sequence featuring a chromatically descending bass line, as in Example 11.43. How did *S* respond to the sequence?

A, based on the chromatic chord sequence in Example 11.44, improvise lyrically, creating a sense of openness. *S,* play on a cymbal, chimes, or ocean drum. What mood did you both create?

As in the first duet of this section, *S,* play on a drum with a strong tango pulse. *A,* support using an eight-measure descending 5th sequence. Then create a transition using a descending chromatic sequence of your choice and modulate to a completely new key. *Hint: The most contrasts in key changes occur between a flat and sharp key (e.g., Gmin to Emin or Amin to C♯min) or vice versa.*

MODAL CLUSTERS

Modal clusters may be used to accentuate rhythmic playing in improvisation. They can also express emotions of suffering (anger, pain, and ambiguous emotions). Played softly, clusters may add atmosphere or colour. In the tango, they are usually derived from the Aeolian scale, ranging from a single added semitone to all of the notes of the scale played together with the palm. Although this technique can be extremely useful in some situations, it is probably best to find a cue from the client's playing that indicates that clusters should be used. While some clients may find it hard to bear such dissonance, others may yearn for it.

Solo (I)

Play the following cluster configurations loudly, softly, solid and broken:

Example 11.45

These clusters add texture and additional colour to the A minor chord and are but a few possibilities.

The first configuration makes use of the D♯ against the 5th of the chord (E). This sonority can pierce through the sound of a loud drum or cymbal crash and can be a useful tool in a high energy improvisation.

The second cluster makes use of the surrounding tones around the 5th of the chord (E).

The F is the added Aeolian 6th, and the 4th (D) is added for extra density.

The final cluster includes the surrounding tones around the 3rd of the A minor chord. The B adds the sound of the 9th. This note, derived from jazz chords, is also characteristic of many tango chords. All of these clusters add density in chords and can be used to increase the level of tension in an improvisation.

Here is a short cyclic progression typical of Astor Piazzolla's compositions, played with added clusters.

Example 11.46

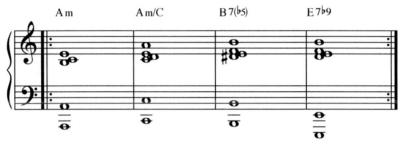

Play it both loudly and softly, without pulse and with a 3+3+2 pulse.

Duet (I)

S, play rhythmically on a drum and cymbal. *A,* support, using a simple chord progression (see Example 11.47) with a walking bass line. After some time, begin to create more intensity and harmonic ambiguity by introducing modal clusters into the same chord progression, as demonstrated in the solo exercises (Example 11.46).

Example 11.47

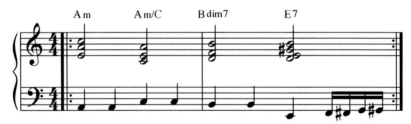

INTEGRATING THE STYLE

Now that we've examined the musical elements of the nuevo tango separately, we can see how they all work together to form the tango style in a more authentic rendition. This section will compare two accompaniment variations based on the same chord progression. Both incorporate a number of stylistic elements previously seen in the above sections. Therefore it is best to practise all the previous exercises before examining this section.

Accompaniment Variation 1

Solo (A)

> The following is a typical tango piano accompaniment using a walking bass line. Play it loudly with a sense of forward motion.

Example 11.48

Its characteristic feel requires the right hand to play chords just after the strong beats, creating excitement and syncopation.

The pattern invites syncopated percussive playing contained by a steady pulse in the bass. Think about situations where this kind of accompaniment would best support a client. What therapeutic aims could it facilitate? What sort of reactions does this accompaniment give you?

The sequence begins at the 4th measure as a II–V–I in Amin (a tonicization of the IV chord in Emin). This pattern is repeated down a whole tone starting in measure 7, leading to Gmaj7 (the relative major of Emin), which finishes with B7 (the dominant), leading back to the tonic. Play it several times and transpose it to the keys of Dmin and Amin.

Improvise or compose other accompaniment patterns that have the same rhythmic feel. Include two or three of the following musical elements: (1) syncopation, (2) modal clusters, (3) chromaticism, and (4) ostinato or walking bass line.

By assimilating the principle and memorizing a few patterns, you will become more flexible not only in creating accompaniments in general, but also in being able to use some of these elements at appropriate times when clinically warranted.

Accompaniment Variation 2

Solo (A)

The next accompaniment follows the same chord progression as the previous one. This time the pulse is a 3+3+2, played in octaves in the left hand. The right hand plays accents after each bass note and provides movement in between:

Example 11.49

The resulting rhythm can be simplified as follows:

Example 11.50

Clap it several times in order to assimilate the rhythmic feel.

Transpose this variation in the key of Amin and Dmin.

Both accompaniment variations can be used as the main A section or refrain of a clinical improvisation.

Improvise on an ABA form, where section A consists of one of the two rhythmic variations presented above in the key of Emin and the B section is a lyrical progression sequence in the key of Gmin. In order to make the contrast, use a minimum of pedaling during the A section.

Creating Your Own Tango Form

As mentioned in the introduction of this chapter, Piazzolla's tangos take on a variety of forms and there are no prescribed rules. However, many of his compositions balance rhythmic and lyrical sections. Most of his tangos also include harmonic sequences. The following are suggestions for possible tango forms. Although it is recommended to approach the tango with an overall form in mind, remember to let clients negotiate the form with you as clinical improvisations unfold, rather than to follow a predetermined plan.

Solo (A)

Create your own rhythmic tango in A minor based on the following scheme:

A (rhythmic), B (descending 5th sequence), A (rhythmic), B (sequence), C (modulation to new key, lyrical), A (rhythmic, original key), B (sequence), coda

Here is a description of how these sections may unfold:

A (rhythmic): This section establishes the home key. The principle harmonies are the tonic and dominant. It may consist of a walking bass ostinato to support a syncopated motive in the right hand. The motive should be played over both tonic and dominant harmonies.

B (descending 5th sequence): This sequence further develops the motivic material. It typically begins on the IV chord (D minor in the key of A) and ends on the dominant chord (V), leading back to the A section.

C (modulation to new key, lyrical): Piazzolla often modulates to a highly contrasting key. Possibilities are C minor, F minor, C major (relative major), or B♭ minor (a half-step higher). This section is considerably longer than the previous sections. Here, the melody is more florid and the theme contains longer phrases, sometimes incorporating musical "sighs," as seen earlier in the chapter. The section may finish in the key it began or modulate back to the original key (A minor) and cadence on its dominant chord (E).

Other possible schemes for tangos are:

1. A (rhythmic), B (lyrical), A (rhythmic), B (lyrical), A (rhythmic)
2. A (lyrical), B (sequence, lyrical), A (lyrical), C (lyrical), A (lyrical),
   B (sequence, lyrical), coda
3. A (rhythmic), B (rhythmic), C (rhythmic), A (rhythmic)

Continue to explore the possibilities, juxtaposing various rhythmic sections and lyrical sections. Try a variety of key transpositions to create harmonic contrast between sections. Piazzolla often used a minor 3rd relationship between two minor keys to create contrast (e.g. A minor to C minor or A minor to F♯ minor).

Duet (A)

CD2
(35)   **S,** play energetically and rhythmically on a tuned percussion instrument (also works with a drum and cymbal). **A,** support at the piano with a tango in ABA form (rhythmic–lyrical–rhythmic) in the key of A minor, where the A section is based on one of the accompaniment patterns demonstrated in the above solo exercises. Try to follow **S**'s rhythms if possible, and then guide the improvisation to a more lyrical B section in the key of C (relative) major. To return to the A section, create a buildup of tension on the V chord (E7) of the A minor key

CONCLUSION

Piazzolla's nuevo tango is a unique style of music capable of expressing a range of emotions such as passion, excitement, anger, frustration, joy, suffering, and intense grief. Its minor sonorities give the music a dark appeal, yet its roots in dance music keep the energy flowing. Indeed, the tango is the "dance of sorrow." Through movement, pain never becomes dull or stagnant. As the tango brings us through endless rhythmic cycles, so we are able to dance with our pain rather than keeping tension inside our bodies. This chapter also shows that music is not composed in a void, but is a part of society and the individual personalities that create it. Astor Piazzolla is a perfect example of a composer who succeeded in putting all of himself and all of his country into his music. He was a progressive individual, eager to absorb musical ideas from a variety of social and cultural sources. You could say that his mentality was one of inclusion rather than exclusion, as he incorporated many world styles into his own music. By studying not only the music but also the life of the composer/performer, you can gain some perspective on human suffering and discover new ways of relating to your clients musically.

PART FIVE

AUTHENTICITY

CHAPTER 12

Finding Your Own Voice

Every improvising clinical musician should aspire to sound unique. Our desire to create different styles and then use them is something to which all music therapists should aspire. Developing our personal style through this process is inevitable, the only questions being those of time and will. The more you follow your own creative process and the more you are passionate about learning music and improvising in sessions, the quicker you will find your own unique path. This is the attitude you must adopt if you pursue the path of a clinical improviser. How can we be creative and unique if we do not first value our own ideas? Thus improvisation is a combination of precise intervention balanced alongside the freedom of personal exploration that is necessary for all artists, be they therapists or not.

Patience and humbleness are also essential qualities required to achieve our own voice. Humbleness, because many students and music therapists think that you can be original immediately. In most cases, such an attitude leads to reinventing the wheel. We believe that it is a mistake to refuse to look to tradition before attempting to break it. It can take many years of study (except maybe for prodigies and geniuses) to become a competent clinical improviser. We would argue that the best improvisers are those who have learned and mastered the conventions of resources and styles over an extended period. This allows them to use the principles they had mastered and manipulate them consciously. We encourage students of improvisation to continuously absorb the music of the artists they love, for there is no doubt something in that music that can be identified with. It is through the accumulated knowledge of the many artists and their styles that you eventually develop a unique voice.

To imitate other artists should never be avoided but instead should be considered one of the quickest ways to achieve your own personal voice. We need willpower to take the time to learn. We must become conscious of how another's music is constructed. This means experimenting on our main instrument, trying to understand what makes a certain song or piece of music work or what makes it so appealing. It is only by doing this that we can achieve uniqueness and apply it clinically. It is not enough to listen to the music we love and hope that somehow we will be able to play it in sessions without practising.

Why is it good to pursue our own musical voice as music therapists? The more we do our own self-searching and discover our own selves, the more easily we will be able to influence clients and inspire them to find their own voices also. Finding our own voice is a journey. Our musical journey often reflects our personal journey, especially when it comes to improvisation. Finding our true identities in music is in a way no different from finding our true selves in real life (Lee, 2008), and although there may be moments of epiphany along the way, this is also a never-ending and often arduous process.

How do we then find a musical identity that will allow an authenticity necessary for our work? How do we combine the specific styles explored in parts one to four of this book, with our own styles to produce an authentic musical self necessary for enlightened clinical improvisations? While this book strives to be a practical, hands-on guide, there is, however, an aspect of learning that cannot be so easily separated into exercises. Combining the building blocks of learning with our personal journey is a complex and ultimately philosophical process. The music we create should be in a style that best suits the needs of the client and not the other way around. We are thus left with a conundrum of how best to adapt our musical knowledge and skills for the moment-to-moment expression of the client and the developing relationship with the therapist. This is not an easy task, because it demands not only the practicalities of knowledge and the ability to create specific styles, but also an understanding of the emotional makeup of the music we use. The specific reasons for every choice and the potential therapeutic connotations of this choice are complex. The "science" of clinical improvisation therefore becomes an ever-changing hierarchical structure that needs to be considered with care and exactness. This can leave even the most seasoned clinical improviser feeling inadequate and in awe of the possibilities ahead.

It is our experience that music therapists do not use specific styles such as jazz, baroque, or world music because they feel they do not have the skill or that the music itself will be too complicated and therefore not appropriate. Also, many therapists keep their individual musical likes separate from their clinical music. We believe that allowing our musical tastes to colour our clinical musicianship will open whole new panoramas, new universes that could dramatically change our view of improvising. If we change this assumption and begin analyzing the content of the music that is important to us, that comes from our own musical journeys, and then adapt it for our work with clients — how significant could this connection be?

The purpose of this part of the book, then, is to provide exercises that have been used by the authors and various educators and clinicians to facilitate the therapist's individual style of improvising. This is often an amalgamation of styles learned combined with the therapist's own experience, learning, and personal likes. These exercises are just a sample of what could be developed, and we are sure that there are educators who have their own library of examples that are similar in design. Allow yourself to be a composer of clinical styles. When considering these examples, be inspired and develop them into specific exercises that will fit your philosophy and clinical population. Have fun in exploring the different elements of music used in therapy. Be specific in the element/aspect you are exploring and think of clinical scenarios where it could appropriately be used. As you allow what you have learned in the beginning stages of this book to meld with your own personal discovery, allow these elements (the realities of specific styles, e.g., classical, jazz, world) to merge with your own discovery of improvised clinical musicianship. In sessions, always play consciously, balancing your judgment between these two polarities and eventually allowing them to combine to produce a form of music-making that is truly your own. This may take many years to achieve, but once discovered it will revolutionize your way of working with clinical improvisation, and this will affect the efficacy of your work and potential therapeutic outcome.

EXERCISES

COMBINING STYLES

Once you have mastered playing in a style, you are then faced with a new set of challenges. Apart from the myriad of therapeutic knowledge and reasoning for choosing a style, there is the challenge of integrating and/or moving between them. How do you balance different styles in a way that will provide a coherent whole necessary for therapeutic balance? From an artistic perspective, music therapists should explore combining both similar and opposing styles to find combinations that are the most effective. How can you move, for example, from improvising in the style of a Bach toccata to an Indian Raga, or from a song in the style of the blues to a romantic lieder? Both examples would seem incongruent, yet it is possible to combine any style with another provided that we are assured of their therapeutic significance and validity. In fact, improvising in disparate styles will bring freshness to your playing and therefore broaden your view of the therapeutic potential available. The following exercise explores a variety of stylistic combinations.

Solo (B–1)

The first step is to practise each style in as many different keys as you can. ABA should always be used as a fundamental beginning to create form. To begin, use simple modes and scales, moving from one tonic mode/scale to another and then from the tonic to dominant. For example:

A Aeolian on A, **B** Middle Eastern on A, **A** Aeolian on A

A Middle Eastern on D, **B** Aeolian on A, **A** Middle Eastern on D

Once you feel comfortable integrating basic modes and scales, try some simple styles in both the tonic and dominant combinations. For example:

A blues in C, **B** raga in G, **A** blues in C

A baroque dance in C major, **B** Korean folk song in G minor, **A** baroque dance in C major

It is also possible to integrate idioms in less-specific music combinations. For example:

A popular song, **B** atonal playing (no defined key), **A** popular song

Once you have mastered improvising from the tonic to dominant and major to minor, try other less-related modulations. Always be specific and conscious in your choice, making note of style combinations that work and those that do not.

Now consider ongoing clinical scenarios. Taking the proviso that every style and idiom has its own distinct artistic and emotional character, consider how integrating each might impact the therapeutic process. Play with precision and dedication, extracting its essence, and then combine one or more to create a clear structure. This should not only be dependent on the styles' artistic merits, but also reflect the aims and objectives of your sessions. Now, if possible, take your practised ideas into actual sessions. Be conscious of everything you play and be aware of how the style is impacting the client(s), their playing, and the process. In your indexing and/or assessment, be aware of how the style of your music affected the therapeutic outcome. How did the client embrace the musical components of a particular style or combination thereof, and how did its expansion into improvising and/or structured interventions/songs become a part of the experience? Consider how you integrated your different styles and how in the future you could be more creative in moving between the different musical polarities. Please note that it is not a good idea to constantly change styles from session to session. Styles should provide consistency and form. Once it is ascertained which style(s) are critical, then they should be repeated and developed, becoming musical/therapeutic "leitmotifs" (Wigram, 2004) within the overall process.

TONE COLOURING

The tone, as a fundamental experience (Lee, 2003; Robbins & Robbins, 1998) that connects the client and therapist, is at the heart of how musical dialogue begins.

The client's opening tone can often be embedded in complex vocal textures or instrumental playing. Spontaneous sounds reflect the emotions of the client entering the session. If the therapist is improvising music as the client enters, the opening tone of their music, either vocally or instrumentally, should be related to the tone of the client as best they are able to do so. The therapist should improvise music that is open and tonally noninferred, since the musical relationship begins the instant that first sounds are created. Precisely hearing, reflecting upon, identifying, and moving forward from the tone into the core of the session is the therapist's challenge. Reflecting upon the interpersonal link between creativity and expression — of the tone — and how it emerges in the evolving relationship is fundamental to the developing process. (Lee, 2003, pp. 79–80)

This simple exercise will help you to explore how to colour a tone in varied ways, potentially leading to more formed experiences/interventions. It will enable you to be free and creative in your response to a client's single note expression.

Solo (B–I)

Take a tone and create ten different chords to colour it. Experiment with tonal and nontonal chords, creating sounds that are unusual and exotic. Find some chords that create tension and others that are calmer and more grounded. Once these are chosen and notated, practise by playing the fundamental tone followed by the chord. Play slowly, if possible with little or no pedal, and listen to the relationship between the tone and chord, keeping the clarity of the sounds intact.

Example 12.1

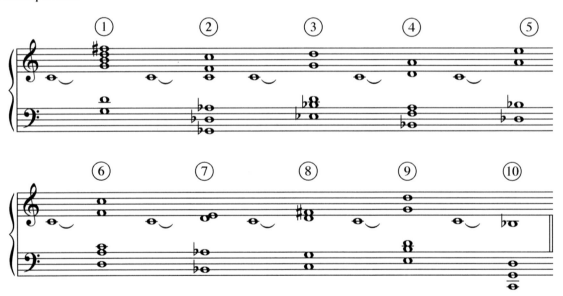

Play each tone in different places on the keyboard, thus creating varied textural landscapes.

Chose four or five chords that you feel go together well that could potentially be the basis for an improvisation or more structured song/intervention.

Create themes and melodies in different rhythmic structures around the chords, forming an A section, and then expand them to include four or five contrasting chords to create a B section in a different style.

Example 12.2

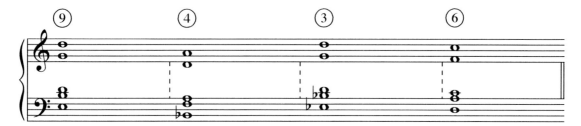

Take a clinical scenario from your work and create a musical experience that could be used in sessions (e.g., a greeting or good-bye song).

Use your chosen chords as the basis for the A section, improvising away from it to create a B section and then returning to A.

Example 12.3

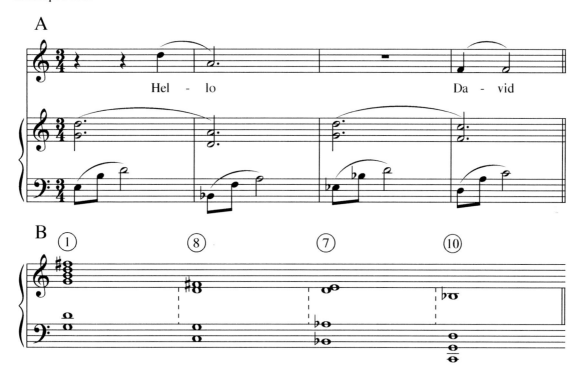

Take other tones and create a library of harmonic ideas and motives based on a single tone. Use these ideas as a base for practising and creating more structured interventions such as songs and repeated themes. Let these themes and ideas become coherent in your playing, incorporating them as structures that could be used as unifying concepts between sessions.

THE ARCHITECTURAL TONIC

Leading on from an improvisation and/or session originating from a single tone, the idea of a unifying tonic was born.

> I discovered that improvisations often originated from a core tone. There seemed to be a fundamental note that acted as an anchor in keeping a tonal sense of structure over the complete improvisation. It occurred to me that if I could identify the core tone, then what might I learn about the client, the client–therapist relationship, and the overall developing work? Was there a connection between the different architectural tonics of each session, and how did these affect my understanding of the therapeutic process? Just as the tonal centre of each movement of a symphony reflects the core of the complete work, so the tonal centres for a group of improvisations in a session or group of sessions could equally influence my understanding of the larger therapeutic picture. The architectural tonic thus became an essential and revelatory component in my continuing perceptions of clinical improvisational structure. (Lee, 2003, p. 157)

The "architectural tonic" is a way of conceptualizing and thinking musically in a session. It provides coherence and form yet promotes freedom in developing thematic ideas. It came out of the insecurities of being able to think theoretically when improvising (e.g., chord progressions, modulation, and transposition), a way to be precise without having to resort to standard musical formulas. It also came from the realization that there were significant tones that had significance in the developing dialogue with clients.

The most important architectural tonic can come from the client's playing, although it can also be heard from within the improvised dialogue between client and therapist. The architectural tonic can come from our clinical listening to/identifying significant tones, either during the session itself or from the reflective act of assessment/indexing. Once it is identified, the therapist can use the fundamental tone and incorporate it as the main structural form of an improvisation, complete session, or series of sessions. The architectural tonic can be imposed before a session or taken from a previous session.

The most powerful architectural tonic normally comes from the client's first utterances, e.g., vocal tones as they enter the room or their first exploration on instruments. This often-unconscious expression can become a powerful tonal representation of the client and their defining needs. All ideas should return to the fundamental tonic, and the session should end with some form of recapitulation of the architectural tonic, which therefore becomes a unifying factor that sits, metaphorically speaking, over the head of the therapist as the session progresses. Every idea should be related in some way to the architectural tonic.

At its most fundamental level, the architectural tonic brings form and cohesion. It is also an excellent way for the therapist to think clearly, balancing the dynamics of the musical and therapeutic processes.

Solo (I–A)

> Choose a tone and create a formed improvisation revolving around that tone. Make written notes of themes in a manuscript book. Use different styles learned from previous chapters in this book, as well as your own unique ideas. Create a symphony of movements from these sketches that could have a direct relation to a hypothetical clinical situation or an individual/group you are working with directly. Practise and refine your ideas until they become second nature.

Now create a clinical symphony, but this time as a free improvisation. Improvise ideas that will act as thematic anchor points as the piece develops. Record your improvisation and listen back, making note of your spontaneous creations and how these may be of use in sessions.

Duet (I–A)

S, choose a group of instruments with different tones and textures, e.g., drum, cymbal, xylophone, and tambourine. Provide *A* with a note that you would like the improvisation to be based on. Begin playing freely. *A,* improvise a clinical symphony around the given tone, creating an experience that is free yet clearly anchored to the tone.

S, choose a single hand chime. *A,* listen to *S* play, then improvise a simple intervention based on the tone. Now incorporate words and create a clinical song.

CREATING SMALL MELODIC THEMES/CELLS

Small melodic themes/cells often become the core of improvisations either consciously or unconsciously. Why is it important for music therapists to know and understand them? How can they be used as a structural basis for improvisations? Also, what do they tell us about the client's expression, the therapist's improvising, and the developing musical relationship?

Melodic themes/cells can come from various sources: as created by the client or the therapist and through the shared dialogue. Through assessment/indexing, they can be further concretised and taken forward for future sessions, thus providing continuity. They can provide unifying ideas that become central to the process and that reflect an accurate compositional voice of the client.

The following examples are of cells that became fundamental in the therapeutic process with two individual clients:

Example 12.4

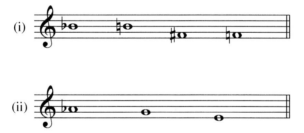

Solo (B–I)

Choose one of the above cells. Play slowly (without pedal), living in each interval. Note how each tone relates to the other. Consider inferred tonal centres and use simple harmonies to colour the tones. Find intervals to create counter cells. At first, try using diatonic harmonies, then move away and experiment with free-floating chords that have no strict key centre. Which do you think reflect the intervals better? Develop the cells into more extended melodies and developed themes. Try in different tempi and time signatures and find rhythmic patterns that will give different colours. Use your voice. At first, stay close to the tones; then, as you become more secure with the sounds, move away and create a complete improvisation. Return to a pure statement of the theme/cell to conclude.

Duet (B–I)

> *S*, play a tuned percussion (e.g., xylophone) instrument to the tones of the above cells. *A*, create an improvisation around *S*'s playing by developing themes as practised above. Use your voice and potentially create a more structured intervention. Also play freely, using the cell as an anchor for your free playing.

> *S*, play a single nontuned percussion instrument (e.g., drum) and repeat the exercise. *A*, note how different it feels to use the cell when improvising with a nontuned instrument.

Solo (B–I)

> Write down a series of random tones. For example:

Example 12.5

> Improvise using only those tones. Create an ABA form with contrasting styles.

Example 12.6

Use the above piece as an A section. Move into a freer improvisation away from the tones but in a similar style (B section), returning to A to complete.

Duet (B–I)

> *A,* try your series in combinations and with different instruments. *S,* play in varied styles, at first keeping strictly to the original order of tones. Make note of the dissimilarity in relationship between improvising with your chosen tones and being free.

Consider identifying themes/cells from your own work and spend time practising and thinking about how you might develop them for future sessions. By practising small ideas, slowly and assuredly, from previous sessions, you will enter the next with greater insight and precision.

CREATING UNIQUE SCALES

There are many scales used in various forms throughout the world. These range from the standard western diatonic scales to the more exotic ones such as the Japanese Han-Nakazora-Choshi scale. Different scale collections (Lateef, 1981; Slonimsky, 1974) can provide music therapists with rich source of data with which to expand and focus their resources. In Appendix D, you will find a Scale Reference as a resource.

Other unique scales can be your own original creations and/or originate from sessions. The most important aspect of any scale is its salient tones. They constitute its musical makeup/form and emotional content. When creating your own scales, experiment with different interval steps, e.g., semitones, tones, and larger intervals. Listen to their combination and the flavours that you can create. Find inspired and exotic harmonies that will further add to the sound of your scale. Use them as a basis for improvising, both as a part of your practice schedule and when comfortable in your sessions. Build your scale repertoire slowly so that when the scales are introduced in sessions, they are done with therapeutic clarity. Build a library of western, world, and then your own original scales. Begin to use them consciously in sessions. Here are two scales that we have created:

Example 12.7

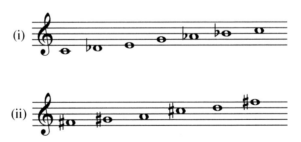

REHARMONISING SONGS

The reharmonisation of songs should be standard technique, especially for those who use song form as their main therapeutic medium. Being able to play songs in different keys and then change their form and style provides an openness of dialogue that is essential for the developing relationship. Being creative in your harmonic realisation of songs is a technique that should be mastered and developed alongside your fluency in learning new repertoire. Standard songs can take on a whole new life if coloured with different sounds and in new keys with nonstandard harmonisations. The world of possibilities then only becomes limited by our own lack of insight and imagination. You should be aware of repeating a song too many times in the same style, be it key, harmonic accompaniment, or mood. This does not mean that we constantly shift our style of playing but rather that a song should be the beginning, a core of endless possibilities, rather than an end once it has been learned. If we do not change and be constantly inspired in our use of songs, then they will become dull and lifeless.

Solo (B)

> Play and sing the spiritual "Amazing Grace." Note the simplicity and clarity of its harmonic realization.

Example 12.8

> Play and sing this new free harmonic realization. Note how the chords do not adhere to any formal harmonic theories but float and seem suspended. Also note how the more dissonant qualities of some chords affect the melody and its emotional impact.

Example 12.9

Now write a series of your own free harmonisations of this song.

Reharmonising songs you already know and creating (and notating) new harmonisations will not only add to the richness of your work but also provide endless opportunities for interpreting and reinterpreting the familiar. Reharmonising standard songs can also be exciting and stimulating both for clients, as they establish their relationship with the song, and for the therapist, as one strives to be innovative.

THINKING LIKE AN ORCHESTRA

How we know and play our instruments in therapy affects how the client perceives and responds to the sounds and potential dynamism. Andrés Segovia's famous quote is a powerful one for therapy: "The guitar is a small orchestra. It is polyphonic. Every string is a different colour, a different voice." The guitar in therapy is so often perceived as a monotone instrument made for playing block chords. This often results in music that has little imagination. If we think of the guitar, however, as an orchestral instrument, one with an infinitesimal collection of sounds and timbres, then new possibilities become available to us. This of course is dependent on skill and requires more than a rudimentary technique.

For music therapists who play single-line instruments, thinking in orchestral terms will be unique to their particular sound and technique. Few studies to date have looked at the clinical applications of orchestral instruments (Schenstead, 2009). Bowing a stringed instrument, for instance, is vastly different from the embouchure needed for woodwind and brass. How orchestral sounds are produced will affect their clinical use and application, as will the technical configurations possible, e.g., flutter tonguing (woodwind) and cross bowing (strings). All of these factors will affect their clinical potential. Many clients will be familiar with the sounds of the guitar or piano, but few will have had direct experience with the more unique textures and timbres of, say, the cello or bassoon. It is the unique textures and presence of such instruments that can make them valid and potentially powerful instruments in therapy.[1]

For piano (keyboard) players, thinking in orchestral terms is easier. The following questions are posed not as definites but as potentials.

How can we create sounds/textures and think like a:

> Full orchestra
> String section/orchestra
> Brass section/band
> Woodwind section
> Harp

If we think of the piano (keyboard) as an orchestral instrument, then how does this change how we use it clinically? Also, how does this also change how we hear? Think of the piano as a:

> Full orchestra
> String quartet
> Chamber orchestra
> Percussion ensemble
> Piano quintet

Some group improvisations could indeed be viewed from the perspective of a piano trio, quartet, quintet, or even orchestra. If we turn our heads to these possibilities, how will it transform how we hear and respond to our clients? The piano is not only a percussion instrument, but also one that has the potential to create a whole range of experiences and textures. When at the piano, you can create, or you can be a part of a symphony, be the support for a dramatic opera, or be a part of the most intimate and spiritual string quartet. If we open ourselves to the endless range of orchestral and chamber possibilities, then the range of therapeutic possibilities becomes endless also.

IMAGE IMPROVISATION

Basing an improvisation on an image is a great way of finding inspiration. Starting points for these improvisations could be a collection of images (e.g., photographs), sounds, texts, or objects. The improvisations are responses to the images or objects not encountered before the moment of improvising. They are an attempt to access sources of inspiration and to experience the spontaneity of original improvisations. As Vaughan (1979) comments, "everyone thinks in pictures before learning to think in words, and new insights and ideas frequently come in the form

---

[1]Our plea to all music therapists who play orchestral instruments is that when entering the field you continue to consider them as your main therapeutic tool. Learning to play the piano and/or guitar are essential skills that all therapists should acquire. If your most fluent musical expression, however, is an orchestral instrument, then make this your focus. Learning to clinically adapt orchestral instruments is a potentially exciting and innovative area of research that could drastically change our aural landscape.

of images" (p. 8). Each improvisation is oriented toward a single or unified "affect." The intention, therefore, is to discover musical correspondence rather than explore musical development or dramatic contrast. Improvisers can give themselves images, or two players, *A* and *S,* can give each other images or objects that have not been seen before.

Points of initiation and continuation comprise an attempt to follow either initial sound images (a clear musical idea) or an intentional imaging process that may be narrative, graphic, tactile, volumetric, dimensional, directional, associative, emotional, sensory, conceptual, or some other response to the image.

This kind of improvisation practice develops responsiveness to outside events and the ability to sound a musical intention clearly and within a short creative moment of one to two minutes: "Like intuition, the creative process is never entirely volitional and involves both letting things happen and taking responsibility for shaping them" (Vaughan, 1979, p.87). It is an effective way to discover toward what sounds and techniques a player gravitates. This is the practising of a musical vocabulary sounded from the psyche. The player does not know until the moment of playing what kind of "image" will arise, what the content will be, or in what ways the "images" will change.

BUILDING A MUSIC-CENTERED LIBRARY OF RESOURCES

Throughout this book, we have repeatedly mentioned the importance of keeping manuscript notations of styles, components, and exercises that you develop. This is important, as we can never remember all of the unique and creative ideas that happen in our practising. Keeping detailed files is like building a collection of clinical compositions. We should be specific not only about the content of each file but also about how we develop practice regimens that will be peculiar to our own individual needs for ongoing work. In Chapter 1, we discussed how to develop a practice schedule that is not unlike that of physically working out. Each file we build will help us in assigning order to our developing resources. Here are some guides to building files that we have found useful:

> Twelve separate files on every note of the diatonic scale (C–B), which includes scales, modes, tone colouring, and simple idioms.

Separate files on:

> World scales
> Harmonic themes and progressions
> Progressions and styles taken from composers, e.g., Schubert: lieder
> Reharmonisations of songs
> Cells/themes taken from sessions
> Original cells/themes

A final file could be that of free associative ideas, themes, melodic motives, rhythmic patterns, and textures. This can be your open compositional/clinical notebook. Keep it with you as a separate resource and jot down any ideas that come to mind as you improvise freely or as a part of more focused exercises. Here you can generate and develop your own ideas. Let your inspiration and imagination guide you, while always thinking about how these ideas could be used in sessions. Think of clients with whom you have worked in the past and clients with whom you are currently working. Think also of potential scenarios and how you might meet them. Make this file one that is full of musical freedoms and potential. We have included five examples of how these notations might look:

Example 12.10

(i) Static chords – slow

(ii) Syncopation – fast and detached

(iii) Accompaniment – lyrical

(iv) Minimalist textures – soundscape

(v) Lyrical harmonic accompaniment

CONCLUSION

Music as a reflection of life is a belief that is at the heart of this book. While on one hand a practical treatise on how to improvise, it is also an expression of the authors' belief in using the elements of music to allow change and reach potential. These two fundamentals are at the core of music therapy and provide the catalyst for all of the other complexities we advocate as part of the therapeutic process. In essence, music therapy is the simplest phenomenon, yet it is also full of complexities, enigmas, and ultimate creative truths. If we are to truly find an indigenous and music-centered theory (Aigen, 2005), then we must first turn ourselves to the study of music itself (Nordoff & Robbins, 2007; Wosch & Wigram, 2007). Learning from and building our musical knowledge through the analysis of precomposed music is just one way to build our musicological repertoire (Lee, 2003). By doing this, we will broaden our horizons and find new ways of being with our clients in music.

The exercises in this book have been refined over many years. They have been used in teaching and also in the personal development of the authors' practice. In preparing them for publication, we have been ultimately aware of how difficult it is to teach improvisation purely from a text. Working in teams helps to balance and share our own awakenings and is why the duet explorations are fundamental. This way of practising also mirrors the therapeutic relationship when taking the roles of soloist and accompanist. Developing your own regime of practising is ultimately a personal one, although we have offered possibilities in Chapter 1. The frequency and intensity of time taken to expand your resources through learning styles must come from a belief that music is central to the process and that music-centered thinking, in part or whole, should be a truth for all music therapists. This belief we can only share as our truth, and one that has led us to a greater understanding of music, therapy, and the potential for change.

This book, then, is not about theories or new approaches in the field. We hope that all music therapists from whatever theoretical backgrounds and clinical biases will find usefulness in this book. How you adapt music in your sessions is a choice dependent on personal philosophy and the clients with whom you work. We hope that the exercises offered give you the opportunity to broaden your musical choices and allow them to become richer, whatever clinical approach you advocate.

Music lives within everyone. It has the ability to inspire us and change our perceptions of the world in inextricable and profound ways. It moves us and provides the time to reconnect our truths with the chaos of the world. For us, it is why we are alive. Music makes sense of our confusion; it is the air we breathe and the reason we struggle to continue. Offering music to others is central to our humanity, and this is why we continually evaluate, reevaluate, and consider its finite workings. This book, then, at its most fundamental level, is an expression of this belief: that the musical components we use in therapy will affect the client's view of their world. Learning to build new resources and styles will add to the richness of our musical palette and create new colours and textures. It is these new textures that potentially hold the underlying truth that connects music and mankind.

As therapists, we strive to achieve perfection in our responses and understanding of the client and their place within the phenomenon we call music therapy. Our responses are always about balance: balance between "art" and "science,"' process and outcome, medicine and psychotherapy. The greatest balance of all, however, is that between music and therapy. These are not so easily divided and can only be fully understood and integrated if our musical skill is equal to that of our therapeutic understanding. This book aims to help music therapists find that balance and integration necessary for a truly balanced practice.

APPENDIX A

LISTENING GUIDE

CLASSICAL[1]

Baroque Era

J.S. Bach: St. Matthew Passion (BWV 244)
J.S. Bach: Mass in B Minor (BWV 232)
J.S. Bach: Goldberg Variations (BWV 988)
J.S. Bach: Well-Tempered Clavier (BWV 846–893)
J.S. Bach: Brandenburg Concertos (BWV 1046–1051)
J.S. Bach: Cello Suites (BWV 1007–1012)

Classical Period

Mozart: The Piano Concertos
Mozart: Requiem (KV 626)
Mozart: The Marriage of Figaro (K 492)
Beethoven: Piano Concertos
Beethoven: String Quartets
Beethoven: Symphonies

Romantic Era

Schumann: Piano Works
Puccini: Turandot
F. Liszt: Piano Works
F. Chopin: Piano Works
A. Bruckner: Symphonies
Brahms: Symphonies
Brahms: Piano Works

20th Century

Bartok: Piano Works
Stravinsky: The Rite of Spring
Copland: Appalachian Spring (1944)
Debussy: Piano Works
Schoenberg: Variations for Orchestra (Op. 31)
Ligeti: Atmosphère

---

[1]Listening suggestions for classical music provide titles only and not specific recordings.

POPULAR

Song

John Lennon: Imagine (1971, 2000), Capitol
Elton John: Blue Moves (1976, 1990), MCA/Rocket
Elton John: Madman Across the Water (1971, 1996), Island
Elton John: Good-bye, Yellow Brick Road (1973, 1996), Island
Mariah Carey: Music Box (1993), Sony
Boyz II Men: Legacy: The Greatest Hits (2001, 2005), UMVD
The Beatles: 1 (2000), Capitol
The Beatles: Abbey Road (1969, 2009), EMI
Billy Joel: Greatest Hits Vols. 1–2 (1998), Sony

Blues

B. B. King: Live at the Regal (1965, 1997), Universal Music Group
Harry Manx: Wise and Otherwise (2002), Festival Distribution, Inc.
Howlin' Wolf: Howlin' Wolf/Moaning in the Moonlight (2001), Universal/MCA
Jimmy Smith: Dot Com Blues (2001), Universal Music Group.
Muddy Waters: Rollin' Stone: The Golden Anniversary Collection (2000), MCA/Chess
Otis Rush: Right Place, Wrong Time (1976, 2008), Hightone
Professor Longhair: New Orleans Piano (1972, 1994), Atlantic
Robert Johnson: The Complete Recordings (1990), Sony
Skip James: Today! (1964, 1991), Vanguard

Jazz

Frank Sinatra: The Columbia Years, 1943–1952: The Complete Recordings (1998), Sony
Ella Fitzgerald: Ella Fitzgerald Sings the Jerome Kern Songbook (1985, 1990), Polygram
Duke Ellington: Duke Ellington and His Famous Orchestra (1992), Hindsight
Miles Davis: Kind of Blue (1959, 1997), Sony
John Coltrane: Giant Steps (1959, 1990), Atlantic/WEA
Julian (Cannonball) Adderley: Somethin' Else (1999), Blue Note
Oscar Peterson: Night Train (1962, 1997), Polygram
Herbie Hancock: Maiden Voyage (1965, 1999), Blue Note
Stan Getz and Charlie Byrd: Jazz Samba (1962, 1997), Polygram
Keith Jarrett: Standards Vol. 1 (1983, 2000), ECM
Brad Mehldau: House on a Hill (2006), Nonesuch

WORLD

India: Ragas

Ravi Shankar: The Sounds of India (1968): (Sitar), Sbme Special Markets
Ravi Shankar: A Morning Raga/An Evening Raga (1968), Angel
Hari Prasad Chaurasia: Darbari Kanada/Dhunin Raga Mishra Pilu (1993), Nimbus
Ali Akbar Khan: Traditional Music of India (1995), Prestige
Dr. N. Ramani: Classical Karnatic Flute (1990), Nimbus

Korea: Folk Music

Voyager: Korean Folk Songs (2007), Columbia River Entertainment Group
The Deep Song of Korea (2007), Buda
Drum and Voices of Korea (2001), WEA
Korea — From the Land of Clear Morning (2009), Buda
Best of Korean Gayageum Music (2007), Arc Music Productions International

Argentina: Nuevo Tango

A. Piazzolla: Adios Nonino (1999), Milan
A. Piazzolla: Tango: Zero Hour (1992, 2007), Nonesuch
A. Piazzolla: Vuelvo al Sur (2008), Warner Spec.
A. Piazzolla: The Lausanne Concert: (2006), Milan/WEA
A. Piazzolla: The Soul of Tango: Greatest Hits: (2000), Milan
Yo Yo Ma: Soul of the Tango: The Music of Astor Piazzolla (1997), Sony
Pablo Ziegler & Emanuel Ax: Los Tangeros: Tangos of Astor (1997), Sony
Astor Piazzolla: Monologos, Dimitris Dimakopoulos (2002), Paradisum

APPENDIX B

INSTRUMENTAL COMBINATIONS

It is important to consider the instruments we offer clients and in what combinations we use them. Each instrument has a particular quality and timbre that gives it certain advantages or disadvantages depending on the type of intervention and/or experience being offered. A reed horn, for example, gives a very different sensory experience than playing a piano or drum. It can be good to facilitate physical aims, such as increasing lung capacity, or simply for creating an atmosphere. On the other hand, it could be overstimulating for some autistic clients. Here are four types of combinations to consider:

Therapist	Client
	Drum and Cymbal
	Bongo or Djembe
1. Piano (and voice)	Small Percussion
	Xylophone or Metallophone
2. Guitar (and voice)	Voice
	Guitar
3. Single Line (and voice)	Chimes
	Ocean Drum
4. Drum (and voice)	Hand Bells
	Piano
	Autoharp or Lyre
	Reed horn

With this list, feel free to combine any of the client's instruments with any of the therapist's instruments, for a total of 48 possibilities. There are many more combinations possible. These suggestions are only the beginning.

Note that when using a percussion instrument such as a drum, it may be more difficult to create musical form, as there is no possibility of harmony or melody. The voice may need to take a more active role in such cases. It may be useful to support clients who already have a good grasp of form and who are able to improvise music on their own. On occasion, it is useful to sing a song or improvise vocally while being supported with the simplicity of a drumbeat.

It is often better to choose instruments that complement one another. The piano is probably the most flexible instrument for the therapist, as it can be rhythmic, harmonic, and melodic, and it is able to create the most varied moods, from lyrical to lively.

The guitar offers textural possibilities not available at the piano. It can be especially useful for lyrical, soft music and the improvisation of songs or tonal music. It can create the right mood at the beginning and end of sessions. It is usually less intimidating, yet it offers the possibility of an open and flexible musical direction.

Single line instruments can be especially useful for creating musical dialogue, as the melodic phrase takes on a prime importance. They can be considered an extension of the natural voice. Generally, they also allow therapists to be mobile and physically flexible. There tends to be less musical clutter when using this approach, as it is easier to be free from harmony and rhythm.

APPENDIX C

JAZZ SCALES AND MODES

Below are jazz scales (or modes) presented in order of brightest sonorities to darkest in the key of C. As a general rule, when compared to a major scale, jazz scales with more lowered tones are perceived as dark (e.g., Phrygian and Locrian), while those with more raised tones are bright (e.g., Lydian). For most scales, key notes are identified in brackets above in order to show which note(s) must be emphasized in order to evoke the quality of the scale. Here are the possibilities for scales used to improvise on major, minor, diminished, and dominant 7th chords.

On Major Chords

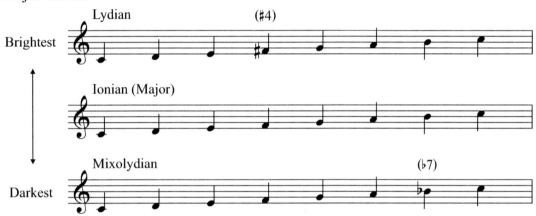

On Minor Chords

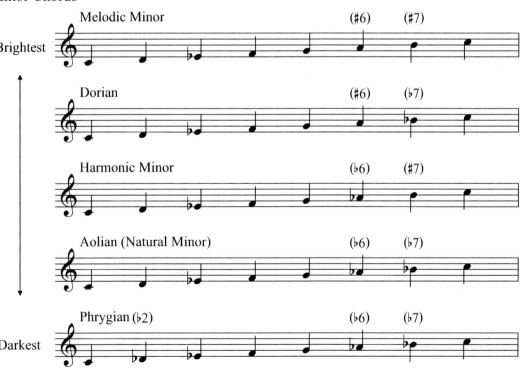

On Half-Diminished Chords

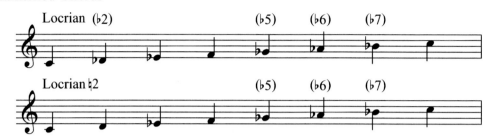

On Diminished Chords

On Dominant Chords

Special Dominant Scales

APPENDIX D

SCALE REFERENCE

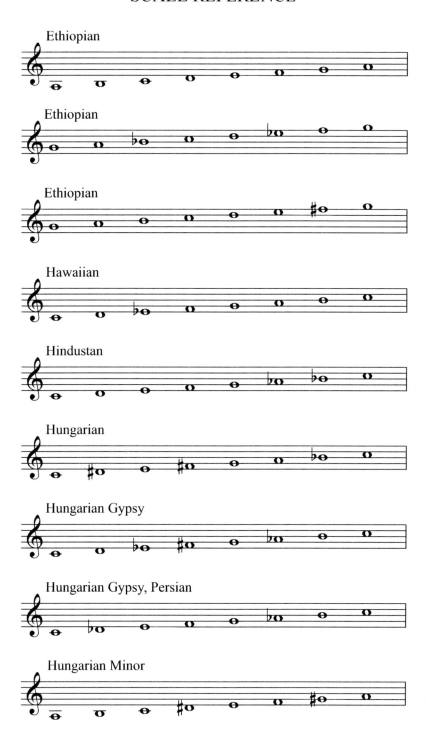

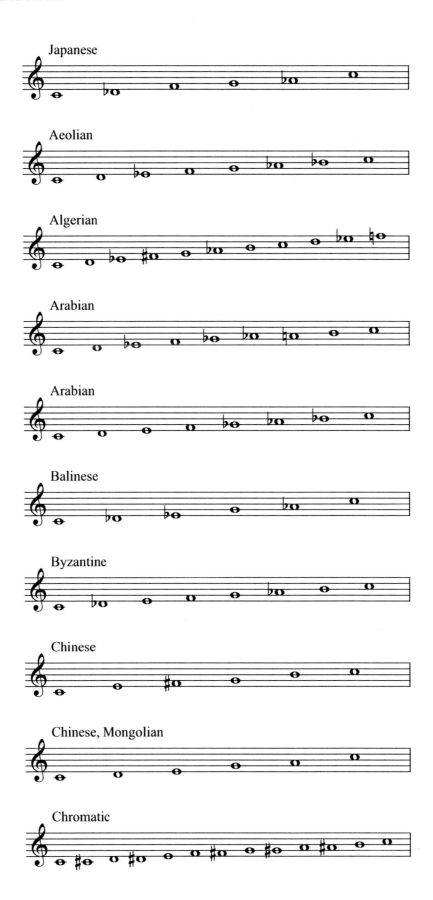

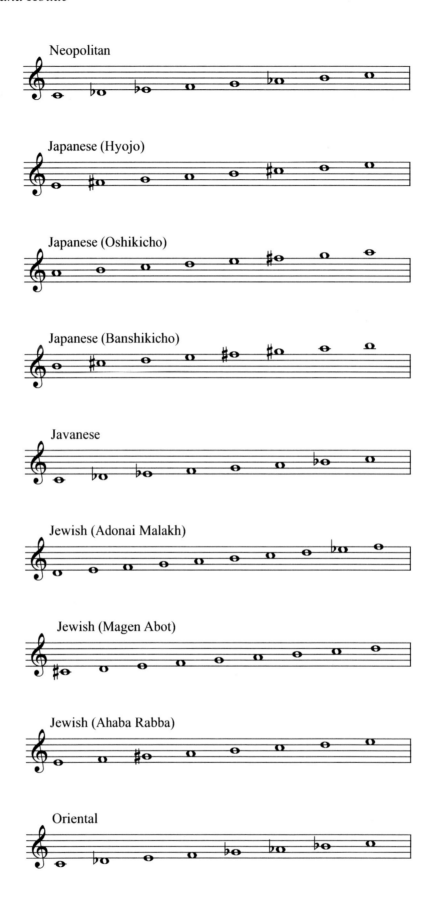

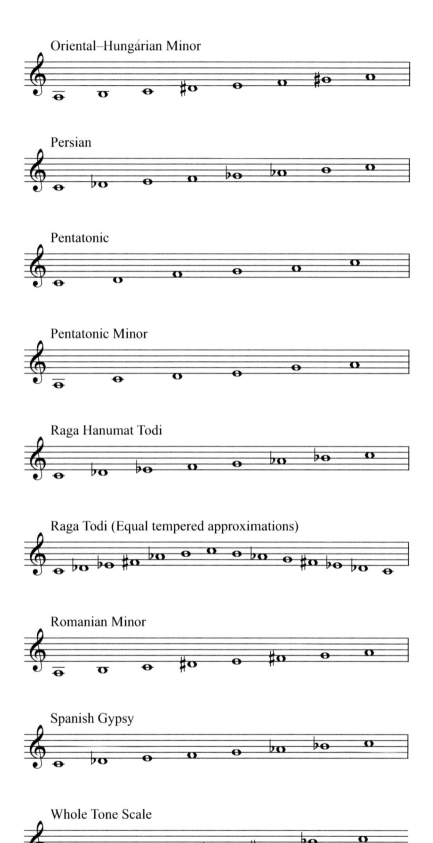

BIBLIOGRAPHY.

A History of Jazz, (n.d. p.1) Retrieved, July 2nd 2010 from
http://www.historyjazz.com/jazzhistory.html

Ahonen, H. (2007). *Group analytic music therapy.* Gilsum, NH: Barcelona Publishers.

Aigen, K. (1998). *Paths of development in Nordoff-Robbins music therapy.* Gilsum, NH: Barcelona Publishers.

Aigen, K. (2002). *Playin' in the band: A qualitative study of popular musical styles as clinical improvisation.* New York: Nordoff-Robbins Center for Music Therapy, New York University.

Ansdell, G. (1995). *Music for life: Aspects of creative music therapy with adult clients.* London: Jessica Kingsley Publishers.

Austin, D. (2009). *The theory and practice of vocal psychotherapy: Songs of the self.* London: Jessica Kingsley Publishers.

Austin, D., & Dvorkin, J (1993). Resistance in individual music therapy. *The Arts in Psychotherapy, 20*(5), 423–429.

Azzi, M. S., & Collier, S. (2000). *Le grand tango: The Life and music of Astor Piazzolla.* New York: Oxford University Press.

Baker, F., & Wigram, T. (2005). *Songwriting: Methods, techniques and clinical applications for music therapy clinicians, educators and students.* London: Jessica Kingsley Publishers.

Baker, R. M. (2004). *A brief history of the blues.* Retrieved May 28, 2007, from http://thebluehighway.com/history.html.

Barlow, W. (1989). *Looking up at down: The emergence of blues culture.* Philadelphia: Temple University Press.

Benward, B., & Saker, M. (2003). *Music in theory and practice.* New York: McGraw-Hill.

Berliner, P. (1994). *Thinking in jazz: The infinite art of improvisation.* Chicago: The University of Chicago Press, Ltd.

Big book of ballads. (n.d.). Milwaukee, WI: Hal Leonard Corporation.

Blumenfeld, A. (1992). *The blues, boogie and barrelhouse piano workbook.* Katonah, NY: Ekay Music, Inc.

Bor, J. (1999). *The raga guide: A survey of 74 Hindustani ragas.* Monmouth, UK: Nimbus Communications International Limited.

Brackett, D. (2009). *Pop, rock, and soul reader:* New York: Oxford University Press.

Braheny, J. (2006). *The craft and business of songwriting.* Palm Coast, FL: Writer's Digest Books.

Brooks, L., Koda, C., & Brooks, W. B. (1998). *Blues for dummies.* Foster City, CA: IDG Books Worldwide, Inc.

Bruscia, K. E. (1998). *The dynamics of music psychotherapy.* Gilsum, NH: Barcelona Publishers.

Bruscia, K. E. (1998b). An introduction to music psychotherapy. In K. E. Bruscia (Ed.), *The dynamics of music psychotherapy* (pp. 1–15). Gilsum, NH: Barcelona Publishers.

Bukofzer, M. (1975). *Music in the baroque era.* London: J. M. Dent & Sons Ltd.

Chailley, J. (1963). *Tristan et Isolde de Richard Wagner.* Paris: Centre de documentation universitaire.

Cuellar, C., & Perez, Z. (Eds.) (2003). *100 years of popular music: '90s.* Warner Bros. Publication.

Dale, R. (2004). *Teach yourself: Jazz.* London: Hodder Headline Ltd.

Danielou, A. (1987). *The ragas of northern Indian music.* New Delhi, India: Munshiram Manoharlal Publishers

Day, R. (Ed.). (2003). *The music of Paul McCartney: 1963–1973.* London: Wise Publications.

Dean, R. T. (1989). *Creative improvisation: Jazz, contemporary music and beyond: How to develop techniques of improvisation for any musical context.* Philadelphia: Open University Press.

De Nora, T. (2000) *Music in everyday life.* Cambridge University Press.

Everett, W. (2000). *Expression in pop-rock music: A collection of critical and analytical essays.* New York: Routledge.

Feist, J., & Lindsay, S. G. (2005). *The songwriter's workshop: Harmony.* Boston, MA: Berklee Press.

Foster, D. (1996). *Best of David Foster* (2nd ed.). Milwaukee, WI: Hal Leonard Corp.

Frederick, R. (2004). *A brief history of love songs.* Retrieved February 1, 2010, from http://www.soundexp.com/history.html#troubadours.

Freed, I. (1958). *Contemporary piano music by distinguished American composers.* Bryn Mawr, PA: Theodore Presser Company.

Frith, S. (1990). *On record: Rock, pop, and the written word.* New York: Routledge.

Frith, S. (2004). *Popular music: Critical concepts in media and cultural studies.* New York: Routledge.

Garred, R. (2006). *Music therapy: A dialogical perspective.* Gilsum, NH: Barcelona Publishers.

Gordon, A. D. (1995). *100 ultimate blues riffs for piano/keyboards.* Lawndale, CA: A. D. G. Productions.

Hillier, P. (1997) *Arvo Pärt.* Oxford University Press.

Hodge, D. (2006). *The complete idiot's guide to playing bass guitar.* New York: Penguin Group (USA), Inc.

Hodson, R. (2007). *Interaction, improvisation, and interplay in jazz.* New York: Routledge.

Hong, J. S. (1987). Composition technical characteristics in church music of Na Woon-Young. *Church and Divinity, 3,* 321.

Houde, M. (2007). *Blues improvisation resources: An analysis and synthesis of the aesthetics of the blues and applications in clinical improvisation.* Retrieved April 26, 2010, from Laurier Centre for Music Therapy Research website, http://www.wlu.ca/soundeffects/researchlibrary/MarcHoude.pdf

John, E. (1991). *Elton John anthology.* Milwaukee, WI: Hal Leonard Corporation.

John, E. (1994). *Elton John ballads.* Milwaukee, WI: Hal Leonard Corporation.

John, E. (2006). *Essential Elton John: A step-by step breakdown of Elton John's keyboard styles and techniques.* Milwaukee, WI: Hal Leonard Corporation.

Josefs, J. (1996). *Writing music for hit songs.* London: Music Sales.

Jun, I. P. (2002). The aesthetics of Korean traditional music in view of the aesthetics of Korean visual arts. *Korean journal of musicology, 9,* 161–198.

Jun, I. P. (2006). Retrospect and prospect of creative Korean traditional music for sixty years. *Ewha music journal, 10(2),* 67–88.

Kaufmann, W. (1968). *The ragas of north India.* Bloomington, IN: Indiana University Press.

Kivy, P. (1990). *Music alone.* Ithaca, NY, & London: Cornell University Press.

Kostka, S., & Payne, D. (2004). *Tonal harmony.* New York: McGraw-Hill.

Lamb, B. (n. d.). *About.com: Top 40/pop: What does top 40 mean?* Retrieved December 21, 2009, from http://top40.about.com/od/popmusic101/a/top40.htm.

Lateef, Y (1981) *Repository of scales and melodic patterns.* Fana Music: Amherst, MA

Lee, C.A. (1989). Structural Analysis of Therapeutic Improvisatory Music. *Journal of British Music Therapy* 3 (2), pp. 11-19.

Lee, C.A. (1990). Structural Analysis of Post-tonal Therapeutic Improvisatory Music. *Journal of British Music Therapy* 4 (1), pp. 6-20.

Lee, C.A. (1992). *The Analysis of Therapeutic Improvisatory Music with People Living with the virus HIV and AIDS.* Unpublished doctoral thesis, City University, London.

Lee, C.A. (1995), The Analysis of Therapeutic Improvisatory Music. In A. Gilroy and C. Lee (eds) *Art and Music: Therapy and Research.* London: Routledge

Lee, C.A. (1996). *Music at the Edge: The music therapy experiences of a musician with AIDS.* London: Routledge.

Lee, C.A. (2000). A Method of Analyzing Improvisations in Music Therapy. *Journal of Music Therapy, 37(2),* 147-167.

Lee, C.A. & Khare, K. (2001). The Supervision of Clinical Improvisation in Aesthetic Music Therapy: A music-centered approach. In Michele Forinash (Ed.), *Music therapy supervision* (pp.247-270). Gilsum, NH: Barcelona Publishers.

Lee, C. (2003). *The architecture of aesthetic music therapy.* Gilsum, NH: Barcelona Publishers.

Lee, C.A. (2003). Reflections on Working with a String Quartet in Aesthetic Music Therapy. (online) *Voices: A World Forum for Music Therapy,* 3(3). 2003. Accessed May 6, 2010, at http://www.voices/Voices3(3)lee.html.

Lee, C.A. (2006). Aesthetics of Creativity in Clinical Improvisation. In Deliege and Geraint (eds), *Musical Creativity. Multidisciplinary research in theory and practice.* (pp.238-251). Psychology Press: East Sussex.

Lee, C.A. (2008). Reflections on Being a Music Therapist and a Gay Man. (online) *Voices: A World Forum for Music Therapy,* 8(3). 2008. Accessed May 6, 2010, at http://www.voices/Voices8(3)lee.html.

Lee, C.A. (2010). *Improvising in Styles: A Workbook for Music Therapist's, Educators and Musicians.* Gilsum, NH: Barcelona Publishers.

Lee, M. G. (2004). Problems in studies of Jangdan. *Korean journal of musicology, 11,* 11–41.

Leikin, M-A. (2008). *How to write a hit song.* Milwaukee, WI: Hal Leonard Corp.

Levine, M. (1989). *The jazz piano book.* Petaluma, CA: Sher Music Co.

Levine, M. (1995). *The jazz theory book.* Petaluma, CA: Sher Music Co.

Love songs of the '90s (2nd ed.) (1995). Milwaukee, WI: Hal Leonard Corp.

Mahler, S,. Pine, F., & Bergmann, A (2000). *The psychological birth of the human infant.* Basic Books: New York.

Marsalis, W. (2008). *Moving to higher ground: How jazz can change your life.* New York: Random House, Inc.

Masden, C. K., & Geringer, J. M. (2008). Reflections on Puccini's *La Bohème:* Investigating a model of listening. *Journal of research in music education, 56,* 33–42.

McGrath (2008). *Indian Ragas in Music Therapy.* Retrieved on May6th from Laurier centre for Music Therapy Research Website: http//www.wlu.ca/soundeffects/researchlibrary.

Mereni, A-E. (1996). Kinesis und katharsis: The African traditional concept of sound/motion or music: Its application in, and implications for, music therapy (Parts I and II). *British journal of music therapy 10*(1), 17–24.

Mereni, A-E. (1996). Kinesis und katharsis: The African traditional concept of sound/motion or music: Its application in, and implications for, music therapy (Part III). *British journal of music therapy 11*(1), 20–23.

Monson, I. (1996*). Saying something: Jazz improvisation and interaction.* Chicago: The University of Chicago Press, Ltd.

Montello, L. (2003). Protecting this child: psychodynamic music therapy with a gifted musician. In S. Hadley (Ed.), *Psychodynamic music therapy: Case studies.* Gilsum, NH: Barcelona Publishers.

Nattiez, J-J. (1990). *Music and discourse: Toward a semiology of music.* Princeton, NJ: Princeton University Press.

Nidel, R. O. (2005). *World music: The basics.* New York: Routledge.

Nordoff, P., & Robbins, C. (2007). *Creative music therapy: A guide to fostering clinical musicianship.* Gilsum, NH: Barcelona Publishers.

O'Brien, E. (2006). Opera therapy and performing a new work with cancer patients and professional singers. *Nordic journal of music therapy, 15*(1), 82–96.

Oclander, J. I. (n.d.). *History of the tango: A dance, a culture, a way of life.* Retrieved October 17, 2009, from http://www.cartage.org.lb/en/themes/Arts/music/occidetalmusic/Modernoccidental/ballroom/tango/History/History.htm.

Oliver, P. (1997). *The story of the blues: The making of a black music.* London: PIMLICO.

Overduin, J. (1998). *Making music. Improvisation for organists.* New York & Oxford: Oxford University Press.

Piazza, T. (2005). *Understanding jazz: Ways to listen.* New York: Random House (Jazz at Lincoln Center).

Pollock, M. (2003). *Musical improv comedy: Creating songs in the moment.* Hollywood, CA: Masteryear Publishing.

Priestley, M. (1994). *Essays on analytic music therapy*. Gilsum, NH: Barcelona Publishers.

Rebennack, M. (Dr. John). (1998). *Dr. John teaches New Orleans piano, Vol. 1*. Woodstock, NY: Homespun Listen and Learn Series.

Rebennack, M. (Dr. John). (1998b). *Dr. John teaches New Orleans piano, Vol. 2*. Woodstock, NY: Homespun Listen and Learn Series.

Robarts, J. (2003). The healing function of improvised songs in music therapy with a child survivor of early trauma and sexual abuse. In S. Hadley (Ed.), *Psychodynamic music therapy: Case studies*. Gilsum, NH: Barcelona Publishers.

Robbins, C., & Robbins, C. (1998). *Healing heritage: Paul Nordoff exploring the tonal language of music*. Gilsum, NH: Barcelona Publishers.

Roig-Francoli, M. (2008). *Understanding post-tonal music*. New York: McGraw-Hill.

Rooksby, R. (2005). *How to write songs on keyboards*. Hastings, UK: Outline Press Ltd.

Ruud, E. (1995). Improvisation as liminal experience: Jazz and music therapy as modern "rites de passage." In C. B. Kenny (Ed.), *Listening, playing, creating: Essays on the power of sound* (pp. 91–117). Albany, NY: State University of New York Press.

Rudd, G. (2006). *Music therapy: A dialogical perspective*. Gilsum, NH: Barcelona Publishers.

Saavedra, G. (1995). *Piazzolla: A sad, current and conscious tango*. Retrieved October 17, 2009, from http://www.piazzolla.org/interv/index.html.

Sairam, T. V. (2005). *Raga therapy*. Chennai, India: Nada Centre for Music Therapy.

Sarnecki, M. (2002). *Harmony: Book 1*. Mississauga, ON: Frederick Harris Music Co., Ltd.

Schenstead, A. (2009) *Performing Musical Liberation: The flute and the self in improvisation and music therapy practice*. Retrieved on May 6th, 2010 from Laurier Centre for Music Therapy Research Website: http//www.wlu.ca/soundeffects/researchlibrary/AmandaSchenstead.pdf

Schmidt-Jones,C (2008). *The music of the romantic era*. Retrieved Feb. 1, 2010, from http://cnx.org/content/m11606/latest/.

Scorsese, M., et al. (2003). *The blues: A musical journey*. New York: Harper Collins Publishers.

Scruton, R. (1997). *The aesthetics of music*. Oxford: Clarendon Press.

Shoenberg, A. (1954). *Structural foundations of harmony*. New York: Norton.

Shankar, R. (2007). *My music, my life*. San Rafael, CA: Mandala Publishing.

Shipton, A. (2007). *A new history of jazz* (2nd ed.). New York: Continuum International Publishing Group Inc.

Shuker, R. (1994). *Understanding popular music*. New York: Routledge.

Slominsky, N. (1986) *Thesaurus of scales and melodic patterns*. New York: Macmillan Publishing Company.

Starr, E., & Starr, N. (2008). *The everything bass guitar book*. Avon, MA: F+W Publications, Inc.

Stige, B. (1992) *Culture-centered music therapy*. NH: Barcelona Publishers.

Strong, J. (2006). *Drums for dummies* (2nd ed.). Hoboken, NJ: Wiley Publishing, Inc.

Summers, L. (1996). *Music the new age elixir*. Prometheus Books: Amherst, NY.

Sutro, D. (2006). *Jazz for dummies* (2nd ed.). Hoboken, NJ: Wiley Publishing, Inc.

Todd, J. (2002). *Worlds of music: An introduction to the music of the world's peoples* (4th ed.). Florence, KY: Wadsworth Group.

Turek, R. (2007). *Theory for today's musician*. New York: McGraw-Hill.

Turry, A. (2005). Teamwork: Therapist and cotherapist in the Nordoff-Robbins approach to music therapy. *Music therapy perspectives*, *23*, 53–69.

Vaughan, F.E. (1979) *Awakening Intuition*. New York: Anchor Books.

Warner, T. (2003). *Pop music: Technology and creativity*. Burlington, VT: Ashgate Publishing.

Weissman, D. (2005). *Blues: The basics*. New York: Routledge.

Wigram, T. (2004). *Improvisation: Methods and techniques for music therapy clinicians, educators and students*. London: Jessica Kingsley Publishers.

Wosch, T & Wigram, T. (Eds) (2007). *Microanalysis in music therapy*. London & Philadelphia: Jessica Kingsley Publishers.

AUTHOR AND COMPOSER INDEX

SUBJECT INDEX